The Council on Foundations

Who We Are

The spirit of the Council on Foundations and its members is based on the earliest American values. Since this country's founding, philanthropy has been a core value of its people. The Council can trace its founding to 1949, with the organization of the National Committee on Foundations and Trusts for Community Welfare.

The Council on Foundations is a membership organization that serves the public good by promoting and enhancing responsible and effective philanthropy. The Council's members include more than 2,000 independent, family, community, public, and operating foundations, as well as corporate foundations and giving programs, in the United States and around the world. In 2002, these organizations held an estimated $289 billion in charitable assets and made grants of an estimated $17 billion.

For more than 50 years, the Council on Foundations has helped foundation and corporate grantmaking staff and board members in their day-to-day grantmaking activities. Through research, publications, conferences and workshops, legal services, and a wide array of other services, the Council addresses the important issues and challenges that face foundations and corporate community involvement leaders.

In an environment of significant change and potential, the Council on Foundations in the twenty-first century supports philanthropy worldwide by serving as

- A trusted *leader*: promoting the highest values, principles, and practices to ensure accountability and effectiveness in philanthropy;

- An effective *advocate*: communicating and promoting the interests, value, and contributions of philanthropy;

- A valued *resource*: supporting learning, open dialogue and information exchange about and for philanthropy; and

- A respectful *partner*: collaborating within a network of philanthropic and other organizations working to promote responsible and effective philanthropy.

The Council on Foundations' work is guided by a set of enduring values:

- The field of philanthropy must uphold the public's trust.

- Philanthropy is a cornerstone of a democratic society and is essential to the success of the nonprofit sector.

- Responsible and effective philanthropy depends on accountability, integrity, and respect for others.

- Inclusiveness and diversity in their many forms are fundamental to the responsiveness and effectiveness of the Council and the field of philanthropy.

The Council's effectiveness requires an ongoing commitment to quality, communication, collaboration, discovery, reflection, and learning.

Inclusive Practices at the Council on Foundations

The Council adopted the following statement of inclusiveness in 1996, and in pursuit of these goals supports research, community outreach, fellowships, and other special programs:

The Council on Foundations was formed to promote responsible and effective philanthropy. The mission requires a commitment to inclusiveness as a fundamental operating principle and calls for an active and ongoing process that affirms human diversity in its many forms, encompassing but not limited to ethnicity, race, gender, sexual orientation, economic circumstance, disability, and philosophy. We seek diversity in order to ensure that a range of perspectives, opinions and experiences is recognized and acted upon in achieving the Council's mission. The Council also asks members to make a similar commitment to inclusiveness in order to better enhance their abilities to contribute to the common good of our changing society.

This book, *Opening Doors: Pathways to Diverse Donors*, is one of several activities that the Council has undertaken to promote greater awareness of the value and importance of diversity to philanthropy. For information on other projects on diversity in philanthropy, and to find out more about the Council on Foundations, please visit us as www.cof.org or contact us by letter or by phone at 1828 L Street, NW, Suite 300, Washington, D.C. 20036; (202) 466-6512.

Opening Doors

Diana S. Newman

with contributions from Mindy Berry,
Jessica Chao, Henry A. J. Ramos,
and Mary-Frances Winters

Foreword by Emmett D. Carson

Opening Doors

Pathways to Diverse Donors

JOSSEY-BASS
A Wiley Company
San Francisco

Published by

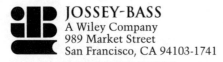

JOSSEY-BASS
A Wiley Company
989 Market Street
San Francisco, CA 94103-1741

www.josseybass.com

Jossey-Bass books and products are available through most bookstores. To contact Jossey-Bass directly, call (888) 378-2537, fax to (800) 605-2665, or visit our website at www.josseybass.com.

Substantial discounts on bulk quantities of Jossey-Bass books are available to corporations, professional associations, and other organizations. For details and discount information, contact the special sales department at Jossey-Bass.

We at Jossey-Bass strive to use the most environmentally sensitive paper stocks available to us. Our publications are printed on acid-free recycled stock whenever possible, and our paper always meets or exceeds minimum GPO and EPA requirements.

Jossey-Bass also publishes its books in a variety of electronic formats. Some content that appears in print may not be available in electronic books.

Library of Congress Cataloging-in-Publication Data

Newman, Diana S., 1943-
 Opening doors: pathways to diverse donors / Diana S. Newman; foreword by Emmett D. Carson.—1st ed.
  p. cm.—(The Jossey-Bass nonprofit and public management series)
 Includes bibliographical references and index.
 ISBN 0-7879-5884-0 (alk. paper)
  1. Charitable uses, trusts, and foundations—United States. 2. Multiculturalism—United States. I. Title. II. Series.
HV91 .N468 2002
361.7'068'1—dc21   2002005438

HB Printing   10 9 8 7 6 5 4 3 2 1   FIRST EDITION

The Jossey-Bass
Nonprofit and Public Management Series

Contents

List of Tables, Figures, and Exhibits   xiii

Foreword   xv
    Emmett D. Carson

Preface   xix

Acknowledgments   xxix

About the Author   xxxiii

About the Contributors   xxxv

1. How Changing Demographics Are Changing Philanthropy   1

2. Understanding Diverse Giving Patterns   25

3. Embracing Diversity and Inclusiveness   67

4. Building Awareness and Cultivating Prospects   85

5. Turning Diverse Prospects into Donors   105

6. Advancing Donor Investment Through Major Gifts   131

7. Encouraging Gift Planning and Endowment Building   157

8. Achieving Success Through Collaboration   183

9. Realizing the Potential of Diverse Donors   197

References   207

Resources   215

Index   227

List of Tables, Figures, and Exhibits

Tables

Table 1.1	United States Population Projections	10
Table 1.2	Age of United States Population by Race and Ethnicity (2000)	12
Table 2.1	Percent of Home Ownership by Race and Ethnicity of Householder	27
Table 2.2	Survey of Minority-Owned Business Enterprises: Nonfarm Businesses (1997)	29
Table 2.3	Distribution of Net Worth of Households by Asset Type (1991)	30

Figures

Figure 1.1	Traditional Donor Pyramid of Giving	16
Figure 1.2	Continuum of Philanthropy: African American, Asian American, Latino	19
Figure 1.3	Cycles of Giving: Native American	23

Exhibits

| Exhibit 4.1 | Alaska Native Heritage Center: Annual Report Cover | 91 |

Exhibit 5.1	Mexican Fine Arts Center Museum: Gala Invitation	112
Exhibit 5.2	Asian Pacific Fund: Growing Up Asian in America	115
Exhibit 5.3	Asian American Federation of New York: New Heritage of Giving, Dr. Procopio Yanong	127
Exhibit 6.1	Native American Rights Fund: Gift Acknowledgment Card	153
Exhibit 7.1	Asian American Federation of New York: New Heritage of Giving, Francis Y. Sogi	159
Exhibit 8.1	African American Philanthropy Initiative	192

Foreword

Emmett D. Carson
President and CEO, the Minneapolis Foundation

Despite considerable progress in some areas of race relations, we in the United States continue to find it difficult to have candid discussions about how and why people of different races and cultures respond differently to similar situations. This difficulty arises from two competing beliefs: (1) everyone should be treated exactly the same, and (2) race and culture matter. The dilemma of how to navigate these two competing philosophies is especially challenging for nonprofit organizations that, in general, believe they are more responsive on the diversity issue than either business or government because they treat all groups, regardless of racial or cultural background, the same. *Opening Doors: Pathways to Diverse Donors* makes a powerful case that race and culture matter in how nonprofit organizations shape their fund development efforts to attract gifts from diverse donors.

Using 2000 census data, *Opening Doors* notes that 30 percent of the nation's population consists of diverse racial groups and that the percentage is even higher in many communities. These new demographic realities mean that soliciting funds from diverse communities is no longer optional for nonprofit organizations—it is a matter of their future survival. Successful donor solicitation efforts will require tailoring traditional approaches to be culturally appropriate.

The goal of *Opening Doors* is to increase the comfort level of nonprofit boards, chief executives, and development officers with reaching out to diverse populations and to provide specific examples of how to do so. Unfortunately this will likely be difficult reading for many in these ranks who have justified their lack of outreach to diverse racial groups based on two erroneous beliefs, often unspoken.

First, there is a continuing belief, despite a growing body of research to the contrary, that diverse racial and ethnic groups have few, if any, traditions of giving. Because of this, there is no need for nonprofit organizations to expend limited financial and human resources (in fact, it would be wasteful) in reaching out to people who have no tradition or capacity to give. *Opening Doors* may help to finally put these falsehoods to rest by its documentation of the changing demography of the United States coupled with increasingly detailed research on the rich giving traditions of different racial and ethnic groups.

The second equally troubling assumption is that fund development departments often appear to operate with the not-too-subtle belief that white donors are indifferent at best, and hostile at worse, to being solicited by a fund development officer who is not white. As the United States becomes more diverse, it will be interesting to see if this perverse logic will result in greater job opportunities for diverse development professionals who have often found it difficult to gain employment and advancement in the fund development ranks.

What makes *Opening Doors* a unique contribution to the nonprofit literature is that it provides specific examples of how a wide range of nonprofit organizations have been able to successfully broaden their fundraising base by reaching out to African American, Asian American, Latino American, and Native American donors. Although other publications have previously presented a small portion of this information with regard to a specific racial or cultural group, this book assembles all of this information in one place. A real strength of the book is that it shows how different racial and cultural groups can have different reactions to the same fundraising approach and compares their traditions side by side.

The examples the book provides are important in helping nonprofit organizations recognize that by treating everyone the same they may unintentionally offend potential donors rather than encourage their participation. The book takes the familiar fundraising pyramid and explains how its hierarchical formulation may lead to cultural miscues when fundraisers attempt to reach out to diverse donors. It details how traditional fundraising methods such as face-to-face appeals, direct mail, major gifts, special events, and planned giving can be successful in attracting gifts from diverse donors, with some important adjustments for cultural sensibilities.

One of the most important contributions of the book is that it emphasizes the importance of having a diverse board and staff with a mission that is relevant to the community that the organization solicits. *Opening Doors* reinforces the crucial point that successful fund development occurs from effectively carrying out and communicating the organization's mission. Nonprofit organizations must walk the talk if they are to be successful in soliciting diverse donors.

Diana Newman is to be commended for forthrightly addressing the heretofore largely taboo issues of race and culture in fund development and providing a variety of relevant examples that nonprofit organizations can learn from. Some will suggest that the strategies outlined in this book, different approaches for different racial and cultural groups, are too complicated for most fund development departments to implement. In addition, as Newman herself points out, there is significant diversity within the broad racial categories examined in the book, and further research is likely to uncover even greater levels of complexity. As with most things, generalizations are starting points for dialogue, and readers should not view this work as suggesting that every person in each racial and ethnic group will respond the same way each and every time. Unfortunately some will use such arguments to justify keeping the doors of their nonprofit organizations closed to diverse donors.

Those of us who recognize that the United States will become only more diverse in the years ahead should view such criticisms for what they are—further excuses to continue to ignore the potential of communities of color in supporting the mission of nonprofit organizations. We shouldn't be too concerned. As *Opening Doors* makes clear, nonprofit organizations that fail to adopt new fundraising approaches to garner the support of this nation's increasingly diverse population are not likely to remain in operation much longer. For those that do, the future is bright, and the opportunities seem to be unlimited.

Preface

A practical guide for fundraising practitioners and students of philanthropy, this book focuses on ways to raise funds from prospective donors who are African American, Asian American, Latino, or Native American.

Fundraisers in the United States direct their development efforts, with few exceptions, to whites. By and large, charitable organizations do not raise funds—and do not attempt to do so—from the breadth of the ethnically and racially diverse populations they serve.

This book provides background about the cultural and charitable histories of each broad segment and examines the donors' motivations for giving, sharing, and volunteering. Although we are acutely aware that broad generalizations can be misconstrued or might promote stereotypes, we recognize two reasons that nonprofit organizations do not reach out directly to diverse cultures: they lack understanding of cultural differences, and they fear making mistakes or causing offense. This book deals with those concerns head-on.

Another reason that the fundraising arms of most charitable organizations do not reach out to people of racially diverse backgrounds is the widespread perception that such people—with the exception of some Asian populations—are more likely to be recipients of charity than participants in philanthropy. Yes, substantial poverty and economic disadvantage remain in many ethnic groups. At the same time, the increasing wealth and expendable income of some individuals and families in the same populations, along with their greater acculturation and social mobility, make them attractive candidates for philanthropy.

Based on research with diverse donors and organizations across the country that have successfully garnered ongoing support from such donors, this book presents real-life examples of strategies and materials that have worked, embellished by anecdotes and first-hand experiences.

OPPORTUNITIES AND POTENTIAL

In the next fifty years, according to the U.S. Census Bureau, the racial and ethnic makeup of the United States population will dramatically shift from a large majority (69 percent) of non-Hispanic whites—referred to in this book as whites or Caucasians—to a population of approximately one-half whites and one-half all other ethnicities and races. This population change will not take place equally in all areas of the country, and in some communities people of diverse backgrounds are already the majority (U.S. Bureau of the Census, 2000h). This shift has had and will continue to have a tremendous impact on nonprofit organizations—in the services they provide and the clients they serve, in the composition of their boards and staff, and in the missions, policies, and strategies they pursue to accomplish goals.

The income levels in each of these diverse populations are rising at a faster pace than those of the population as a whole. Members of diverse populations owned nonfarm businesses that brought in revenues of nearly $600 billion in 1997, the most current data available (U.S. Bureau of the Census, 2001l). Other indicators of financial wherewithal—such as employment rates, education, and home ownership—are expected to continue increasing. We describe these data in more detail in Chapter Two.

At the same time, nonprofit organizations are increasingly dependent upon voluntary support from the private sector to fund operations, special projects, capital improvements, and endowments. We know from *Giving USA 2001* that more than 80 percent of charitable contributions come from individuals—either during their lifetimes or through estate plans (Kaplan, 2001). Yet nonprofits rarely consider or approach as donors these rapidly growing and increasingly affluent segments of the diverse U.S. population— already more than 30 percent of the total.

Ethnically and racially diverse people can make excellent donor prospects because, in general, they are likely to have only recently acquired their wealth and are unlikely to have made long-term charitable commitments outside of their own communities.

BACKGROUND

The impetus for this book came from a 1999 report published by the Council on Foundations, *Cultures of Caring: Philanthropy in Diverse American Communities*. The idea and funding for the report originated from the Ford, W. K. Kellogg, and David and Lucile Packard Foundations. The report's five authors (of which I was one) interviewed affluent donors in four broad communities—African American, Asian American, Latino, and Native American—about why they give, how they select the organizations they support, and what they think about setting up endowments. The authors also interviewed eighty community foundations about their experiences in attracting diverse donors to establish endowment funds.

Cultures of Caring affirmed the large and growing potential of philanthropy in diverse ethnic communities. Each of the four groups discussed in the report has made impressive gains in indicators of economic success in the United States: rising in education and income levels, attaining management positions and ownership of businesses, and increasing the number of professionals. In addition, as diverse individuals and families continue their rich history of charitable activities, they increase their involvement in formal philanthropy through faith-based giving and contributions to colleges and universities, ethnic organizations, and mainstream institutions.

Opening Doors expands the work of *Cultures of Caring*, which focused on wealthy donors and large contributions, to include charitable gifts of all sizes—both current and deferred—for operating, capital, and endowment purposes. In addition this book includes the results of new research with more than fifty charitable organizations: information, stories, and examples from organizations successfully attracting and expanding volunteer and financial support from diverse donors. We have included many quotes throughout the book from individuals who were interviewed during the research for *Cultures of Caring* and this book. If not otherwise credited, quotations in this book should be assumed to come from these interviews.

Although numerous excellent books and articles on charitable activities in each of the ethnic cultures exist, many of which are listed in the References and Resources, few materials discuss practical ways to attract philanthropic support in all four broad ethnic segments. This book is not a handbook with explicit instructions but rather a guide that includes broad principles as well as insights and examples from nonprofit organizations that are attracting and sustaining gifts from diverse communities.

AUDIENCE

We offer *Opening Doors* primarily for those who work or volunteer in a broad range of charitable organizations: hospitals and health care agencies; colleges and universities; arts and cultural institutions; grassroots and neighborhood organizations; churches, synagogues, and mosques; day care centers; nursing homes; social service agencies; community foundations; and many others. It is focused toward board members, CEOs, development professionals, and others who want their organizations to be relevant and thriving in the years ahead and to be representative of the communities they serve.

This book will be helpful for the relocating seasoned development professional, entry-level development officer, campaign chair or committee member, and newly recruited board member.

Both mainstream and ethnic-specific organizations will find useful and innovative ideas on the following pages. Organizations that actively reach out to donors in diverse local populations are often organizations—such as the Native American Rights Fund, the Mexican Fine Arts Center Museum, Associated Black Charities, or the China Institute—that directly serve a specific community. Mainstream organizations seldom focus efforts to attract and cultivate donors from diverse racial and ethnic groups. The primary audience for this book consists of white professionals and white board members, although many members of other cultures and ethnicities are uneasy and inexperienced in seeking funds from members of their own communities. This book offers ideas and suggestions about how to begin or enhance your organization's efforts to attract diverse donors.

In addition those who care about philanthropy—leaders, contributors, activists, and legal and financial advisers—will want to learn about diverse donors and the giving styles and philosophies that influence whether such donors will choose to give to already established charitable organizations. Scholars and teachers will use the book as a resource for courses on philanthropy, volunteerism, fundraising, and ethnic studies.

OVERVIEW OF THE CONTENT

Chapter One serves as an introduction to the book, demonstrating the large and growing economic and philanthropic potential in diverse populations. Both the numbers of diverse people and their affluence are increasing at rates faster than those of the general population. The chapter describes some of the common elements of diverse cultures in terms of historic philanthropy and their motivations for giving money, time, and talent. It also defines important terms we will use in the book and presents the continuum of philanthropy and the cycle of giving as models by which to gauge philanthropic readiness and activity.

Chapter Two begins with an overview of demographic information and indicators of wealth for each group. Drawing heavily from the research for *Cultures of Caring,* we describe the four large population groups—African American, Asian American, Latino, and Native American—in terms of the philosophy, customs, traditions, and current practices of each culture.

Chapter Three sets forth elements of organizational commitment necessary for successful outreach to diverse donors. It begins with the personal commitment to diversity on the part of the organization's leadership and includes the composition of the board and staff, the roles of trustees and volunteers, accessibility issues, and the organization's mission, inclusiveness, programming, and strategic plans.

Chapter Four describes some of the values and cultural sensitivities in diverse populations. It suggests ways to build awareness of the services and programs that the nonprofit organization offers while respecting ethnic differences. It renders an account of techniques for cultivating prospective donors that organizations have used successfully to reach diverse populations.

Chapter Five demonstrates ways to turn prospects into donors through personal meetings, house parties, special events, and direct mail, with candid stories from people in the trenches who have successfully attracted diverse annual donors. It also presents suggestions about printed materials and methods for seeking gifts from diverse businesses.

Chapter Six lays out culturally effective ways to encourage small donors to become large donors. Through customized approaches and real-life stories, we explore some of the nuances of successfully seeking large gifts.

Chapter Seven focuses on gift planning and endowment building. It lists both the reasons for and the challenges to starting gift planning programs in diverse communities, paying particular attention to how sensitive the ethnic group may be to the subjects of estate planning and charitable giving. We review and give many examples of gift planning strategies and characteristics of planned gift donors.

Chapter Eight discusses methods to identify appropriate partnerships between nonprofit organizations—both mainstream and ethnic-specific—and other groups in diverse cultures. Such collaborations establish trusted relationships, initiate discussions of issues and needs in common, and sponsor joint programs that benefit all members of the collaborations as well as the diverse populations.

Chapter Nine concludes the book by offering specific ways to stimulate philanthropy in diverse U.S. populations. It presents examples of organizations and groups of organizations that are sponsoring workshops and seminars about philanthropy and planned giving for diverse people. This chapter also reviews the steps along the pathways to diverse donors that previous chapters covered.

At the end of the book are References, a list of publications used in its preparation; Resources, a list of contact information for organizations that provide networks, training, materials, and information related to fundraising and diverse cultures; and Further Reading, a list of additional publications on these topics.

LANGUAGE AND WORD USAGE

We chose carefully and thoughtfully the words we used to describe ethnically and racially diverse populations in this book, and yet we are aware that many people may take exception to specific usages.

Terminology

We use the term *diverse* rather than referring to *minorities* (because some groups are the majority in their local areas) or *people of color* (because some individuals are affronted by categories based on skin tones) to describe people from the many ethnicities and races other than Caucasian. Even so, we know that individual African Americans, Asian Americans, Latinos, and Native Americans may not identify themselves or their families as diverse. Please bear with us as we struggle to find appropriate terms that are both descriptive and innocuous.

Another controversial word used in this book is the adjective *mainstream*, which we mean to imply use primarily, but not exclusively, by Caucasians. You will find such phrases as *mainstream fundraising practices* (such as annual funds, direct mail, and capital campaigns) and *mainstream organizations* (hospitals, universities and colleges, and arts organizations, for example).

The words we use to identify the four broad population groups that are the focus of the book—African Americans, Asian Americans, Latinos, and Native Americans—are themselves controversial. We recognize that some individuals within these population groups do not find these terms descriptive or even appropriate. Just as some Americans may—or may not—consider themselves Caucasians, whites, or European Americans, individuals may prefer to refer to themselves as black, Hispanic or Chicano, or American Indian, or may prefer noting their nationality or tribal affiliation, such as Japanese American, Hopi, or Cuban American. Furthermore, some individuals will identify with various labels depending on the cultural, social, or political context. For example, a Mexican American may refer to himself or herself as Mexican in terms of cultural identification, as Hispanic when dealing with governmental agencies, and as Latino in reference to social justice issues.

Thus the same terminology may please some people while offending others. The best way to protect against offense is to ask the people to whom you are referring which terms they prefer—and to keep asking as the social and political context changes. Donors appreciate candor and interest in their culture. Because many diverse communities have experienced racial discrimination and even violence, you may expect them to be sensitive about the words you use to address and describe them. As members of these communities become more familiar with you and your institution, some of the sensitivity and distrust will decrease.

Ethnic and Racial Categories

The broad categories we employ in this book—African American, Asian American, Latino, and Native American—are indeed simplistic. Although each category describes people who have common characteristics, each racial and ethnic group is composed of numerous distinct nationalities and tribes that have their own traditions, religions, customs, and history. This book is a first cut at describing fundraising strategies aimed at non-Caucasians and has of necessity lumped very diverse cultures into the four main headings. We anticipate that future works will describe specific fundraising techniques and activities particularly appropriate for specific nationalities and regions.

Please note that the ethnic and racial categories we use in the book are not the same race and ethnic labels that the U.S. Census Bureau uses. We include the census terms so that the reader will recognize them as such when we use them in this book. The census terms are *white; Spanish, Hispanic,* or *Latino; black* or *African American; American Indian* and *Alaska Native; Asian;* and *Native Hawaiian and other Pacific Islander.* Although the exact difference in the meaning of the two sets of terms is not critical in the context of fundraising from diverse communities, we must acknowledge the fact that this book uses terms that differ from those the census uses. The census nevertheless provides significant data leading all nonprofits to consider the need to expand their fundraising strategies to include prospective donors from the four diverse cultures that we identify.

May 2002   Diana S. Newman
Columbus, Ohio

This book is dedicated to all those working to make their organizations open and welcome to people from diverse backgrounds as donors, board and staff members, service providers and receivers, suppliers, and vendors.

It is also dedicated to my husband, Dennis, and our three children, Barbara Newman LaBine, John Newman, and Elizabeth Newman, who remind me daily of the value of diverse points of view.

Acknowledgments

Many people from many backgrounds and diverse experiences across the United States have contributed to this collaborative effort. I am indebted to all the individuals with whom I have had conversations, meetings, discussions, and conferences for helping me along this journey. Their insights, openness, honesty, and trust continue to amaze, humble, and invigorate me.

The colleagues with whom I worked on *Cultures of Caring* have been intimately involved with this book. They provided suggestions of and introductions to people who have firsthand fundraising experiences in specific ethnic communities for me to interview. The people they recommended gave me additional suggestions of organizations that have done effective work with diverse donors. Thus I was able to contact an increasing network of people across the United States engaged in the extraordinary work of promoting philanthropy to current and prospective donors of richly diverse backgrounds. I am deeply grateful to the scores of nonprofit CEOs and development directors who took time from their busy schedules to talk with us and share their thoughtful insights and experiences.

The following individuals were particularly helpful in identifying effective ways to reach prospective donors in African American communities: Mark Dennis (The Alford Group), James T. Ellis (Detroit attorney), Dr. Walter Earl Fluker (Morehouse College),

Jean Fountain (Minneapolis Foundation), Lea Gilmore (Association of Baltimore Area Grantmakers), Mellody Hopson (Ariel Capital Management), Erica Hunt (Twenty-First Century Foundation), Annette Jefferson (J. Ashburn Jr. Youth Center), Rev. Paul Martin (Macedonia Baptist Church), William Merritt (National Black United Fund), Calvin Pressley (Boulé fraternity), Pier C. Rogers (Associated Black Charities of New York), Erika Seth (Associated Black Charities of Maryland), Lorraine Holmes Settles (The AFRAM Group), Pat Solomon (Michigan consultant), and Sullivan Robinson (Congress of National Black Churches, Inc.).

Those with whom I spoke about practices engaging Asian donors include David Baker (On Lok Senior Health Services), Barnett Baron (Asia Foundation), Anni Chung (Self-Help for the Elderly), Vishakha N. Desai (Asia Society), Jane T. Eng (Chinatown Health Clinic), Robbie Fabian (California consultant), Margaret Fung (Asian American Legal Defense and Education Fund), Ilean Her (Council on Asian Pacific Minnesotans), Irene Hirano (Japanese American National Museum), Gail Kong (Asian Pacific Fund), Cao O (Asian American Federation of New York), Moira Shek (Asian Americans/Pacific Islanders in Philanthropy), Penelope Haru Snipper (Minnesota consultant), Gwynne Tuan (China Institute), and Minoru Tonai (Japanese American Cultural and Community Center).

The following people ably described the Latino communities, motivations for giving to charities, and techniques for cultivating contributions to charities: Diana Campoamor and Michelle Sargent (Hispanics in Philanthropy), Lorraine Cortés-Vasquez (The Hispanic Federation), Pete Garcia (Chicanos por la Causa), Adam Martinez (Baylor College of Medicine), Kate McLean (Ventura County Community Foundation, Destino 2000 Fund), Ana Gloria Rivas-Vasquez (Carollton School of the Sacred Heart), Lili Santiago de Silva (El Museo del Barrio), Beatriz Olvera Stotzer (New Economics for Women), Carlos Tortolero (Mexican Fine Arts Center Museum), and Raul Yzaguirre (National Council of La Raza).

Native Americans who shared their wisdom include Cynthia Adams (Grantstation.com), Alice Azure (United Way of Southeast Connecticut), Sherry Salway Black (First Nations Development Institute), Barbara Bratone (American Indian College Fund), Donna Chavis (Native Americans in Philanthropy), Michelle Henderson (American Indian Business Leaders), Roy Huhndorf (Alaska philanthropic leader), Diane Kaplan (Rasmuson Foundation), Tia Oros (Seventh Generation Fund for Indian Development), Barbara Poley (Hopi Foundation), Mary Lu Prosser (Native American Rights Fund), Carla Roberts (Arizona Community Foundation), Joanne Stately (Two Feathers Fund of the Saint Paul Foundation), Thomas Sweeney (National Museum of American Indians), and Diane Wyss (National Indian Gaming Association).

I also talked with numerous people at mainstream organizations about their efforts to reach diverse constituencies and donors. Those whose contributions were particularly helpful include Augusta Rivera Campbell (St. Jude Children's Research Hospital), Viney Chandler (United Way of Metropolitan Tarrant County), Steve Coulter (San Francisco Public Library), Mary Foote Davis (Chicago Historical Society), Gary Dollar (United Way of Greater St. Louis), Dorry Elias (Minority Executive Directors Coalition), Margaret Epstein and Deborah Thomas (Greater New Orleans Foundation), Heime Garcia (Bill and Melinda Gates Foundation), Mary Kaufman-Cranney (YMCA of Greater Seattle), Dean Owen (WorldVision), Sheryle Powell and Katina Fullen (United Way of Central Ohio), Bill Pratt (Montana Community Foundation), Marissa Robich and Cara Storm (San Francisco Museum of Modern Art), Steve Suda (Stanford University), Charlene Tarver (Georgetown University), and Joe Young (Chicago Symphony Orchestra).

The prior work of my colleagues, Mindy Berry, Jessica Chao, Henry A. J. Ramos, and Mary-Frances Winters, in *Cultures of Caring* informed this book, particularly in the background descriptions of each of the four cultural segments we describe in Chapter Two. They each reviewed the first draft of this manuscript and offered many helpful comments and suggestions. Working with them has broadened my understanding of this complex topic and deepened my appreciation of their knowledge and experience.

Johanna Vondeling, editor at Jossey-Bass, led me through the mystery of publishing a first book. Jenny Ledman designed the figures in Chapter One. Most of all, I owe a particular debt of gratitude to Joanne Scanlan, senior vice president of the Council on Foundations, for recommending that I write this book and for serving as the project coordinator with Jossey-Bass and the four contributing writers.

To all of the above and many more, I offer my sincere thanks for your help and encouragement.

—D.S.N.

About the Author

Diana S. Newman is principal of Philanthropic Resource Group, a consulting firm that provides strategic planning, evaluation, and fundraising services for nonprofit organizations and financial institutions, specializing in gift planning and endowment building. She attended Oberlin College and is a certified fundraising executive. Prior to establishing Philanthropic Resource Group, Newman was vice president for advancement for the Columbus Foundation, one of the ten largest community foundations in the United States. She was also the founding director of the Ohio Historical Foundation, the fundraising arm of the Ohio Historical Society.

Newman is an author, with Mindy Berry, Jessica Chao, Henry A. J. Ramos, and Mary-Frances Winters, of *Cultures of Caring: Philanthropy in Diverse American Communities*, funded by the Ford, W. K. Kellogg, and David and Lucile Packard Foundations and published by the Council on Foundations in 1999. She has written articles appearing in such national publications as *Planned Giving Today* and *Journal of Gift Planning*.

Newman was a cofounder of the original Leave A Legacy program in Columbus, which was adopted as a national model in 1996 by the National Committee on Planned Giving and is now offered in more than 150 communities across North America. In addition Newman is a member of the faculty of the Community Foundations Institute at the Center on Philanthropy at Indiana University and wrote the curriculum for its course, Community Foundation Fundamentals.

She served on the board of trustees for the National Committee on Planned Giving, chairing its Leave A Legacy Committee. She served on the Central Ohio board of trustees for the Association of Fundraising Professionals and as president of the board for the Central Ohio Planned Giving Council, as well as on the boards of numerous other local and regional organizations. A frequent presenter at international, national, and regional conferences, Newman consults with a variety of organizations, including community foundations, regional associations of grantmakers, nonprofit organizations, and financial institutions.

About the Contributors

MINDY BERRY is vice president of The Alford Group Inc., a consulting firm that offers organizational and fund development advice to the nonprofit sector. She received a master's degree in public policy from Georgetown University and also studied at the London School of Economics and Political Science. Berry is coauthor, with Rebecca Adamson, of *The Wisdom of the Giveaway* (2000), a curriculum guide published by the Center for the Study of Philanthropy at the City University of New York. With Jessica Chao, she is the coauthor of *Engaging Diverse Communities for and Through Philanthropy* (2001). Berry served in the federal government in the Office of the Secretary of Labor and as a senior policy analyst at the National Endowment for the Arts. Her experience in the nonprofit sector includes management, research, development, board membership, and teaching service in such organizations as Independent Sector, Georgetown University, the Washington Child Development Council, and the Supreme Court of the United States.

JESSICA CHAO is an independent consultant offering services in organizational development, institutional planning, and program research, assessment, and design. A graduate of Barnard College, she received a master's degree in education from Columbia University's Teachers College. Chao was formerly the vice president of the Wallace–Reader's Digest Funds, where she developed one of the largest private sector arts and culture programs in the country. With Berry, she is the coauthor of *Engaging Diverse Communities for and Through Philanthropy*. Her other professional experiences include positions at the Public Broadcasting Service and the Cultural Alliance of Greater Washington. She is currently a member of the advisory committee of the National Center for Family Philanthropy. Formerly, she was a board member of the New York Regional Association of Grantmakers, Asian Americans/Pacific Islanders in Philanthropy, and the Ridgewood Arts Council.

HENRY A. J. RAMOS is principal of Mauer Kunst Consulting, a firm specializing in program development and research for foundations, businesses, and nonprofit organizations. He holds degrees in political economics, law, and public administration from the University of California, Berkeley, and Harvard University. Ramos is the author of the book *The American GI Forum: In Pursuit of the Dream, 1948–1983* (published in 1998, a historical recounting of the nation's oldest Latino veterans' and civil rights organization), and the editor, with Diana Campoamor and William A. Diaz, of *Nuevos Senderos: Reflections on Hispanics and Philanthropy* (1999), both published by the University of Houston's Arte Público Press. Ramos's recent clients include the California Endowment, the Carnegie Corporation of New York, the Ford Foundation, Nike, and the W. K. Kellogg Foundation. He serves on the boards of directors of the Mexican Museum of San Francisco, the Soros/Emma Lazarus Fund, and Hispanics in Philanthropy.

MARY-FRANCES WINTERS is president of the Winters Group, Inc., a consulting firm specializing in research, strategic planning, training, and public speaking, with emphasis in ethnic and multicultural issues. She received undergraduate and M.B.A. degrees from the University of Rochester. Prior to founding the Winters Group in 1984, Winters spent eleven years at Eastman Kodak Company. She serves on the boards of trustees of the University of Rochester (as its first African American female trustee), Roberts Wesleyan College (which presented her with an honorary doctorate in 1997), Chase Manhattan Bank, and the Greater Rochester Chamber of Commerce. She has served on the boards of the Rochester Area Community Foundation, United Way, and the national board of directors of Girl Scouts of the USA, among others.

1

How Changing Demographics Are Changing Philanthropy

African American, Asian American, Latino, and Native American communities represent both significant portions of the United States population and substantial amounts of untapped wealth. This book provides background, information, and insights to engage diverse individuals and families in the fundraising programs of charitable organizations.

It is important for nonprofit organizations to include these four ethnic and racial groups in their fundraising programs for two reasons: (1) the population of the United States is becoming increasingly diverse, and (2) the income and wealth of these diverse populations are significant and growing.

After making the case for engaging prospective donors, this chapter introduces the four broad population groups that are the focus of the book and provides documentation of their diversity, size, and dramatic growth. It also provides fundraising models as alternatives to the traditional donor pyramid of giving. Chapter Two discusses the significant wealth and philanthropic influence of members of diverse population groups.

THE SCOPE OF THE ISSUE

Nonprofit organizations raised more than $168 billion from individuals in 2000 (Kaplan, 2001). Most of these organizations sought gifts from the white, non-Latino population that this book will refer to as Caucasian or white. Nonprofit organizations will (and should) continue to raise funds from this large group. Caucasians represent nearly 70 percent of the U.S. population and control much of its wealth (U.S. Bureau of the Census, 2001e). This book, however, is designed to take fundraising beyond present practices and to explore new groups of prospective donors and new ways to reach them.

The census of 2000 established that more than 30 percent of the total U.S. population is nonwhite, and that number is likely to approach 50 percent by the middle of this century (U.S. Bureau of the Census, 2000a). Although not all areas of the country are equally affected by all ethnic and racial groups, nearly every state and county will experience (or already has experienced) tangible population changes.

This book helps you develop new strategies necessary to enlarge your donor base and diversify your donor pool. It gives you information about the philanthropic backgrounds and motivations of the four distinct and diverse groups. It provides examples of fundraising programs that have worked for other organizations in these diverse communities. Some of these will work for you and your organization.

WHY YOUR NONPROFIT SHOULD ENGAGE DIVERSE PROSPECTIVE DONORS

The mission of your organization, as a public charity, is what distinguishes it from other organizations in the nonprofit sector. It speaks to a wide range of stakeholders and constituents, at least some of whom are members of these four significant population groups.

Yet the fundraising departments of mainstream organizations—and, frankly, many ethnic-specific organizations—largely ignore these diverse populations, whom they frequently consider recipients rather than contributors and providers of services. This characterization is both shortsighted and misleading. These are populations that are growing in numbers, influence, and wealth.

If a nonprofit organization is going to thrive in the twenty-first century, it must not only recognize and serve diverse cultures but also

The mission of your organization, as a public charity, is what distinguishes it from others in the nonprofit sector

raise substantial portions of its monies from them. It cannot continue to exclude ethnically and racially diverse prospective donors, who represent 30 percent of the United States population.

In order to attract and include any or all of these diverse populations, an organization must create a development plan that is appropriate to the specific group it wishes to approach. This is simply good fundraising practice. The organization cannot assume that programs it has used effectively with white donors will also work for new and different populations. To develop new fundraising programs, it must explore the philanthropic backgrounds and interests of the people it wishes to attract. The organization must be willing to let go of its standard operating practices and procedures in order to find new and exciting strategies designed to work in new environments.

This is a new and emerging field in the philanthropic landscape. Most of the successful programs we describe in this book are less than ten years old. The work of the original innovators is still taking shape, and measurable results are sometimes limited. Opening doors to engage constituents and encourage contributions in diverse populations is a work in progress. Join us as we explore the pathways to diverse donors.

A NATION OF INCREASING DIVERSITY

The U.S. Census Bureau (2001e) reported that the United States was home to 281.4 million people. Of this number, 69 percent are Caucasians. Traditional fundraising strategies have been geared to the Caucasian segment of the population. To state it differently, nonprofit organizations have not given attention to more than 30 percent of the current population.

According to the 2000 census, the makeup of the current population is as follows:

Non-Hispanic White	69.1 percent
Non-Hispanic Black or African American	12.6 percent
Spanish, Hispanic, or Latino	12.5 percent
Non-Hispanic Asian and Other Pacific Islander	3.9 percent
Non-Hispanic American Indian and Alaska Native	1.0 percent

A fundamental premise of this work is that 30 percent of the population is significant and substantial, a percentage too large for responsible nonprofit organizations to ignore. It is significant not only in its size but also in the growth pattern it has experienced. While the U.S. Caucasian population grew 5.3 percent between 1990 and 2000, the non-Hispanic African American population grew 21.1 percent, and the non-Hispanic Asian population increased by 74.3 percent. Hispanics, classified by the census as an ethnic group regardless of race, increased by nearly 58 percent (U.S. Bureau of the Census, 2001j).

Caucasians accounted for 69 percent of the people living in the United States in 2000, down from 76 percent in 1990. By contrast, the U.S. minority populations exploded. In the last ten years, the minority population grew 43 percent to 86.9 million people, or 31 percent of the total population (U.S. Bureau of the Census, 2001j).

This impressive growth is, for Asians and Latinos, linked significantly to recent immigrants and their children. The U.S. Census Bureau estimated in 1999 that 88 percent of Asian and Pacific Islander students had at least one foreign-born parent. Likewise, 65 percent of Hispanic students had at least one foreign-born parent. This is in contrast to 11 percent of African American students and 7 percent of non-Hispanic white students. These statistics suggest a significant and continuing growth in both

Asian and Hispanic populations (Asian American Federation of New York, 2001a).

African American Demographic Data

The nation's African American population totaled approximately 35.5 million at the start of this century. The African American population is young, with an estimated median age of 30.4 years as of November 2000, more than five years younger than the median for the U.S. population as a whole (U.S. Bureau of the Census, 2001k).

The African American population is young, with an estimated median age of 30.4 years as of November 2000, more than five years younger than the median for the U.S. population as a whole.

Nationwide 53 percent of African Americans resided in the central cities of metropolitan areas. The majority of them (54 percent) lived in the South, with 19 percent each in the Northeast and the Midwest, and 8 percent in the West (U.S. Bureau of the Census, 2001c).

In 2000 79 percent of African Americans age 25 and over had completed at least high school, and 17 percent had earned at least a bachelor's degree. About one million African Americans had an advanced degree—for example, a master's, Ph.D., or J.D. (U.S. Bureau of the Census, 2000d).

Asian American Demographic Data

Asian Americans have almost doubled their numbers in each of the past four decades. They now total 10.9 million compared with 250,000 in 1940 (U.S. Bureau of the Census, 2000c).

Stella Shao (1995) broadly defines more than twenty countries as the Asia-Pacific region: the area from Japan to Iran, and from Central Asia to New Zealand, Australia, and the Pacific Islands. The following list from Shao (p. 30) identifies major Asian and Pacific Islander groups.

Asian Groups by Ethnicity	Pacific Islander Groups by Ethnicity
Chinese	Polynesian
Filipino	Hawaiian
Japanese	Samoan
Asian Indian	Tongan
Korean	Other Polynesian
Vietnamese	Micronesian
Cambodian	Guamanian
Hmong	Other Micronesian
Laotian	Melanesian
Thai	Other Pacific Islander
Other Asians	

Asian Americans are diverse in many important ways including culture, language, religion, economic class, immigrant or citizenship status, and length of time in the United States. They came to this country for a broad range of reasons—from seeking political asylum or religious freedom to career advancement, from escaping war or poverty to building businesses or expanding family fortunes. Likewise each immigrant wave experienced acceptance (or the lack thereof) by mainstream Americans in different degrees and ways, many enduring racist violence and outright discrimination. Most experience the "perpetual foreigner" syndrome, which Jessica Chao (2001) describes as the assumption by some people that those who do not look Caucasian or who speak with an accent must be foreigners rather than U.S. citizens.

The United States experienced a rapid increase in Asian immigrants after the passing of the Immigration Act of 1965 (which lifted restrictive Asian quotas), the end of the Vietnam War, the opening of relations with the People's Republic of China in 1979, and later immigration regulations that favored letting in people of specific highly skilled professions and occupations. By 1990 approximately 68.2 percent of Asian Americans were foreign-born, with a high of 93.9 percent among Laotians and a low of 28.4 percent among the Japanese (Shinagawa, 1996). Asian Americans had a median age of 30 years in 1990, younger than the national median of 33 years. Only 6 percent of Asian Americans were 65 years old or older, compared with 13 percent for the total population (U.S. Bureau of the Census, 1993a).

Although the gateway cities of Honolulu, New York, San Francisco, and Los Angeles have the most concentrated Asian American populations, large communities also exist in Chicago, Houston, Washington, D.C., and in many urban and suburban areas of the West Coast. The mix of ethnic groups varies from region to region and city to city. Six out of ten Asian Americans reside in California, New York, Texas, and Hawaii (U.S. Bureau of the Census, 2000b).

Latino Demographic Data

The 2000 census counted 35.3 million Latinos, or 13 percent of the total U.S. population. This is an increase of 13 million people (58 percent) since 1990 (U.S. Bureau of the Census, 2001f).

Latino Group	1990 Population	2000 Population	Increase
Mexican	13.5 million	20.6 million	52.9 percent
Puerto Rican	2.7 million	3.4 million	24.9 percent
Cuban	1 million	1.2 million	18.9 percent
Other Hispanics	5.1 million	10 million	96.6 percent

Among Latinos permanently residing in the United States, 80 percent are U.S. citizens; most of the others are documented immigrants who have obtained permission to live and work here as permanent residents. At present, the United States has the fifth largest Hispanic population of any country in the world (Wagner and Deck, 1999).

Of those with Latino backgrounds, 63 percent are of Mexican descent; 12 percent are Puerto Rican; and about four percent are

Cuban. Nearly 15 percent of Latinos in the United States are recent immigrants and refugees from Central America. Many Latino families can trace their roots back hundreds of years in what is now the Southwestern United States, California, and Florida prior to the acquisition of these territories from Spain and Mexico. Whereas 25.7 percent of the U.S. population was under 18 years of age in 2000, fully 35.0 percent of Hispanics were 18 or younger. The median age for Hispanics was 25.0 years, 10.3 years below the median for the entire U.S. population. These figures vary dramatically by nationality, from Mexicans, with a median age of 24.2 years, to Cubans, at 40.7 years (U.S. Bureau of the Census, 2001f).

Although Latinos from different countries share the same language, word meanings and usage differ from country to country, as do traditions and philosophies of life. Moreover immigration patterns, education, and income—all of which have a direct effect on philanthropic engagement—also vary.

Native American Demographic Data

Approximately 2.5 million American Indians and Alaska Natives make up 1 percent of the U.S. population (U.S. Bureau of the Census, 2001j). Communities of Native Americans differ in lineage, language, location, size, histories, means of survival, religion, and social and political systems.

Approximately 2.5 million American Indians and Alaska Natives make up 1 percent of the U.S. population.

Currently, the United States government recognizes 556 tribes, of which 226 are in Alaska. States recognize an additional two hundred tribes. The five largest tribes, if we combine the Cherokee, Navaho, Chippewa, Sioux, and Choctaw peoples—account for approximately 40 percent of the Native American population (U.S. Bureau of the Census, 1995a).

According to the 1990 census, 22 percent of Native Americans live on reservations and trust lands. Patterns of movement in and out of reservations are fluid, depending on economic and personal circumstances. The incidence of poverty remains disproportionately high in Native communities. For example, the three-year (1996–1999) average poverty rate for Native Americans was 25.9 percent, compared to 11.6 percent for the national population. In 1990, fully 39 percent of Native Americans were under 20 years old, compared to 29 percent of the total U.S. population. The median age of the Native American population was 26 years, considerably younger than the U.S. median age of 33 years (U.S. Bureau of the Census, 1993b).

Four states—California, Texas, Oklahoma, and Florida—account for 34 percent of the nonfarm business firms owned by Native Americans; three other states—Alaska (10.6 percent), Oklahoma (5.4 percent), and New Mexico (5.2 percent)—have the largest percentage of firms owned by Native Americans (U.S. Bureau of the Census, 2001b).

Projections for the Future

The U.S. Census Bureau projects that the population in 2050 will total 403 million people:

Non-Hispanic white	52.8 percent
Non-Hispanic black or African American	13.2 percent
Spanish, Hispanic, or Latino	24.3 percent
Non-Hispanic Asian and other Pacific Islander	8.9 percent
Non-Hispanic American Indian and Alaska Native	0.8 percent

If the projection proves true, the percentages of both the Asian and Latino populations will have doubled in fifty years. The percentage of African Americans will increase by less than 1 percent, and the white population will drop by more than 16 percent. The Native American population is predicted to drop from 1 percent to slightly under 1 percent in the same time period (see Table 1.1).

Table 1.1. United States Population Projections.

	2000	2050	Increase
Total population	281.4 million	403.7 million	44%
African American	34.7 million	53.5 million	54%
Asian American	10.9 million	35.8 million	228%
Latino	35.3 million	98.2 million	178%
Native American	2.3 million	3.2 million	39%
White, non-Hispanic	194.50 million	213.0 million	10%

Source: U.S. Bureau of the Census, 2001e, 2001h.

The impact of the predicted population growth will have greater significance in some geographic areas than in others. Other than Native Americans, the non-white population is overwhelmingly found in urban areas. Latinos are concentrated in California, Texas, Florida, and New York. Nearly all Asian Americans live in gateway cities, primarily in the large metropolitan areas of San Francisco, Los Angeles, and New York City, although the 2000 census shows that the growth rate of Asian Americans was especially strong in rural and outlying areas. The so-called minority population in 2025 will exceed the white non-Hispanic population in Hawaii, California, New Mexico, Texas, and the District of Columbia, according to the Minority Business Development Agency of the U.S. Department of Commerce (U.S. Bureau of the Census, 2000g). Other populous states, such as Florida, New York, Illinois, Georgia, New Jersey, and Virginia, will not be far behind. More than half of all Native Americans live in six states: Oklahoma, California, Arizona, New Mexico, Alaska, and Washington.

This demographic and U.S. census data may not apply to your local community. For instance, although African Americans and Latinos are the two largest minorities in the country, your community may contain more Asian Americans or Native Americans. Or perhaps the minority may be the majority of the population in your particular community, a growing trend in many urban areas.

Although Mexican Americans are the majority of Latinos, your community's Latino population may be primarily Costa Ricans. Likewise although the Chinese and Filipinos are the largest ethnic groups of Asian Americans, the Asian Americans in your area may be Hmong—who are among the smallest groups of Asian Americans in the United States. Although African Americans are often thought of as descendants of U.S. slaves, a specific African American community may consist primarily of recent African or Caribbean immigrants. And Native Americans have roots in many tribes with very different customs, languages, histories, and geographical origins.

Finally all four racial and ethnic populations are younger than the U.S. Caucasian population. According to Melissa Therrien and Roberto Ramirez (2000), 35 percent of Latinos were under eighteen years old, and only 5 percent were sixty-five or older; for Caucasians, the corresponding proportions were 25.7 percent and 12.4 percent. In 2000 the median age for all Asians was 30.1 years compared to 35.3 years for the U.S. population. This varied greatly across groups of different national origins, with Japanese, among the oldest of the Asian American subgroups, having a median age of 36.3, and the Hmong, among the most recent refugees, with a median age of 12.5 years (see Table 1.2).

These data indicate that we cannot assume the continuation of white European-based cultural traditions and practices for much of the U.S. population in the future.

These data indicate that we cannot assume the continuation of white European-based cultural traditions and practices for much of the U.S. population in the future.

PHILANTHROPY DEFINED

Merriam-Webster's Collegiate Dictionary (10th ed.) defines *philanthropy* as "goodwill to fellowmen; especially active effort to promote human welfare." Yet many mainstream organizations and fundraisers apply

Table 1.2. Age of United States Population by Race and Ethnicity (2000).

	Under 18	Over 65	Median Age
Total population	26.0%	12.0%	35.3
African American	32.5%	7.9%	29.5
Asian American	28.6%	6.2%	30.1
Latino	35.0%	4.9%	25.8
Native American	33.6%	6.3%	28.7
White, non-Hispanic	22.6%	15.0%	38.6

Source: U.S. Bureau of the Census, 2000a.

the word only to major financial contributions. Many members of diverse communities associate philanthropy only with wealthy white men—such as Andrew Carnegie and John D. Rockefeller. This book uses the term *philanthropy* as *Merriam-Webster* defines it.

Multiple Meanings of Philanthropy

Philanthropy includes sharing of time, skills, and money; giving to meet immediate needs; and promoting behavior that mitigates the effects of future problems and takes advantage of future opportunities. A compelling need or crisis stimulates immediate generosity and well-executed programs that address critical issues. A donor's passion and commitment about an issue, a movement, or an idea stimulates longer-term philanthropy.

In this book we contrast institutional philanthropy with personal philanthropy. By *institutional philanthropy* (sometimes called *organized philanthropy* or *formal philanthropy*), we mean philanthropy governed by an organization's formal policies and procedures, as differentiated from the charitable activities of individuals in direct response to immediate needs. Institutional philanthropy, in simplistic terms, involves relatively wealthy individuals giving gifts of money to favored nonprofit institutions (in which they often serve as board members or advisers), private foundations, community foundations, or other charitable entities.

In some communities, philanthropy used to mean *noblesse oblige*, the responsibility of the rich to provide charity to the deserving poor. Today, according to African American philanthropist Jean Fairfax (1995, p. 10), philanthropy is "a communal enterprise, a manifestation of a community whose members care for one another."

James Joseph, former president of the Council on Foundations, writes that in the annals of American philanthropy, "the real heroes were the ordinary people who, with meager resources, accomplished extraordinary deeds. Mired in poverty, racked by frequent epidemics, and oppressed by vicious racism, the poor reached out to the poor, sharing what little they had with each other" (1991, p. 7).

"'Philanthropy' in the Native sense means the tradition of sharing and honoring," writes Rebecca Adamson (1999, p. 8), president of First Nations Development Institute, "which is generally not a question of altruism or charity but of mutual responsibility. In this worldview, both giver and receiver benefit from the gift. To share wealth is a responsibility of every caring member of a community."

When we use terms such as *charitable giving* and *philanthropy*, we are describing what James Joseph calls "voluntary activity for the well-being of the community rather than private action to achieve individual wealth" (1995, p. xiii). We include gifts of time and money, daily acts of kindness and caring, and the more public formal acts of institutional philanthropy.

In *Philanthropy in Communities of Color* (1999), authors Smith, Shue, Vest, and Villareal described philanthropy as a form of social exchange, in which donor and recipient trade both tangible and intangible resources. Intangible resources received by donors might include personal satisfaction; discharge of moral, social, or familial obligations; and increased social standing. Thus philanthropy is an articulation of the donor's values. The act of giving time, treasure, and talent is a measure of what is important in all diverse cultures.

Traditions of Philanthropy

When we asked diverse donors to describe the traditions of philanthropy in their families or communities during interviews for *Cultures of Caring* (Council on Foundations, 1999), they often told us that there were no traditions of philanthropy. (This is true for white donors as well, who usually did not grow up within wealthy families.) However, when we asked about how friends help each other or share their good fortune, the responses were robust and filled with specific examples of giving and volunteering at all levels of the income spectrum, not just the affluent.

Immigrants have a strong tradition of helping others in informal yet direct ways. A U.S. family sends a portion of its monthly earnings to its native country to support other family members. An aunt pays for her nephew's college tuition. A cousin takes a newly arrived family member into her home while he finds a job and saves to move on his own. These are all examples of informal giving that occur in diverse communities, yet they are not measured in studies of philanthropic giving.

Immigrants have a strong tradition of helping others in informal yet direct ways.

Lorraine Holmes Settles, head of The AFRAM Group, an African American–owned fundraising firm, described examples of charitable giving by African Americans that are not measurable or deductible for income tax purposes but nonetheless are altruistic good works: paying for a relative to go to college, keeping the elderly at home rather than in a nursing home, and raising a child who is not one's own.

Many individuals do not consider the money or the help they give to extended family or to members of their churches or other voluntary associations as philanthropy or even as charitable giving. They view this type of giving as their responsibility as members of the community or as an obligation to give back for the good of the community as a whole. Grassroots philanthropy (both giving and receiving) has a communal orientation as demonstrated in the rent parties of African Americans, the rotating credit circles of Asian Americans, and the potlatches of Native Americans.

Some Caucasians view the giving of in-kind gifts as an excuse for not giving more financially. People in all four diverse communities value volunteering as much or more than contributing money. Adam Martinez, development director for Baylor College of Medicine in Houston, said, "The very foundations of American society must rethink what philanthropy is about so it remains relevant in this new century. We must do a better job of documenting and valuing time and talent."

One of the focus group participants in a study from the Baltimore Giving Project (1999) said, "We never seem to count time as a legitimate aspect of philanthropy. But many of us have given a great deal of time when we had no money to offer. There needs to be a way to account for the giving of ourselves in service."

Your messages—both verbal and written—should communicate that your organization values both institutional philanthropy and personal philanthropy. People use multiple philanthropic strategies and choose to use these strategies under different life circumstances and within different social contexts. One is not better or more generous than the other; they are simply different. We will discuss these concepts more fully in Chapter Two.

Your messages—both verbal and written—should communicate that your organization values both institutional philanthropy and personal philanthropy.

MODELS OF FUNDRAISING

Those of us involved in professional fundraising are familiar with the traditional donor pyramid of giving (see Figure 1.1).

Figure 1.1. Traditional Donor Pyramid of Giving.

Personal solicitation — Planned Gifts

Capital or Major Gifts

Small events
Personalized direct mail
Telephone solicitation — Repeat Donors

First-Time Donors

Mass solicitation
Special events
Telemarketing
Direct mail — Universe of Prospective Donors

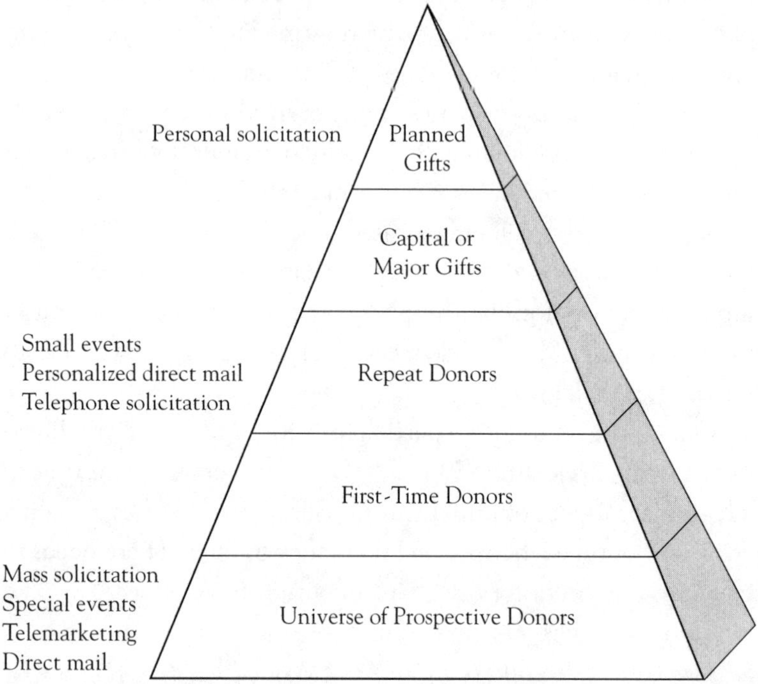

In the traditional donor pyramid of giving, the organization begins its development efforts with a broad base of prospective donors that includes board members and volunteers; clients, patients, students, and visitors who know the organization; selected categories of people based on factors such as interests, zip codes, jobs, and wealth; and the general public. Through advertising, special events, direct mail, telemarketing, and other methods, the organization raises small donations from many people.

Once the donor has made the first gift, that person is a candidate for annual support at increasingly higher levels. After several years of annual support, the donor is ripe to be asked for a larger commitment to a capital campaign or special project. When the organization receives one large gift, the donor may receive a personal visit by an influential person to ask for a major gift and long-term commitment. At the top of the pyramid are those rare donors who will complete gift plans naming the organization as a beneficiary of charitable provisions in wills, trusts, or other types of planned gifts.

New Models Needed for Diverse Ethnicities

The traditional model works well for organizations that raise most of their individual charitable gifts from white donors. Many of the principles embedded in the pyramid are important for all ethnicities of prospective donors, such as the concepts that fundraising is based on personal relationships and that people give because they are asked. As we discussed the patterns of voluntary involvement and motivations for giving with diverse donors and nonprofit executives, however, we heard repeatedly that the standard pyramid of giving did not apply in many cultures. The reasons varied from the pyramid's perceived inaccessibility to its hierarchical nature, from its formality to the implication that those on the top are standing on the backs of those below.

"The pyramid model will never work in Latino communities," said Lorraine Cortés-Vasquez at The Hispanic Federation, "because the model is nearly flat in our community. Most people will give small amounts for at least another generation. For us, volume is the answer, not large gifts." As an example, she described the Puerto Rican Day Parade, New York's largest annual parade, as a wonderful day of pride drawing a million people. "I always think if only I could get each person to do two things: vote and give twenty cents to a charity," Cortés-Vasquez said, "just think of the difference that would make!"

The biggest stumbling block, however, seems to be that the pyramid model does not provide for the element of time: length of time in the United States, amount of time of financial stability and wealth, the lifetime experiences of prospective donors, time of life for the donor and the donor's children, and the donor's number of years of familiarity with the nonprofit organization.

The Continuum of Philanthropy

In a panel presentation for the Council on Foundations in 1999 following the publication of *Cultures of Caring,* Jessica Chao introduced the concept of a continuum of philanthropy applicable to Asian Americans. She later developed the model more fully (2001, pp. 57–79). It has resonated not only with Asian Americans but also with African Americans and especially Latinos (see Figure 1.2).

The continuum of philanthropy model was designed primarily for immigrant populations. As Figure 1.2 illustrates, it starts with families concerned with survival and basic needs, who freely share resources with others in similar circumstances. In the middle are those who are able to help others who have less. On the right are people ready to invest in their communities and in other institutions to accomplish visionary goals.

To progress along the continuum, the individual must attain increased levels of financial, cultural, and social stability. As families make permanent homes and become vested in the community, they move from left to right along this continuum.

Survival

The first phase of the continuum is the struggle through the early immigrant years or, in the case of former slaves, early years of freedom. They share resources—money, goods, skills, and information—with family members and peers.

The first phase of the continuum is the struggle through the early immigrant years or, in the case of former slaves, early years of freedom.

For most the struggle is to establish a home and some foothold on the economic ladder of opportunity. In their isolation and need, people form voluntary associations and mutual aid societies based not only on race and ethnicity, but also on finer distinctions of village of origin, language dialect, clan, or religion. The associations provide a myriad of services including information

Figure 1.2. Continuum of Philanthropy: African American, Asian American, Latino.

		Survive	Help	Invest
Living Stages		Highly personal sharing Known recipients Informal, direct, immediate responses	Personal giving and involvement Ethnic-specific Responsive, compassionate	Ethnic-specific Pan-ethnic and mainstream Formal, proactive, long term, planned
		Increasing cultural, social and financial stability →		
Giving Stages	*Motivation*	Sharing among social and economic peers	Giving to less fortunate Desire to give back Identifying with need Supporting projects	Empowering vision Building the ideal community Producing programs
	Vehicles	Family Voluntary associations Faith-based organizations Mutual aid societies	Family and voluntary associations Ethnic organizations Community causes Faith-based organizations Nonprofit organizations	Ethnic and pan-ethnic organizations Noncommunity causes Mainstream organizations Private and community foundations
	Causes	Family or friends in need Children and elderly Remittances	Family and friends Education Cultural heritage Civil rights or social justice Health Remittances	Colleges and universities Cultural institutions Civil rights or economic development Hospitals and medical research

about housing and jobs, aid to the elderly, rotating credit circles, and support for medical or funeral expenses.

Giving to Help

Once individuals reach a level of financial and emotional stability, they frequently reach out to help others in greater need, an almost spontaneous reaction to deeply felt needs. African Americans, Asian Americans, and Latinos may not feel secure until their children, siblings, parents, cousins, aunts, uncles, nieces, and nephews are also stable. The urge to help is often motivated by a desire to give back and by deep levels of compassion, triggered either by the type of person in need or the type of need.

The giving has no expectation of return, and it will benefit more distant recipients, often through voluntary associations and eventually through nonprofit organizations. U.S.-born Asians and Latinos grow away from the mutual assistance associations and have little connections with the country of origin. As the community's human and social welfare issues become less acute, people may become more interested in civic and civil rights organizations. Interest in relieving poverty, for example, may lead to supporting programs to fight poverty in other communities.

Investment in Philanthropy

As families become stable and finances secure, people begin to visualize the ideal community. People attain the final stage on the continuum of philanthropy when they invest in that preferred future. They identify with and support organizations that can provide solutions rather than with specific needs or the needy. They seek organizations as partners to help them realize their visions for a better community or world. They work not only with the largest and best ethnic organizations but also with mainstream organizations such as universities, research hospitals, museums, and those concerned with social justice and human services.

These investment donors are usually the most affluent and most acculturated, often successful entrepreneurs and professionals. They own property, investments, and assets that they have earned in the United States, and they depend on the wider community for their continued success. They are generally in their sixties and older.

This investment segment is similar to the mainstream wealth holders that Paul Schervish says have "an inclination to be producers rather than simply supporters of philanthropic projects" (1997, p. 31). Through in-depth interviews with mainstream persons of wealth, Schervish isolated three key findings that define motivations for charitable giving: hyperagency, identification, and association.

- *Hyperagency* refers to the capacity of wealthy individuals to establish or substantially control the conditions under which they and others will live. This is the ability to set one's own agenda.

- *Identification* is the donor's ability to identify with the recipients of the contribution, both personally and globally. Schervish calls this "spirituality in the age of affluence" (1997, p. 23).

- *Association* refers to the social networks in which donors learn about the needs of others, both within and beyond their local communities.

These three motivations appear to be applicable in diverse communities as well. Wealthy individuals, Schervish predicts (1997, p. 29), will increasingly entertain two questions: (1) Do I have something I want to accomplish for society? (2) Do I think that philanthropic institutions can do a better job than government in accomplishing it?

The continuum of philanthropy is a useful model but by no means a blueprint of the philanthropic progression of all African American, Asian American, and Latino donors.

The continuum of philanthropy is a useful model but by no means a blueprint of the philanthropic progression of all African American, Asian American, and Latino donors. These broad ethnic groups are much too complex and diverse. Although it is simplistic, we present this model to encourage you to ascertain whether prospects are acting from a motivation to help or a motivation to invest—and to adjust your fundraising programs accordingly.

Native American Model

The Native Americans with whom we spoke also took exception to the traditional donor pyramid of giving model. They view philanthropy as a network of continuous overlapping cycles (see Figure 1.3).

Native Americans often organize on the basis of mutual support, working on projects around the kitchen table or at the community center. Native Americans may be related to everyone else in their community. They must be supportive of one another and share the burden. They are not trying to get to the top of the pyramid.

Yet the Native Americans we interviewed for this book did not relate with the continuum of philanthropy because of its linear nature. Instead they described cyclical fundraising models in terms of the seasons, the circle of life, a cycle of renewal, overlapping rings with many intersections, or a network. They saw all of life's facets inseparably interwoven in a universal web.

Components of Philanthropy

We offer the continuum of philanthropy and the Native American cycles of giving as frameworks for structuring your development plans for diverse communities. Other critical components of philanthropy that you will also want to consider include the following:

Figure 1.3. Cycles of Giving: Native American.

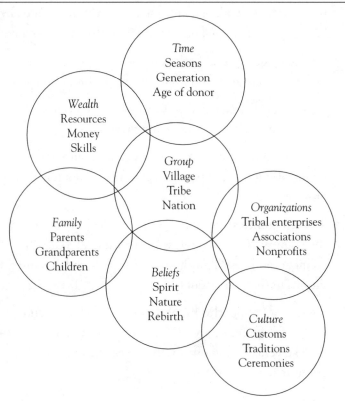

- Acculturation—the process by which people adapt and change in response to living in the United States.

- Multiple generations—the degree of acculturation and ties to the country of origin are affected by the number of generations in this country.

- Financial and social stability—as a self-defined level of stability is achieved, individuals move to the right along the continuum of philanthropy.

- Gifts of money, time, and skills—acknowledge and celebrate all forms of philanthropy.

- Responsibilities for extended family—many individuals support a wide network of family members, whether related by blood or by affection, financially, physically, and emotionally.

- Spiritual and cultural backgrounds—beliefs and values play important roles in philanthropic decisions and actions.

- Ethnic, racial, and tribal customs—many consider long-established practices as unwritten law.

- Maturation of wealth—those for whom wealth and financial stability are recent occurrences often have pressing priorities that tap their resources.

- Ties to countries of origin—people with close ties to the country of origin often send remittances to family members and contributions to individuals and organizations in the home country.

- Newness of philanthropy, philanthropic vehicles, and nonprofit organizations—for many, formal philanthropic vehicles and organizations may be unfamiliar, confusing, and untested.

WHERE WE GO FROM HERE

This is a book about nurturing relationships and raising funds in diverse communities to support the work of nonprofit organizations. Collectively these diverse groups represent more than 30 percent of the total U.S. population at the beginning of the twenty-first century. Each of these broad communities is growing in numbers and in influence. This chapter presents background information and statistical data about the diverse U.S. population groups. It also introduces two philanthropic models that we will discuss in later chapters.

As we shall see, there are many pathways to diverse donors. Chapter Two details the wealth of each broad population segment and its unique history and philosophy of philanthropy.

2

Understanding Diverse Giving Patterns

We present in this chapter the standard indicators of wealth—
household income, education levels, home ownership, asset
accumulation, and business ownership—that demonstrate the
important financial contributions to the U.S. economy of these four
broad populations. This chapter also describes each large and complex population group's philosophy of philanthropy and proposes
brief answers to some basic questions:

Who are the donors?
What kinds of gifts do they give?
Why do they give?
When and where do they make gifts?
How are they likely to make the gifts?

Staff members at nonprofit organizations whom we interviewed for this book and for *Cultures of Caring* (Council on Foundations, 1999) stated that some of the greatest impediments to
involving diverse constituents at their organizations were lack of
understanding of cultural differences, discomfort with the unfamiliar, and fear of making hurtful or embarrassing mistakes. To
avoid showing disrespect or offending anyone, they have often
concentrated efforts to attract support on the most familiar people—
those of their own ethnicity and race. This chapter offers a

To avoid showing disrespect or offending anyone, fundraisers have often concentrated efforts to attract support on the most familiar people—those of their own ethnicity and race.

synopsis of each of the broad cultures to help ease that discomfort and fear.

People from all backgrounds demonstrate the human impulse to give and share. Please remember that individuals do not conform to statistical norms or aggregated data.

Some of the content and conclusions in this book may not apply to your local communities or to specific individuals and families within those communities. We offer it to encourage you to proactively diversify your organization, outreach, and fundraising practices.

INDICATORS OF INCREASING WEALTH

Indicators of wealth among these four population groups demonstrate their increasing potential as prospective donors.

Median Household Income

The U.S. Census Bureau (2001h) gives the 1998–2000 three-year-average median household income by race and Hispanic origin as follows:

Non-Hispanic White	$45,500
African American	$28,700
Asian American	$52,600
Hispanic (of any race)	$31,700
Native American	$31,800

Keep in mind that the income of one-half of each population group is higher than the median and that one-half is lower. Within the broad categories are wildly varying subgroups. For example, the median income for a Filipino American in 1990 was $43,300, whereas the median income for a Southeast Asian American in the same year was $18,300 (Ong and Hee, 1994, p. 36).

Home Ownership

Home ownership is not only an indicator of wealth but also of stability and acculturation. Although non-Hispanic whites (73.8 percent) were 50 percent more likely to own their own homes than blacks (47.2 percent) or Hispanics (46.3 percent) in 2000, the rate of increase in home ownership since 1995 was 4 percent for non-Hispanic whites compared to 10.5 percent for blacks and 10 percent for Hispanics. Home ownership for Asian Americans (52.8 percent) and Native Americans (56.2 percent) increased more modestly between 1995 and 2000 (U.S. Bureau of the Census, 2000f; see Table 2.1).

Education

Educational attainment is another indicator of wealth. As of March 2000 the percentage of each population group, age twenty-five and over, that had completed high school and undergraduate school were as follows:

	High School	Undergraduate School
Non-Hispanic whites	88 percent	28 percent
African Americans	78.9 percent	16.6 percent
Asian Americans	85.7 percent	43.9 percent
Hispanics	57 percent	10.6 percent
Native Americans (1990 data)	66 percent	9 percent

Table 2.1. Percent of Home Ownership by Race and Ethnicity of Householder.

	1995	2000	Increase
African American	42.7%	47.2%	10.5%
Asian American	50.8%	52.8%	4.0%
Latino	42.1%	46.3%	10.0%
Native American	55.8%	56.2%	0.7%
White, non-Hispanic	70.9%	73.8%	4.0%

Source: U.S. Bureau of the Census, 2000f.

Although African American, Hispanic, and Native American rates of completion lag behind those for whites and Asians, the gap has been closing in recent years (U.S. Bureau of the Census, 2000e).

Business Ownership

In 1997 members of diverse populations owned 3,132,000 nonfarm businesses and employed 4,517,000 people in the United States. Those businesses brought in revenues of nearly $600 billion (U.S. Bureau of the Census, 2001l; see Table 2.2).

Ownership of new businesses, often seen as an economic indicator, increased by 7 percent from 1992 to 1997 for all U.S. firms, excluding C corporations, for which prior comparable data are not available. During the same period, business ownership for African Americans rose 26 percent; for Asian Americans, 30 percent; for Latinos, 30 percent; and for Native Americans, 84 percent. Over the same period, receipts for all firms in the United States rose 40 percent, compared to a rise of 33 percent for African American firms, 68 percent for Asian American firms, 49 percent for Latino firms, and 179 percent for Native American firms (U.S. Bureau of the Census, 2001l).

Net Worth

Net worth, the difference between the value of everything one owns and the total amount of one's outstanding debt, may be an important indicator of financial philanthropic activity. If donors usually make philanthropic contributions from reserves of liquid resources (bank accounts, certificates of deposits, stocks, and mutual funds or bonds), as opposed to monthly income sources (jobs, gifts, or investments), then the relationship between assets and philanthropic activity is important.

In an article titled "The Racial Wealth Gap: Origins and Implications for Philanthropy in the African American Community," Dalton Conley (2001) explores the black-white difference in average net worth. The most recent year for which data are available is 1995, when the median household net worth for the highest

Table 2.2. Survey of Minority-Owned Business Enterprises: Nonfarm Businesses (1997).

	African American	Asian American	Latino	Native American
Businesses owned	823,000	913,000	1,199,000	197,000
People employed	718,000	2,200,000	1,300,000	299,000
Business revenues	$71.2 billion	$306.9 billion	$186.3 billion	$34.3 billion
Percentage of 20.8 million total U.S. businesses	4.0%	4.5%	5.9%	1.0%
Percentage of total U.S. business receipts	0.9%	3.7%	2.2%	0.4%

Source: U.S. Bureau of the Census, 2001l.

quintile (one-fifth of the population) for whites was $123,781; for blacks, $40,866; and for Hispanics, $80,416 (U.S. Bureau of the Census, 1995b). We could find no comparable data for Asian American and Native American populations.

In the census's figures on percent distribution of net worth of households by asset type, we can see that whites have slightly more than half of their assets invested in their homes and vehicles (51.7 percent), whereas blacks (78.7 percent) and Hispanics (68.6 percent) have much higher percentages in those two categories. On the other hand, whites (17.2 percent) have a higher percentage of their assets invested in the stock market and retirement accounts than do blacks (4.8 percent) or Hispanics (10.5 percent) (U.S. Bureau of the Census, 2001g; see Table 2.3).

Thus whites may be more likely to make major gifts than diverse donors at the same income level because (1) the white donor has substantially more net assets, and (2) a greater portion of those assets are readily marketable. (For example, it is much easier to make a gift of common stock than, say, a portion of the value of a home.) We discuss more fully in Chapters Six and Seven additional cultural differences that contribute to the disparity in net worth.

AFRICAN AMERICANS

African Americans increasingly realize the importance and advantages of full participation in philanthropy. We base this section on the report written by Mary-Frances Winters (1999) as well as on

Table 2.3. Distribution of Net Worth of Households by Asset Type (1991).

	White	Black	Hispanic
Home	43.7%	61.8%	55.6%
Vehicles	8.0%	16.9%	13.0%
Stocks or mutual funds	8.6%	2.1%	4.3%
Retirement assets	8.6%	2.7%	6.2%

Source: U.S. Bureau of the Census, 2001g.

the writings of Emmett Carson, Jean Fairfax, James Joseph, and others who have researched and written extensively about African American philanthropy.

Indicators of Wealth

African American–owned businesses totaled 823,500 firms employing 718,300 people and generating $71.2 billion in revenues in 1997, as Table 2.2 indicates. The number of African American–owned firms, excluding C corporations, increased 26 percent from 1992 to 1997, compared with a 7 percent increase in this category for all U.S. firms. In 1997 about 1 percent, or eighty-seven hundred, African American–owned businesses had sales of $1 million or more. Nine hundred firms had one hundred or more employees and total receipts of $12.3 billion (U.S. Bureau of the Census, 2001l).

Other indicators of wealth include the following:

- African American home ownership reached 47 percent during the third quarter of 2000, an increase of nearly 4 percent from 1995 (U.S. Bureau of the Census, 2001a).

- The number of blacks in managerial positions within corporations increased from 5.6 percent in 1987 to 6.9 percent in 1997 (U.S. Bureau of the Census, 2001d).

- The number of black households with annual incomes of more than $100,000 increased from 4.0 percent in 1996 to 6.1 percent in 2000, according to census data (U.S. Bureau of the Census, 2001i).

Philosophy

"Black philanthropy is based on a communal notion of philanthropy," said Rodney Jackson, president of the National Center for Black Philanthropy, Inc. "When individuals in the black community support others, the community as a whole—not just immediate recipients—benefits."

"When individuals in the black community support others, the community as a whole—not just immediate recipients—benefits."

"We're a hands-on kind of people," said Pat Solomon, former director of the African American Legacy Program in Detroit. "Don't write a check if you won't come to the event." Solomon said the willingness to give time, energy, and work counts as much as money in the African American community.

James Ellis, a black attorney, pointed out that African Americans have a strong oral rather than written tradition. Personal interactions yield more than written invitations; physical presence means more than sending money. Money alone is sometimes seen as a way of salving the giver's conscience rather than a way of getting in and helping.

Mark Dennis, president of The Alford Group Inc. and an ordained minister, offered eight characteristics of African American philanthropy at the Third National Conference on Black Philanthropy held in May 2001:

1. The "axiom of kinship": shared values and identification with others in the African American community.

2. The power of what Emmett Carson calls "collective giving," where each member contributes to a common pool.

3. The desire to leave something for grandchildren, a legacy; recognition that three generations are always present: the unborn, the current generation, and those who have passed on.

4. The thanksgiving and joy in giving, knowing that "the Lord loves a cheerful giver," an attitude of gratitude.

5. The importance of seeing the "face" of the need and the willingness of leaders to stand up and express the need.

6. Gifts of time and talent are as valued as giving treasure; when people are involved, they tend to invest.

7. Sacrificial gifts happen if it is easier to pay; make giving affordable.

8. Ownership of the gift; claim the gift as your own.

"Blessing others blesses the donor," said the Rev. Dr. Jeremiah A. Wright Jr., senior pastor of Trinity United Church of Christ in Chicago. "The acceptance of gifts brings with it obligations to the receiver. Self-help is an imperative."

"Women are the biggest givers and the best fundraisers in the African American community," said a successful black fundraiser. "We prefer events over planned giving. We will pay a lot to be entertained and listen to good music."

Spirituality

Spirituality has played and continues to play a central role in African American philanthropy.

The Black Church

Historically, African Americans have made the bulk of their charitable donations through church organizations, giving $4.8 billion to churches in 1999, up from $4.3 billion in 1998. The black church tends to be at the center of black philanthropy, perhaps because blacks have consistently controlled it, and it appeals to different socioeconomic strata within the black community. Approximately sixty-five thousand black churches are active in the United States today, typically with congregations of three hundred to five hundred members (Lewis, 2000).

"The church, as historically, remains today the bedrock—the strongest and most influential institution of African American philanthropy. Across history, the black church has maintained a critical role in social welfare and community development for African Americans. In this regard, much giving of time, talent and treasure has been to and through the church. Indeed, theological beliefs undergird and to a great extent dictate giving practices among African Americans. . . . In African American communities, theological beliefs support the practice of giving for the present, rather than giving *in perpetuity*" (Partnership for African American Endowment Development, 1999, p. 6).

"Philanthropy is part of the spiritual journey," said Rev. Paul Martin, senior pastor of Macedonia Baptist Church in Denver, one of the thirty-five African American "mega" churches (defined by Mary-Frances Winters as those with two thousand or more members). His congregation supports staff of twelve full-time and nine part-time employees. It offers forty-two ministries of outreach to the community, including a community development corporation, the Macedonia Village Project, which is a separate 501(c)(3) organization. It has a $100,000 scholarship endowment fund created through the American Baptist Foundation and sponsors an annual educational fair for high school students. In 2000, Rev. Martin said, 55 percent of the fifteen hundred giving units (usually individuals or families) tithed, meaning that they gave 10 percent of their earnings to the church. "Tithing," Rev. Martin said, "helps people focus on one gift." Many in his church also give to missions work, often in the form of in-kind contributions to the church's food pantry and clothing bank.

African American Muslims

"Charity is one of the five pillars of Islam," writes philanthropist Jean Fairfax of Phoenix (1995, p. 15).

> Consideration of how American Muslims, and especially African American Muslims, fulfill this religious duty should be included in any discussion about pluralism in philanthropy. Although we tend to focus on Christian churches when we think of black religious institutions, the Muslim community in America is diverse and important. It encompasses immigrants,

diplomats, students, employees of multinational corporations who are temporarily
assigned here, and African
Americans. The American

*"Charity is one of the five
pillars of Islam," writes
philanthropist Jean Fairfax.*

Muslim community is considered one of the most
important and rapidly growing in the world of Islam. As
Islam has grown over the centuries, indigenous cultures
have often shaped the ways in which the faithful fulfill
their religious obligations.

Philanthropy

Early in their experience in the United States, African Americans
recognized the critical importance of banding together economi-
cally, not only for survival but also to enhance their collective identity. Now known as *cultural capital,* this sense of group consciousness
serves as an economic resource to support economic and philanthropic efforts.

Once philanthropy in the African American community has
moved from the survival stage on the continuum, it focuses on
social and economic empowerment as well as on helping others
cope and succeed in the broader culture. This concentration on
building community self-sufficiency and cultural capital travels
along the continuum of philanthropy from direct personal giving to
more structured and formalized contributions.

History

African Americans have a history of self-help, voluntarism, and
charitable giving dating back to their arrival on the North American continent in the 1600s, when they eagerly shared their meager
belongings. By the late 1700s, African Americans began to engage
in organized philanthropic activities to provide for their own basic
needs, usually conducted through the black church or organizations
associated with the church (Carson, 1989).

Beginning with the Prince Hall Masons, founded in 1781, fraternal and mutual aid societies flourished during the 1800s and early 1900s, among them the ancient Egyptian Arabic Order, the Improved Benevolent Protection Order of Elks, the Masons, and the Eastern Star. Sororities and fraternities became popular social and philanthropic vehicles in the early 1900s (Carson, 1989, pp. 24–25).

During this same time period, civil rights organizations such as the National Urban League and the National Association for the Advancement of Colored People were formed. During the 1930s and 1940s, organizations such as the National Council of Negro Women and the United Negro College Fund emerged to focus on the issues and needs of women and youth. The most influential institutions in the African American communities were—and remain—civil associations, fraternal orders, and churches rather than businesses and financial institutions. After the 1960s African Americans increasingly focused on developing more formal mechanisms for charitable giving, such as the Black United Funds, funds in community foundations, and very recently, private foundations and giving circles. Today more than one million college-educated African Americans belong to historically black Greek organizations.

"Traditional philanthropy within the Caucasian community has often been from 'rich to poor,'" according to the Partnership for African American Endowment Development (1999, p. 3). "Black philanthropy is more often a sharing among equals. African American philanthropy is derived from a distinctive notion of family as an inclusive and permeable institution. Therefore, much of African American giving is to family, neighbors, and needy strangers as a general obligation, rather than as philanthropy." Historically and currently, philanthropy and benevolence within the African American community draws no distinction between gifts of money and gifts of labor.

"Therefore, much of African American giving is to family, neighbors, and needy strangers as a general obligation, rather than as philanthropy."

As wealth increases, interest in pooling resources and in making a greater overall impact with charitable gifts also increases. African Americans prefer to establish their own charitable vehicles, at least in part as a result of a continuing mistrust on the part of many African Americans toward white-controlled mainstream institutions.

Who the Donors Are

African Americans of all economic classes contribute to the church and support family members. Most black donors to other causes are the first generation in their families to reach the middle and upper financial brackets. Some are highly paid entertainers and sports figures, but most are business owners and entrepreneurs. Most have multiple financial and social responsibilities to extended families and friends as well as to associations and organizations.

What Kinds of Gifts They Give

The largest annual gifts usually support the church and major educational organizations, such as historically black colleges, the United Negro College Fund, and other scholarship funds. In addition to immeasurable in-kind contributions of time, goods, skills, and expertise, financial gifts are usually cash from current income, although wealthy donors also contribute gifts of appreciated assets.

Why They Give

"Philanthropy is not about wealth. It is about giving back," said Cleo Glen-Johnson-McLaughlin, president of the Black United Fund of Texas. The rich history of sharing whatever one has with family and friends continues to be the dominant motivation for charitable giving. Even among the more affluent, tax advantages play a lesser role than the desire to give back and share. African Americans most frequently support the following causes:

- Emergency and immediate assistance to family and friends
- Religion

- Education and scholarships

- Civil rights

- Youth programs, especially programs for at-risk youth

- Human services

- Health care and research, especially in areas such as substance abuse, diabetes, heart disease, and sickle cell anemia

- Community and economic development

Donors most often cite the first four items, generally in that order. A personal connection to the cause and the organization are important.

On another level, some affluent African Americans see charitable giving as a valuable opportunity for networking. Philanthropy provides opportunities to pursue business and social contacts.

When and Where They Give

In its African American research project, the Baltimore Giving Project (Winters, 1999) found a strong belief among affluent local African Americans that blacks tended to give many small amounts of money over time, whereas white donors were more likely to give one large gift. There was a sense that blacks do not wait until they have accumulated wealth to contribute and that they often give to multiple interests. Tangible causes, annual appeals, and impulse giving appear to be the most common approaches.

African Americans interviewed for *Cultures of Caring* contributed to numerous organizations and causes, including local scholarship funds, alma maters, the Urban League, local chapters of the American Cancer Society and the American Heart Association, the United Negro College Fund, the YWCA, the Black United Fund, and the United Way.

How They Give

African Americans make gifts through a wide range of charitable vehicles (Berry and Chao, 2001, p. 30):

- Direct giving through family, friends, and community members

- Black churches

- Mutual aid societies

- Fraternities, sororities, and social or civic groups

- Historically black colleges, black scholarship funds, and other higher education institutions and scholarship funds

- African American civil rights organizations

- Community human service organizations

- Black federated campaigns, united charitable funds, and community foundations

These donors generally make financial contributions and volunteer on a situational and personal basis, rather than on an abstract or organizational level (Hall-Russell and Kasberg, 1997).

In sum African American donors give in small increments over time, spontaneously, for immediate causes, by cash or check, and in time and talent. The tax benefits of giving are not an important considera- tion for them. African American communities are moving from a survival model to a model of community self-sufficiency and eco- nomic empowerment.

In sum African American donors give in small increments over time, spontaneously, for immediate causes, by cash or check, and in time and talent.

ASIAN AMERICANS

The Asian American population has surpassed the size of the U.S. Jewish population. Its rate of growth, primarily due to immigration, is faster than that of Latinos (U.S. Bureau of the Census, 2001j).

Jessica Chao's research and writing in *Cultures of Caring* and in her essay, "Asian American Philanthropy" (2001), provide much of the background for this section.

Indicators of Wealth

Asian Americans were 3.9 percent of the U.S. population in 2000; businesses owned by Asian Americans made up 4 percent of the nation's 20.8 million nonfarm businesses and generated 2 percent of all receipts. The number of Asian American–owned firms, excluding C corporations, increased 30 percent from 1992 to 1997, compared with a 7 percent increase for all U.S. firms. Receipts from these firms rose 68 percent to $161 billion in 1997, compared with a 40 percent increase for all U.S. firms over the same period (U.S. Bureau of the Census, 2000b).

In 1997 businesses owned by Asian Americans in the United States totaled about 913,000 firms, employed more than 2.2 million people, and generated $306.9 billion in revenues, according to the most recent data available from the U.S. Bureau of the Census (2000b).

Aggregate data from the Census Bureau and other sources obscure the diversity of economic reality among Asian Americans. The census data indicates that Asian Americans are now outpacing white Americans in terms of average total household income. There is, however, great variation among the various Asian ethnicities. Affluence was more concentrated among people of Japanese, Asian Indian, Chinese, Filipino, and Korean descent, and poverty was more concentrated among various Southeast Asian ethnicities (U.S. Bureau of the Census, 1993a).

Philosophy

Stella Shao, a fundraising consultant in California and founding board member of Asian Americans/Pacific Islanders in Philanthropy, writes that "the Asian American culture of giving is based on commonly held beliefs in the value of compassion, the importance of relationships with families and communities, and in the reciprocity of gift-giving and relating, ceremonially and ritualistically carried out at each occasion throughout life. . . . Asians give because of their understanding that benevolence, compassion, interdependence, and basic respect for humankind are necessary ingredients to living, first in their families, then in their own ethnic communities, and then in the greater society" (1995, p. 56).

The meaning of money and its uses may vary depending on the ethnicity of the donor. "The way in which money is handled is different in the different Asian cultures," said Penelope Haru Snipper, cochair of the Asian Pacific Endowment for Community Development. "In China success is measured by money, much as it is in the U.S. Money is the goal. In Japan people live behind closed gates. No one in the outside would know how much wealth the family had. A person would not broadcast wealth. In Hmong societies, a culture with no written language, bartering counts more than money. A sack of rice is valued more than the equivalent amount of money. In many Asian cultures a man would not talk with a woman about money." (This last belief can be an issue if the development officer is a woman.)

"Well-to-do Asians are fairly assimilated in the professional Western world," said Vishakha N. Desai, senior vice president and director of the museum at the Asia Society. "Philanthropy, however, is more emotional. [Asian Americans] want to know what in their Asian-ness connects them to a project."

Dignity and prestige are important in Asian cultures, often associated with the concept of "face."

Dignity and prestige are important in Asian cultures, often associated with the concept of "face." As an example, an Asian would be reluctant to ask directly for a charitable gift. If the answer was no, both the person who was asked and the person doing the asking would lose face. We will discuss methods to avoid making direct solicitations in Chapter Four.

Asian donors, regardless of the size of the gift they make, expect a personal thank-you letter, preferably from the CEO or a board member. Etiquette is important because it is a matter of face, and relationships cannot be built without face. Similarly, deciding who contacts the prospective donor about the gift is very important. The initial letter should come from someone respected in the community, a friend. The merits of the organization will come later.

Philanthropy

Asian Americans have a long tradition of exchanging gifts and caring for family members, which extends to their ethnic communities and sometimes to the community at large.

Who the Donors Are

Asian American donors are usually first-generation Americans who have made their wealth through entrepreneurial businesses. Although most are sixty years old or more, some entrepreneurs in their forties and fifties make major charitable contributions. In recent years, some wealthy Asian American donors have established private foundations, and a few have established donor advised funds in community foundations.

Here's how a donor advised fund works. An individual, family, or corporation establishes a donor advised fund with a charitable gift to the community foundation, for which the donor takes an income tax deduction at the time the fund is established. The donor, from time to time, makes nonbinding recommendations for distributions from the fund to local, regional, and national charities.

What Kinds of Gifts They Give

In the early immigrant years, Asian Americans share gifts of time, money, knowledge, and skills. Once the donor is sufficiently acculturated to help those less fortunate, the gift is usually cash or stock. For the few individuals of high net worth, gifts may include setting aside a percentage of equity in a company before it goes public to

donate to a charity after the initial public offering, loaning employees to a nonprofit organization for months or years, or annually giving a steady percentage of stock to a charitable fund that will grow
as the value of the stock grows.

Why They Give

Asian Americans feel a personal obligation to assist family, friends,
and community members in need. First-generation immigrants send
money to their countries of origin in the billions of dollars each
year, including to countries like Vietnam and Bangladesh. They may
send contributions directly to family members and friends or to
relief organizations and governmental agencies. Filipinos report that
Filipino Americans send approximately $8 billion to the Philippines
annually (Berry and Chao, 2001).

"Compared with those of mainstream America, giving practices
among Asian Americans are more focused, ethnic-specific, ritualis-
tic, and institutionalized. Giving is often related to specific occasions and causes that will help preserve Asian culture and assist in
the survival of Asian people in a foreign, and at times hostile, environment" (Shao, 1995, p. 56).

According to Gail Kong of the Asian Pacific Fund, Asian Americans often give to universities because they feel an obligation to
give back. Steve Suda at Stanford University reports that some
Asian Americans are motivated by the desire to be associated with
a specific institution or cause at the institution, whether or not they
are alumni.

Charitable causes that Asian Americans are likely to support
include

- Emergency and financial aid to family and friends

- Causes and organizations in countries of origin

- Education

- Health and human services for the elderly

- Youth development

- Cultural heritage and appreciation

- Social justice and human rights

When and Where They Give

"The arts, culture and appeals for the country of origin are important to foreign-born Asians," said Vishakha Desai at the Asia Society. The prospective donor who is interested in the immigrant experience in the United States may find pan-Asian organizations, serving the interests of people from multiple Asian countries, and social issues such as health care, community centers, and civil rights more appealing.

Asian American donors make gifts at all stages along the continuum of philanthropy, although they are more likely to make substantial gifts after they reach a level of what they determine to be financial stability. Asian American donors that we interviewed support schools of business, finance, or law in U.S. universities; scholarship funds to attract students from Asian backgrounds; projects and programs in countries of origin; private and community foundations, art museums, cultural centers, and health care organizations.

How They Give

Asian American immigrants provide assistance to individuals and families and build associations and infrastructure to support the community. As they settle and establish themselves in their new country, immigrants continue to give directly to friends and relatives and through various ethnic and faith-based associations. As they become more acculturated and financially secure, they make the transition to more formal nonprofit organizations, both ethnic-specific and mainstream. Here are some vehicles for their charitable giving (Berry and Chao, 2001, p. 36):

- Family and close networks of friends

- Mutual aid associations defined by ethnicity, village, province, dialect, or surname

- Faith-based institutions including churches, temples, and mosques

- Alumni, professional, and business associations

- Asian ethnic nursing homes

- Community centers and cultural institutions

- Asian American and ethnic-based social justice organizations and civic associations

- United funds (for example, United Way, Black United Fund) and community funds (for example, Asian Federation of New York, National Council of La Raza)

- Mainstream organizations that focus on community programs.

Asian American immigrants would be more likely to support those vehicles for charitable giving at the beginning of the list, such as mutual aid associations and alumni, professional, and business associations related to specific ethnic subgroups. U.S.-born generations would be more likely to give through those organizations listed near the end of the list, such as social justice and community funds (Berry and Chao, 2001).

Asian American immigrants provide assistance to individuals and families and build associations and infrastructure to support the community.

Family and friends are both sources of philanthropic giving and receivers of gifts. As Asian Americans become more financially secure and assimilated, the vehicles for charitable giving move from individuals whom the donor knows to philanthropic institutions.

In summary, the following are key observations about Asian American giving:

- Gift size increases with greater acculturation.

- Donors give in response to specific requests by respected individuals.

- Donors carefully plan their gifts.

- Gifts provide both immediate and long-term impact.

- The concept of "face" is important (see Chapter Four).

- Prestigious institutions provide donors a sense of acceptance by the wider community.

LATINOS

Latinos are people of Spanish or Latin American descent. The word *Latino* is an umbrella term for diverse and distinct subgroups, each with its own characteristics, issues, and philanthropic traditions. The Catholic Church and experiences of discrimination in housing, jobs, and politics have served as unifying forces for Latinos, even though they are diverse both ethnically and geographically, as Chapter One describes. Much of this section relies on the research and data of Henry Ramos (1999), along with *Engaging Diverse Communities for and Through Philanthropy* by Mindy Berry and Jessica Chao (2001).

Indicators of Wealth

Latino-owned businesses totaled 1.2 million nonfarm firms, employed over 1.3 million people, and generated $186.3 billion in revenues in 1997, as Table 2.2 indicates. Approximately 2 percent of those firms (26,700 firms) had sales of $1 million or more. The eleven hundred firms with one hundred or more employees generated revenue of $28.3 billion. Receipts of Latino-owned firms rose 49 percent over five years, from $77 billion in 1992 to $114 billion in 1997, compared with a 40 percent increase for all U.S. firms of the same type over the same period (U.S. Bureau of the Census, 2001l).

Latino-owned businesses totaled 1.2 million nonfarm firms, employed over 1.3 million people, and generated $186.3 billion in revenues in 1997.

With these statistics, it is easy to envision a time in the near future when substantial numbers of Latino businesspeople and professionals will have the stability and financial security to expand their philanthropic giving and volunteering. Whether and to what degree they become active philanthropists will depend largely on the efforts that current philanthropic leaders and institutions make today to promote expanded Latino participation.

Philosophy

"My personal vision of the meaning of philanthropy is that life is larger than we are," wrote Olga Villa Parra (1999, p. 77), a consultant and former executive director of the Midwest Council of La Raza. "Life will go on long after we are gone. Life is a gift from God. Life does not owe us anything. On the contrary, we owe it much, because it is an opportunity to do something larger than ourselves; that is, do deeds, help our families, offer whatever we can pass on for the benefit of others."

In Latin American cultures, philanthropy provides benefits to both donor and recipient. The donor receives a sense of comfort in knowing that these good works may offset past misdeeds or missed opportunities, and the feeling of being right with the world (or with God). The recipients of philanthropy can benefit from improved health, productive livelihood, richer cultural experiences, or greater opportunities to improve themselves. "In the end, a significant transaction occurs between donor and donee, and vice versa," wrote Charles Rodriguez (1999, p. 48), executive director for development and public affairs at the University of Texas Health Science Center in San Antonio. "Philanthropists gain emotional, psychic, and social satisfaction (and perhaps even financial satisfaction in the form of a tax benefit from the IRS), where donees have their personal situations and aptitudes enhanced, perhaps for the rest of their lives."

Bea Stotzer, board president of New Economics for Women, an organization that provides affordable housing for women and single parents in Los Angeles, said, "In other communities, services are provided based on deviant behavior (kids on drugs, teenage mothers, and so on). The Latino community seeks to support and reinforce assets, not deficits. Latinos want to work together to make life better; there is a great sense of hope, of deciding together."

Stotzer finds that Latinos define success by simple solutions to complex problems. She recently facilitated a neighborhood meeting at which the group decided that the two most pressing issues were to get a mailbox and to get a police observation station in the neighborhood. "Next year, they'll want a post office," she quipped.

"For U.S. Hispanics, the entire cosmos—including the earth below and the heavens above—is an intrinsically relational reality," wrote the late Roberto Goizueta, former CEO of Coca-Cola, "where . . . each member is necessarily related to every other member. . . . To be an isolated, autonomous individual is, literally, to have no humanity, no identity, no self; it is to be a no-thing, a no-body" (1995, p. 50).

Latino cultures highly value dignity—both one's own and that of family members and friends. A person's word is sacred, and the individual has an obligation to help others in a quiet and noncompetitive way. Many Latinos manifest this in a hesitancy to claim credit, admit weakness, or deal with rejection (Royce and Rodriguez, 1999, p. 20).

Religion

One-third of the membership of the Catholic Church in the United States is Latino (Miranda, 1999, p. 60). Many of the Latino individuals we interviewed consider giving to the Catholic Church an integral part of their lives; they see their contributions not as charitable giving or philanthropy but rather as an ongoing responsibility.

In recent years Protestant evangelical churches have significantly increased in Latino followers, and other Christian organizations are becoming increasingly attractive to Latinos. For example, World Vision, one of the nation's leading Christian charities and a supporter of ministries in developing countries, now receives some 17 to 20 percent of all its contributions from U.S. Latino donors, according to its director of public relations, Dean Owen.

Empowerment and Nonprofit Organizations

The oldest Latino nonprofit organizations were established during the civil rights movement in the 1960s, and fully half of all formal nonprofits are fewer than ten years old. Although Latino nonprofits still represent less than 1 percent of the nation's more than one million tax-exempt organizations, they are developing at a rate of more than three hundred per year, double their growth rate from 1985 to 1989 (Campoamor, 1999, p. 15).

The oldest Latino nonprofit organizations were established during the civil rights movement in the 1960s, and fully half of all formal nonprofits are fewer than ten years old.

Much of the Latino nonprofit sector's short history of voluntary action was inspired by individuals' experiences in the labor movement and a desire for political empowerment. In the 1960s and 1970s, with the help of several mainstream private foundations, some major Latino civil rights and educational organizations were established, including the National Council of La Raza, the Mexican American Legal Defense and Education Fund, and the Puerto

Rican Legal Defense and Education Fund. Community development and social services organizations developed shortly thereafter
(Cortés-Vasquez and Miranda, 1999).

Philanthropy

Although examples of informal charity and social giving through family networks date back to the 1500s in Latino cultures, philanthropy—
as practiced in the United States—is a relatively unknown concept.
In large measure, this is because Latinos come from nations where
governments and churches, rather than private and nonprofit organizations, have traditionally played the central roles in providing
social and human services as well as arts and culture. The dominant
role of state and church institutions in Latin American social welfare has been the largest impediment to Latino familiarity and comfort with U.S. philanthropic models (Ramos, 1999).

"Many Latinos—especially newer immigrants—do not give
because they either do not relate to the organization seeking funds,
or because they believe government or the church should provide
the needed service or intervention," said a Chicago-based Mexican
American in an interview.

"Family-driven, church-based giving is what largely defines Hispanic philanthropy, said a Cuban American tax attorney from
Miami. "Typically, this giving is highly informal and personalized."

In recent years, as more Latinos feel financially secure and stable, Latino giving reflects an increasingly wider spectrum of philanthropic vehicles and practices.

Who the Donors Are

Latinos are primarily in the early and middle stages of the continuum
of philanthropy. Although many share freely with one another as they
struggle to obtain an economic foothold, others have reached the stage
of helping others who have less. They are generally the first generation in their families to have reached a level of financial stability, and
they have many competing interests for their discretionary funds.

Those few who have obtained significant wealth often are responsible for a large number of extended family members, are asked to participate and contribute to every nonprofit, both ethnic and mainstream, and are still growing their businesses and investments. Many are not yet ready—emotionally, mentally, or financially—to make large or long-term philanthropic commitments, and many are concerned about diminishing their capacity to address more immediate community needs in the current hostile environment that confronts many Latinos nationwide. "Latinos and Giving, 1999" (Cortés-Vasquez and Miranda, 1999), published by The Hispanic Federation, reports that giving by Latinos to nonreligious institutions and charitable causes increases with educational attainment and income.

What Kinds of Gifts They Give

Much Latino giving is directed informally to family members and communities outside the United States. Carlos Tortolero of the Mexican Fine Arts Center Museum in Chicago said in our interview that the third largest source of revenue in Mexico (after oil and tourism) is *remittances*, financial support or gifts that individuals in the United States send to family members, agencies, or the government in their countries of origin. Fernando Ascencio (1993) determined that the total amount of remittances sent from the United States to Mexico during 1990 alone was $3.2 billion. This type of giving is particularly responsive to natural or economic crises that directly affect the donors' families, communities, or countries of origin. A 1998 collaborative fundraising effort to benefit the Central American and Puerto Rican victims of Hurricanes George and Mitch, spearheaded by The Hispanic Federation, raised $1.2 million within a few months.

Much Latino giving is directed informally to family members and communities outside the United States.

Latinos also give to those who are significantly impoverished or otherwise disadvantaged, both in the United States and abroad.

They provide personal caretaking services for the young and old, rather than relying on institutions. The most significant portion of Latino giving supports their churches—both Catholic and evangelical Christian churches. Interviewees reported a preference for supporting Latino causes, mainly through direct cash contributions from current income and volunteer service at the board of directors' level.

Why They Give

The Latinos we interviewed for *Cultures of Caring* consistently expressed their chief motivation for participation in philanthropy as a sense of personal responsibility—a desire to give back to the Latino communities from which they came and, in the process, to help accelerate Latino rights and opportunities within the United States. Many sense an increasing anti-Latino trend in the United States—as evidenced by new laws and policies in states such as California. They view participation in philanthropy as an important vehicle to mitigate such sentiments. Philanthropy can serve as "an increasingly important bridge to the mainstream," said a Cuban American interviewee, "enabling mainstream leaders to see us increasingly as societal givers rather than mere takers."

As we have said, many foreign-born Latinos feel a strong motivation to give by helping family members and communities in the home country. Latino culture is oriented toward the family, heavily influenced by the Catholic Church, and intensely driven by a sense of ethnic and community pride. Causes that are particularly appealing to Latinos include

- Emergency and financial assistance to family and close friends, both in the United States and abroad

- Religion

- Family-related issues including, especially, children, youth, and the elderly

- Community rights and economic opportunities

- Scholarship funds, education, and youth development

- Cultural heritage or preservation and the arts

- Health care and human services

- Disaster relief in home countries

When and Where They Give

A significant number of the wealthy and influential Latinos interviewed for *Cultures of Caring* reported that they were as likely to support mainstream organizations that address Latino issues and needs as they were to support Latino nonprofit agencies. In fact, many felt that participation in mainstream organizations was their most appropriate focus, because those organizations afforded them unique opportunities to influence mainstream thinking on behalf of Latino community interests.

"The opportunities I have to engage in leading mainstream philanthropic institutions as a major donor and trustee are not about just writing a check or volunteering time," said Mexican American donor from Los Angeles. "They are much broader and necessarily more strategic. These opportunities are about gaining access and influence on behalf of Latinos. They are about responsibility to my family and my [ethnic] community."

The donors interviewed for *Cultures of Caring* supported organizations including the American Heart Association, the March of Dimes, the Houston Museum of Fine Arts, and the Florida Symphony, as well as the University of Notre Dame and St. Mary's College in San Antonio, Texas. A 1996 nationwide independent survey showed that the Latinos polled donated as frequently to United Way campaigns as white Americans did ("Market Research," 1996, p. 11).

Age also affects Latino giving, according to the report "Latinos and Giving," 1999. The youngest and the oldest give the least, and the thirty-five- to forty-nine-year-old age group gives the most. Almost half of Latinos from ages eighteen to twenty-four do not

Age also affects Latino giving. . . .
The youngest and the oldest
give the least, and the
thirty-five- to forty-nine-year-old
age group gives the most.

give to any institution; 42 percent of Latinos in this age range report giving to the church. Among those older than fifty-four, 42 percent do not give to any cause or institution. In contrast, within the thirty-five- to forty-nine-year-old age group, 72 percent give, and 28 percent do not. In this age group, 53 percent contribute to a church, 26 percent to a nonchurch institution, and 19 percent to a charitable cause (Cortés-Vasquez and Miranda, 1999).

How They Give

Michael Cortés (2001), assistant professor of public policy at the University of Colorado at Denver, describes charity among Latinos as including "an element of traditional Latin-American *personalismo*, in which personal, intimate, one-to-one relationships shaped the nature and extent of giving" (p. 14). Cultural values such as the importance of one's word, the intrinsic worth of each person, obligation, giving back, family, and trust shape Latinos' highly personalized and informal patterns of philanthropy.

Much of Latino giving is directed to people, the church, or voluntary organizations. Preferred vehicles for giving include the following (Berry and Chao, 2001):

- Family and friends

- Church

- *Mutualistas*, mutual assistance associations

- Civic associations, chambers of commerce, and business and professional associations

- Latino civil rights and social justice organizations

- Latino community development corporations and other community organizations

- Latino community funds and federated campaigns

- Mainstream nonprofits that address Latino needs

Family and friends are both the recipients of gifts and the vehicles through which charitable gifts are made. As Latinos travel across the continuum of philanthropy, the methods of giving also change, from hand-delivered gifts (financial and in-kind) to checks to established nonprofit organizations.

The following characteristics summarize Latino charitable giving in general:

- Donor seeks personal, hands-on participation.

- Giving is family-driven and church-based.

- Focus is on concrete and visible causes and projects.

- Donor was asked to give by a credible individual.

- Current needs and opportunities are of paramount importance.

- Contributions are given directly to recipients.

NATIVE AMERICANS

The term *Native American* in this book includes American Indians and Alaska Natives. The information in this section relies heavily on the work of Mindy Berry (1999), her work with Jessica Chao (2001), and the work of Sherry Salway Black (2001).

Indicators of Wealth

Native American-owned businesses totaled 197,300 firms, employed 298,700 people, and generated $34.3 billion in revenues in 1997, as Table 2.2 indicates. The vast majority of Native American–owned firms, 88 percent, were sole proprietorships (unincorporated businesses owned by individuals). The U.S. Census Bureau excluded some businesses not owned by individuals, such as those owned by tribes, from the survey (U.S. Bureau of the Census, 2001l).

The number of Native American–owned firms, excluding C corporations, increased 84 percent from 1992 to 1997, compared with a 7 percent increase for all U.S. firms. Receipts of such firms rose 179 percent, to $22 billion in 1997, compared with a 40 percent increase for all U.S. firms over the same period (U.S. Bureau of the Census, 2001l).

Nationwide, reservations hold 4 percent of U.S. oil and gas reserves, 40 percent of uranium deposits, and 30 percent of western coal reserves, among other natural resources. In recent years reservations have generated new wealth from mineral extraction, gaming enterprises, and a growing array of entrepreneurial ventures, such as banks, resorts, retail establishments, and other Native-owned businesses.

Nationwide, reservations hold 4 percent of U.S. oil and gas reserves, 40 percent of uranium deposits, and 30 percent of western coal reserves, among other natural resources.

Philosophy

"Differences in philosophies that separate non-Native people from their counterparts in the Native world are vast," according to Rebecca Adamson (1999, p. 9), president of First Nations Development Institute. "Non-Native socioeconomic activities are based on a philosophy of personal property rights and ownership, market economics, the accumulation of wealth, and consumerism. Traditional Native American societies rely on communal ownership, communal economies, redistribution of wealth, and spirituality and its connection to humans and to nature."

Interdependence

For Native Americans, "the good of the community takes precedence over the good of the individual" (Joseph, 1995, p. 27). The survival of the tribe is of primary importance—not the well-being of particular individuals. The group gives significance to the individual, not the individual to the group (Black, 2001, p. 43). Because the entire tribe usually owns the assets, philanthropy is often communal. The tribal council or leadership often makes philanthropic decisions. Gifts include money, time, talents, and goods.

Sharing the earth's abundance is central to Native American values. For Native Americans, who believe that everything belongs to the earth and nature and that everything is inherently interconnected and spiritual, giving connects the individual to his or her ancestors and to nature. "The fundamental appreciation of interdependence between all elements in creation, that all reality participates or shares in one form of life, lies at the root of the Native sense of responsibility for other people and tribal willingness to share" (Black, 2001, p. 46).

Redistribution

Rather than accumulating wealth, Native Americans redistribute what they have. One traditional method of redistribution common among many Native American tribes is the potlatch. A *potlatch* or "giveaway" refers to the custom of giving one's belongings to others. Before the arrival of European goods, typical items given away at potlatches were food, shawls, blankets, and necklaces. Such items of value are gathered over a long period of time to be given away during powwows or celebrations in honor of births, anniversaries, marriages, birthdays, deaths, and other special occasions. Sometimes the giver gives away nearly all of his or her possessions. In such instances, seeing how little the giver has left at the end of the potlatch, recipients of the gifts return some items out of kindness. The giver and the receiver are equally honored in the exchange (Black, 2001).

"Native Americans are incredibly generous with what they have," said Barbara Bratone, development director at the American Indian College Fund. "Wealth is measured not by what you have, but in terms of what you give away and how you care for the well-being of the tribe and its members." Native Americans approach giving from the perspective of stewardship rather than ownership. They give as much as it takes to sustain the system, without disturbing the balance.

Mutual Responsibility

The distinction between sharing and charity is critically important to understanding Native American giving. "Philanthropy in the Native sense means the tradition of sharing and honoring," writes Sherry Salway Black (2001, p. 42), "which is a question of mutual responsibility. To share wealth is a responsibility of every caring member of a community."

Donna Chavis, executive director of Native Americans in Philanthropy, described a contribution in terms of a birthday present: "the gift giver expects nothing in return and both the giver and receiver are equally honored."

"By accepting the gift, the recipient validates and honors the giver's responsibility to give," according to Native American Jeannette Armstrong (Wells, 1998, p. 29). "It's not a shameful thing or a social stigma to receive a gift. What you're actually doing is helping the giver by receiving—because they may be rebalancing their poor luck, or their hardships. Since they are receiving blessings in giving, and doing a good thing in terms of their own feelings, the recipient is doing them a service by receiving in an honorable way."

> *"By accepting the gift, the recipient validates and honors the giver's responsibility to give."*

Reciprocity

"In Native giving, there is always an understanding of broad reciprocity . . . that requires that the gift must continue to be given, to be passed on," said Rebecca Adamson (Wells, 1998, p. 36), president of First Nations Development Institute.

This is probably the pan–Native American value that underpins all the different forms of tribal giving. Every tribe has different forms, different rituals, different ceremonies, different understandings of what a gift is, how a gift is given. But you see in all those different kinds of ceremonies the understanding that gift-giving is really reciprocally based—that you give to someone, and that person is expected to give—but not merely as a quid pro quo back to you. . . . That is the reciprocity of it—the gift is given, the beneficiary is expected also to give—not necessarily back, but on, so the gift is always alive.

In Alaska, individuals do not have a long history of donating to community projects, other than for immediate needs. Native corporations, however, are different. According to Diane Kaplan in Anchorage, they give more generously and more long-term because they realize that their grandchildren's grandchildren will live on the same land. Their unique long view is expressed vividly in the slogan of the NANA Corporation: "Doing Business in Alaska for 10,000 Years."

The symbol of the circle appears frequently in Native American cultures from the recycling of materials and goods among tribal members in the potlatch, to the traditional cycle of knowledge that has helped to perpetuate Native societies for hundreds of generations, to the cycles of renewal during the earth's seasons, and to the interlocking spheres of influence within each nation and among all Native cultures. Thus the individual is connected to all other individuals, life forms, and the mother earth.

Unique Philanthropic Structures

Since the 1970s, Native Americans have established an increasingly wide range of mainstream philanthropic vehicles. These vehicles include mainstream institutions such as college foundations, funds at community foundations, service organizations, and payroll deduction programs. Other forms of philanthropy are unique to Native cultures, such as tribal foundations, tribal enterprise giving programs, tribal government giving, and giving by intertribal consortia. Tribes have a special relationship with the U.S. government to interact as sovereign nations with laws and regulations that govern many aspects of commercial and business activity.

Internal Revenue Code Section 7871

In 1982 Congress passed the Indian Tribal Governmental Tax Status Act, codified as Section 7871 of the Internal Revenue Code, treating tribal governments as state governments for a variety of specified tax purposes including private foundation rules and the tax deductibility of charitable contributions. In effect the act affirmed tribal self-regulated sovereignty rather than dependence upon exemptions from state tax regulations. First Nations Development Institute, through its program called Strengthening Native American Philanthropy, encourages the establishment of Native organizations under Section 7871. The Hopi Tribal Council, for example, provided the initial investment of $10 million in 2000 to help establish the Hopi Education Endowment Fund as a 7871 organization.

Alaskan Regional Corporations

Other vehicles for philanthropic giving were established in the early 1970s in Alaska. When the U.S. government wanted to lay the Alaskan pipeline, it reached an agreement with Alaska Natives in the Alaska Native Claims Settlement Act of 1971. The agreement divided the tribes into twelve regional corporations, with members of each tribe as the shareholders of the corporations. Some of these corporations have become very successful commercial enterprises. The largest is CIRI, which was started with $34 million and 2 million acres of land, oil, and gas and by the end of 2000 was worth $1.2 billion even after substantial dividends were paid to shareholders. Some of the regional corporations have formed private foundations and public charities from the proceeds of farming, energy-related, or other businesses. Some have contributed a por-

tion of legal settlements from land claims and lawsuits to scholarships and special community needs.

Tribal Gaming

Tribal gaming generated $9.6 billion in gross income in 1999, more
than 10 percent of the total U.S. gaming industry. Of 561 federally
recognized Indian nations, 196 are involved in gaming. Although
only one tribe in ten produces significant revenue from gaming, a
few tribal gaming operations have seen spectacular success—such
as the Mashantucket Pequot tribe in Connecticut and the Shakopee
Mdewakanton in Minnesota—but these operations are the exception
rather than the rule. In fact, these
two tribes, located near major urban   *Tribal gaming generated*
areas, have benefited the most from   *$9.6 billion in gross income in*
the gaming boom generating 40
percent of all Indian gaming rev-   *1999, more than 10 percent of*
enue (National Indian Gaming   *the total U.S. gaming industry.*
Association, 2001).

"Native Americans are fundamentally givers," according to
Diane Wyss of the National Indian Gaming Association. This organization and the First Nations Development Institute recently completed a survey and reported that the gaming tribes gave over $68
million to charity in 2000. By comparison, other forms of gaming—
namely, Las Vegas and Atlantic City casinos—donated $58 million
in that same year to charity.

Philanthropy

Although many of the philanthropic practices of Native Americans
are similar to those of Caucasians, significant differences and
nuances exist.

Who the Donors Are

Donors in Native American communities are often the tribes themselves or tribal enterprises, although individuals, families, and
extended clan also give, but usually in undocumented gifts as part

of their daily lives. The elders or the tribal council often make the grantmaking decisions. Very recently some tribes have established tribal foundations with grantmaking programs.

Wealthy Native Americans who do not live on reservations are more likely to give individually. "The age of the donor and the newness of the donor's wealth are also influences on Native giving," according to Adamson (2000, p. 5). "The younger the donor, the greater the tendency to seek advice, give incrementally, and target their donees carefully. The more recent the acquisition of wealth, the more the donor tends to engage in giving on a gradual basis. The age of the donor and newness of wealth may be helpful predictors because the median age of the American Indian population (26 years old) is below that of the U.S. population as a whole (33 years) and personal giving both on and off reservations is derived primarily from recent or first-generation wealth."

What Kinds of Gifts They Give

As we have said, Native American gifts take many forms, including time, skills, food, goods, services, and money. "If you give the most you can," said Tia Oros with the Seventh Generation Fund, "that is more valuable than a large gift that is insignificant to the giver." Monetary gifts are generally fairly small.

Because their wealth is new, donors tend to be cautious and very selective in their giving, usually starting with a small gift to assure that the recipient uses it wisely before giving a substantial gift.

Tribal enterprises are just beginning to develop partnerships with nonprofit organizations and to institute matching funding for projects and causes. Increasingly they are making in-kind gifts and sponsoring various public and community events. Although Native Americans highly value in-kind contributions as symbols of support, they can also view monetary gifts from individual donors, tribes, and enterprises as a modern way of giving back to ancestors, the land, and the spirits.

Why They Give

When asked why they give, individuals from the successful gaming tribes responded with reasons such as sharing, reciprocity, and bettering the tribe. The charities they fund are primarily designed to serve youth, education, health, and elders. "Taking care of each other is an important value," said Diane Wyss. According to her organization's survey (National Indian Gaming Association, 2001), tribal councils generally select recipients, with 40 percent of the dollars going to non-Indian organizations. Tribes give 75 percent on an as-needed basis, and 21 percent of the tribes have a foundation or fund. Tribes that have accumulated substantial assets from commercial enterprises have been more likely to fund visible mainstream institutions such as the United Way, Special Olympics, local museums, and relief organizations.

Native Americans are not interested in funding administrative costs but are supportive of small projects, according to Barbara Poley, executive director of the Hopi Foundation. Individuals who live on reservations tend to give to and through the family, and to the community through the tribe itself. Those who live off the reservation tend to give to Native-run nonprofits and funds or to mainstream nonprofits that focus on Native issues (Berry and Chao, 2001).

Charitable causes likely to receive Native American support include the following (Berry and Chao, 2001, p. 39):

- Education and scholarships

- Cultural preservation and the arts

- Economic development

- Youth

- Emergency aid and disaster relief

- Health care

- Services for the elderly

- Development of human, economic, and environ-mental assets

- Rehabilitation services, especially substance abuse counseling

When and Where They Give

Native Americans give primarily to address current and immediate needs. The more traditional tribes tend to give to local issues, whereas the more progressive tribes give more to pan–Native American and mainstream types of interests. Native Americans who were interviewed mentioned gifts to the Smithsonian Institution, United Way, scholarship funds, tribal and mainstream colleges and universities, and cultural centers.

How They Give

Native Americans often, both individually and tribally, make gifts personally and directly to the recipient. Individuals tend to make anonymous gifts and are generally very modest about their giving, so publicity about gifts may be inappropriate. More formal and structured gifts typically take place through legal structures that the tribe or the U.S. government sanctions. The following is a list of methods or vehicles by Native Americans make gifts, with the more traditional listed first:

- Family, friends, and tribal members

- Tribally focused membership organizations

- Native American nonprofits

- Tribal enterprises and businesses

- Tribal governments

- Tribal foundations

- Tribal college funds

- Community foundations and the United Way

Family, friends, and tribal members can be both the vehicles through which gifts are given and the recipients of the gifts. It appears that as philanthropic practices evolve from communal giving to more institutional giving, a parallel transition

Native American individuals tend to make anonymous gifts and are generally very modest about their giving, so publicity about gifts may be inappropriate.

occurs from using voluntary charitable vehicles to the more structured and formal vehicles of nonprofit organizations.

We can broadly summarize giving by Native Americans and their tribes as follows:

- Both the giver and recipient are equally honored.

- Donors give incrementally and gradually.

- They give directly to the recipient for immediate needs.

- The tribe and tribal consortia often make the gifts.

- Donors select recipients carefully.

- Gifts are often in-kind.

WHERE WE GO FROM HERE

Standard indicators of wealth demonstrate the increasing importance and clout of the four diverse populations. Donors of diverse ethnic backgrounds are often first-generation Americans, college graduates (generally), and entrepreneurs who have limited disposable income—as well as complicated and multiple responsibilities to parents, siblings, children, and others. As they become affluent, they first take care of the needs and desires of those closest to them: family, friends, neighbors—a pattern that a number of scholars have also observed in philanthropy among whites—and only then make gifts targeted for projects that address their communities' current needs.

Often members of ethnic groups who are the most likely prospective donors are focused on generating or accumulating wealth. Concurrently they are helping to meet immediate needs in their communities, including giving considerable support to religious, spiritual, and educational organizations.

Organizations that seek to expand their prospective donor pools to include new ethnicities and races must first assure that their internal policies and practices encourage diversity within the organization. We will explore this issue further in Chapter Three.

3

Embracing Diversity and Inclusiveness

Public charities must fully embrace the diversity of the local community in their missions, policies, and practices. This is a critically important concept for organizations seeking to engage people of diverse backgrounds in their fundraising programs. The nonprofit organization's mission, as established by its board of trustees, drives its programs, including fundraising and development. In order to fully realize its mission, the organization must closely align policies and practices with both its mission and the composition of the population it serves. Through inclusive practices that permeate the entire organization, the organization opens the door to diverse prospective donors.

As we discussed in Chapter One, donors move on the continuum of philanthropy from sharing with family members and peers at the survival stage to giving to others at the helping stage. During

Through inclusive practices that permeate the entire organization, the organization opens the door to diverse prospective donors.

this transition, their giving patterns evolve from giving gifts directly to known recipients to contributing to associations and organizations that provide services to members of the community. Such donors require that the organizations have proven records of effective service and that the organizations have earned their trust.

Likewise, as donors move from the helping to investing stages on the continuum, they seek organizations and institutions to which they have relationships and in which they have confidence, nonprofits that serve members of their racial and ethnic groups and that involve their ethnicity at every level. Diversity must go beyond tokenism and number counting to become part of the institutional ethos.

"People make different assumptions about organizations that are grounded in the community," said Pier Rogers, former chief operating officer of Associated Black Charities in New York City. "One is that they will be more sensitive to the needs and issues of the community."

To become and maintain an organization reflective of the local population requires a long-term commitment to building relationships and trust, often despite entrenched tensions and suspicions from all sides. The organization must critically examine the ways its institutional practices and procedures hinder or facilitate effective inclusion of diverse communities. It must then develop an institutionwide diversity plan to attract nontraditional participation. Board and staff composition, provision of programs and services, and commitment of leadership (both board and staff) are areas that require attention and action before the organization can address fundraising and donor relations.

ORGANIZATIONAL COMMITMENT

The Minority Executive Directors Coalition of Kings County, Washington, refers to inclusive practices as *cultural competency*. It developed and adopted a working definition of cultural competency, which its member organizations use as a guideline in their efforts to become fully inclusive agencies. It states, in part, "Cultural Competency is defined as a set of behaviors, attributes and policies enabling an agency (or individual) to work effectively in cross cultural situations" (Minority Executive Directors Coalition, 2001). It also lists three guiding principles:

1. Commitment to social change

   Acknowledgment that institutional racism exists at all levels of the service delivery system

   Recognition that cultural differences exist between and within groups and that people of color cannot and should not be measured against the dominant culture

2. Accessibility to services, training and funding

   Elimination of barriers to service

   Decentralization of points of entry to access services

3. Relevance of service delivery

   Congruence of services with client's culture, environment, class, language, concept of time, spiritual and religious beliefs, and worldview

   Involvement of and respect for traditional and nontraditional resources within the community.

This is one example of an organization's commitment to diversity and to encouraging its member organizations to be inclusive. In order for any organization to fully diversify both its practices and its composition, it must begin with the full commitment of the organization, as defined by the board of directors.

Mission Statement

Often the board expresses its commitment directly in its mission statement. The following examples from mission statements of community foundations that have decided to embrace diversity demonstrate the variety and breadth of such missions:

"We are committed to equality of opportunity for all and the elimination of any injustice, prejudice or indifference that denies or delays its attainment."

"A community is far more than a geographic locale. It consists, rather, of relationships among a group of people whose lives are inextricably linked, and who, for all of their differences, have many customs, aspirations, and values in common. The Foundation seeks to reinforce these shared values, encourage mutual respect, develop practices of common concern, and enable all people to realize their full potential."

"To further its mission, the Foundation seeks to reinforce these common values—by nurturing a sense of community, encouraging mutual respect, and enabling people to take responsibility for their own lives. At the center of the Foundation's work is a conviction that no community can flourish, or even endure, unless each of its members is treated fairly."

"We strive to protect and enhance the unique resources of our area—its diversity of race and culture, its richness of artistic creation and appreciation."

"We seek to enhance human dignity by providing support for community members to exercise personal responsibility and participate actively in determining the course of their own lives and the life of the community."

"We seek to establish mutual trust, respect, and communication among the Foundation, its grantees, and the community within which they operate."

By adopting a formal statement, the board codifies its intent, gives direction to the staff, and notifies the organization's constituents of the importance it attaches to this issue.

Organizational Policies and Operations

The commitment to diversity must be more than a token gesture. The organization's structures, policies, and day-to-day activities must reflect this commitment. The organization must create a work environment that treats diverse people as professionals in their own fields, while allowing them to incorporate their knowledge of and commit- ment to their communities in their work. Such practice directly bene- fits the operations and program activities of the organization.

The commitment to diversity must be more than a token gesture. The organization's structures, policies, and day-to-day activities must reflect this commitment.

The Hispanic Federation, for example, has established board cri- teria, responsibilities, and a code of conduct that it applies to its own board and shares with its member agencies. Set up to be a model nonprofit organization, demonstrating the best of business practices as well as the compassion of charitable organizations, the federation practices the principles it advocates in its technical assis- tance to its member organizations. This level of organizational com- mitment is required to move forward with a diversity agenda that your various stakeholders will embrace: board and staff members, clients and patients, governmental entities, funders, and others.

"The best strategy to achieve diversity in organizations is to stop talking about it and do it," said Wilma Mankiller ("Foundations of Diversity," 1995, p. 1), the former principal chief of the Cherokee Nation of Oklahoma. "People in staff and board positions, particu- larly leadership roles, should come from as diverse a group as possi- ble. Diversity should not be perceived as something that will occur as the result of an overall policy statement or a general mandate. It should permeate everything the organization does."

The organization must make a focused commitment over time that is appropriate and sensitive to the specific ethnic community it wishes to attract before it can realize significant results. "It is too fre- quently said that Hispanics don't give as a summary dismissal for why many nonprofit organizations in the United States have not been as successful as they would like in raising funds from this increasingly expanding and affluent group," writes Ana Gloria Rivas-Vazquez (1999, p. 129), formerly vice president of the Carollton School of the Sacred Heart in Miami and author of numerous articles about

Latino philanthropy. "But this myth ignores a cultural framework where giving has different meaning and expression than it does in the Anglo culture, and it belies the fact that few nonprofits have developed effective strategies designed to reach Latino donors."

TRUST

We cannot overstate the importance of trust. A relationship of trust between your organization and its potential donors is essential to members of every community. In diverse communities, whose trust may have been violated in the past, the organization must earn trust over time. Relatively small steps, however, can begin that process now. Donors in ethnically diverse communities pay attention to whether your organization is accessible and whether it follows through on its commitments to the community. Donors of diverse ethnic backgrounds are acutely aware of the presence of your organization's president and board members at neighborhood and community functions, and they monitor closely the composition and diversity of your board and staff.

"Latino philanthropy is mediated by personal exchange relationships based on trust," according to Michael Cortés (1995, p. 28).

"Latinos often seek a personal guarantee from an individual they trust that their donations will indeed be used in ways they value."

"Trust is the cumulative product of personal relationships based on mutual assistance and exchange. Latinos are like other ethnic groups in this respect. But fundraisers should not assume that their institution's mission and reputation are enough to gain the trust of Latinos. Latinos often seek a personal guarantee from an individual they trust that their donations will indeed be used in ways they value."

"I would never give money to tribal government because of lack of trust and historical problems," said a prominent Native American who left the reservation as a young child. "But I do support the tribal college, radio station, health clinic, and relief efforts."

Janet Pearce, CEO of the United Way of Southeast Connecticut, established relationships with the Mashantucket Pequot Tribal Nation and the Mohegan tribe shortly after she was appointed president in 1989 and before the tribes' large casinos were operating. Twelve years later, members of the tribes and representatives of the tribal casinos serve on the United Way board, its allocation panels, and as campaign chair.

Some organizations, particularly those in poor urban areas, have found themselves on the brink of closing and have made the conscious decision to become active fundraisers as a matter of survival. One such example is St. Elizabeth's School on the South Side of Chicago. St. Elizabeth's is a Catholic elementary school serving an African American community with four hundred students, none of whom pays full tuition and only 20 percent of whom are Catholic. Sister Maureen Carroll credits four survival techniques for the school's recent fundraising successes: (1) prayer, (2) a clear mission that confirms its commitment to the neighborhood, (3) staying true to the mission, and (4) trust and belief in the institution. Already well known and trusted in the community when it began its fundraising efforts, St. Elizabeth's has moved from $40,000 in annual gifts to $250,000 in each of the past three years, primarily by providing formal development training to existing staff (white, African American, and Latino) and learning to become more self-supporting rather than relying solely on the Catholic diocese. By contacting former students and involving businesses in the local community, it is building a base for larger gifts in the future.

Trust, confidence in the organization, and accountability go hand in hand and are very important to donors deciding whether to give to a particular cause. "Before asking for financial support, it is very important to have a relationship of familiarity and trust," said Bea Stotzer at New Economics for Women. "For us [Latinos], it is an issue of reputation and outcomes." Providing the potential donor a personal association with the organization or with the individual soliciting the donation is the most effective way to generate trust.

INTERNAL DIVERSITY

Prospective donors from diverse backgrounds pay close attention to the diversity of your organization itself.

Trustees and Volunteers

Trustees drive the degree of internalization and integration of diversity within nonprofit organizations. Organizations whose trustees are committed to diversity carefully examine trustee selection and development processes, hiring practices, professional development opportunities for staff, program offerings, and management practices.

Only 0.5 percent of the members of nonprofit boards of directors are Latino, despite Latinos' large and rapidly growing presence in the United States (Sanchez and Zamora, 1999). "More and more Latinos are capable of serving on nonprofit boards and giving," said a Mexican American entrepreneur in Los Angeles. "But there are still so relatively few of us that those who exist are overwhelmed by the demands and expectations placed upon them. We need to expand the pie. Leadership development is what is needed most."

"Acknowledging the close relationship between volunteering and giving, we must recruit more African Americans for membership on important nonprofit boards, both national and local. The black community is largely an untapped source for nontraditional financial support," writes Jean Fairfax (1995, p. 19), a black philanthropist and author in Phoenix. "Representative numbers of blacks on the board are key to developing their trust. But for them to play a vital role in outreach to potential black donors, these individuals must themselves be trusted by the community."

"To play a vital role in outreach to potential black donors, African American board members must themselves be trusted by the community."

"Many Latinos identify their volunteerism as a critical turning point in their philanthropic development," writes Leo Estrada (1990,

p. 35), "since it provides opportunities to meet and get to know [mainstream] corporate, political, and community leaders [and to] learn from [these individuals] about styles of leadership and giving."

In Asian cultures most of the volunteers in nonprofit organizations are women. This is particularly true of immigrants and refugees, as the men often work two or three jobs and simply have no time to volunteer. As Asian Americans become more acculturated, the men are more likely to serve in board or leadership positions.

When you seek diverse board members, be selective in choosing people by consistently looking for such characteristics as a good reputation, ability to work with others, specific skills that your organization needs, and belief in the vision. Do not flatter people onto the board just to fill a quota. In other words, use essentially the same standards you use with mainstream candidates, while remaining flexible about fundraising expectations. We do not mean to imply that you waive or lower fundraising expectations but rather that you expand them to include nonmonetary gifts.

Staff

Staff members in all departments of the organization must represent the ethnic and racial composition of the local area. Most diverse organizations accomplish this by making a concerted effort to attract qualified, diverse applicants.

The Chicago Symphony Orchestra, for example, has instituted a residency program for administrative staff. It offers part-time employment to diverse students, providing them with valuable experience in the workplace and gaining fresh new perspectives for the orchestra. Before publicizing job openings outside the organization, the orchestra first notifies current and former participants in the residency program. The Chicago Civic Orchestra, a training orchestra of young professionals, has increased recruitment of diverse candidates. The symphony orchestra, on the other hand, has difficulty actively diversifying because only one or two positions turn over each year, and all auditions are blind to prevent favoritism or prejudice. (At a blind audition, judges can hear the music but cannot see the musician or even know the performer's identity.)

The San Francisco Museum of Modern Art established a diversity committee through its human resources department in the 1990s to oversee the diversity of the staff. Now that the museum's staff is diverse, the committee plans activities to increase all staff members' sensitivity to others and celebrate the diverse workforce. Examples of some recent programs include a staff art exhibit, softball team, baby photo contest, pizza party, wellness programs, and sponsorship of a team at an AIDS walk. The museum's annual International Feast and Fair is its largest staff event, featuring a potluck supper of favorite ethnic foods followed by an arts and crafts fair at which staff members can sell their own work.

Many organizations have changed the way they describe broadening their staff from "diversifying" to "practicing inclusivity." They are not only concerned that the composition of the staff reflect that of the community but also that the unique background, culture, and perspective of each staff member be treated with respect and included in discussions. In learning to appreciate the values and traditions of various cultures, each member of the staff broadens his or her own worldview and increases the likelihood of effective job performance.

PROGRAMS

The programs that your organization offers signal to potential consumers and supporters your level of commitment to reaching diverse populations. Here are a few examples.

Chicago Symphony Orchestra

One of the strategies to diversify the Chicago Symphony Orchestra is to build mutual and engaging relationships with diverse populations, especially Latinos and African Americans. It has four artist-in-residence programs in different communities in which it holds town meetings with leaders to determine how the community perceives the orchestra and what programs the community would be interested in. In each residency, orchestra staff members work directly in the communities. For example, in the Latino community, it sponsors performances of classical musicians with Mexican folk musicians to produce a hybridization of musical styles. The orchestra has also established an advisory council—composed of twenty diverse individuals from the media, financial institutions, arts organizations, foundations, churches, and other local organizations—to provide advice on marketing and programming and "to keep our feet to the fire," said Joe Young, the orchestra's director of community relations.

The orchestra's musical programming has greatly diversified in recent years to encompass works by various ethnic composers. The orchestra gives ticket vouchers to local organizations serving diverse communities. Selected individuals receive tickets to three very different orchestra performances so that they can experience diverse musical styles (classical, jazz, and vocal music, for example).

Greater Seattle YMCA

The downtown YMCA facility in Seattle, close to the International District, was recently remodeled. It opened with outreach to neighborhood seniors who, it quickly learned, wanted their own recreation services and swimming classes. In a nearby housing project with a high percentage of Islamic residents, the YMCA has added specific programs addressing safety since September 11, 2001. It

In a nearby housing project with a high percentage of Islamic residents, the YMCA has added specific programs addressing safety since September 11, 2001.

offers what it calls Culture Jams, discussions and activities for young people to learn methods for coping with terrorism and respecting other cultures.

The Seattle YMCA began its Earth Service Corps in the early 1990s, primarily composed of middle-class white youth. Recently, it has received funding to broaden the racial and ethnic backgrounds of participants by partnering with schools in diverse communities. The YMCA has full-time staff in selected Seattle public schools to provide a more positive environment for children in after-school programs. The YMCA has documented that the schools that participate in the Earth Service Corps have better school attendance rates than those that do not, according to Mary Kaufman-Cranney, senior vice president for financial development. This educational program with measurable results is attractive to corporate funders with a high interest in education.

San Francisco Museum of Modern Art

The 2000 exhibition "Ultra Baroque: Contemporary Voices in Latin Art" gave the San Francisco Museum of Modern Art an opportunity to reach Latino populations. The marketing department sought media sponsorship to reach Spanish-speaking audiences. The bilingual newspaper that became the exhibit sponsor provided a venue to reach prospective visitors. The museum paid for some ads and received others in-kind, all in Spanish. It used the newsprint space to encourage visitation and included a coupon for discounted admission fees. An unprecedented number of Latinos attended the exhibition, and the museum staff hopes they will return in the future now that they have been introduced to the museum.

Although the public relations department already had a relationship with the newspaper and had met with its editorial department, this was the first time that its marketing department worked with the newspaper's marketing department. The newspaper provided the museum with information about upcoming events in Latino communities and offered to distribute museum materials at selected events.

In addition to obtaining the newspaper's sponsorship, the museum purchased advertisements in other Spanish news outlets. The marketing department sent public service announcements to Spanish-language radio and television stations. It sent promotional e-mails to relevant departments at regional colleges and universities, asking professors to consider a class trip to the museum or at least mention the exhibition to students.

ACCESSIBILITY

People of diverse ethnic backgrounds often do not perceive mainstream nonprofit organizations as readily accessible. Indicators of accessibility include such simple matters as the location of the organization's offices and the warmth and approachability of the receptionist, as well as formal policies and criteria. Even if the organization is, in fact, accessible to donors from diverse cultures, the perception is often otherwise. And the perception will effectively keep prospective donors away.

Some of the ways to ameliorate this perception might include offering space for community meetings and events, using ethnically appropriate media (newspapers, radio, billboards, and so on) for public relations efforts and human resource development, and initiating services and programs specifically designed to address the needs of specific ethnicities.

Organizations that have integrated the value of diversity in their institutional procedures and practices generally become more open and accessible. Such organizations are usually led by CEOs and program managers who have made concerted efforts to develop relationships with leaders in diverse communities.

Some of the programs that the San Francisco Museum of Modern Art hopes to undertake in the near future to make the museum more welcoming to diverse visitors include

- Providing multiple language options on the museum's telephone line for basic information and hours of operation
- Greeting visitors with bilingual membership staff
- Offering membership materials in a variety of languages

- Coding the name badges of staff members who are in contact with museum-goers to indicate the languages they speak (perhaps with a pin of the flag of the appropriate country or countries)

In the early 1990s, the Boston Foundation, one of the oldest and largest U.S. community foundations, started the Partnership Program, composed of African American and Latino middle managers from local corporations who want to be more involved in civic leadership. Participants receive training and hands-on experience in community issues, nonprofit organizations, and ways to support local causes and organizations. Graduates of the program become members of the Partnership Fellows Program. They continue to meet at the foundation's offices and offer advice to the foundation's grant-making staff about emerging issues in their communities. These individuals now have firsthand experience with the foundation and will be more likely to contribute in the future.

STRATEGIES OF INCLUSIVITY

Here are some methods to connect diverse individuals with your organization.

In a proactive manner, ethnically and racially diversify all organizational departments and activities to reflect the diversity of your local community, including the composition of the board and its committees, staff, and vendors; establish an inclusive practices committee to set benchmarks and monitor progress.

Develop programs and activities that especially appeal to or recognize the contributions of local diverse communities. Plan programs in collaboration with organizations that serve specific ethnic communities.

Write a multiyear development plan to reach diverse prospective donors, fully fund and staff the effort, integrate the diversity work into all development activities, and carry out the plan.

Recruit and train development staff members from diverse communities and enlist their assistance in developing outreach programs. They bring language and cultural sensitivity in addition to their educational and professional experience.

Rather than placing an ad in a mainstream newspaper and waiting for applicants to arrive, do the following:

Recruit and train development staff members from diverse communities and enlist their assistance in developing outreach programs.

- Place ads in ethnic publications.

- Meet with guidance counselors and place ads on bulletin boards and electronic bulletin boards of colleges, universities, and continuing education sites.

- Meet with instructors and professors of relevant classes to discuss job openings and determine other campus groups of interest to contact.

- Meet with directors of major ethnic institutions, such as cultural centers and neighborhood activity centers, and place ads in their newsletters and on their Web sites and bulletin boards.

- Meet with spiritual leaders in houses of worship, and place ads in their newsletters and on their Web sites and bulletin boards.

- Enlist the help of people already on your staff to suggest other opportunities for advertising and to talk with friends and neighbors about openings.

Provide communication and marketing materials to ethnically diverse populations through such nontraditional venues as billboards, ethnic periodicals, television, radio, and other local media.

Keep in mind that many diverse communities are rooted in oral rather than written traditions.

Provide training and support for staff and board members about philanthropy in diverse ethnic communities. Include all those who work or volunteer for your organization in diversity efforts. To demonstrate the importance of this training, use examples such as the scouting organization that used the concept of camping with Japanese American immigrants who associate the word *camp* with concentrations camps or the receptionist who engaged a Native American in a discussion of why the local Indian mascot was changed. Open up discussion of instances when staff members experienced or witnessed a lack of sensitivity so that everyone in your organization is included in the diversity training, not just the people in one department or at management levels.

Publicize gifts that your organization has already received by highlighting diverse donors (with their permission) in newspapers, on radio and television, and in programs and periodicals that reach consumers in ethnically diverse communities.

Establish an advisory council composed of members of the diverse population you hope to attract. Set clear expectations of the members and the council prior to extending invitations to join the council. Invite people from diverse backgrounds to serve on existing councils and committees.

Some of these strategies can be both expensive and time-consuming; others can cost little or nothing to put into place. If your organization is struggling to justify the expense of such diversification, focus on the long-term benefits of the community's increased awareness of and trust in your organization to show that the return is often worth the investment of resources.

WHERE WE GO FROM HERE

Your nonprofit organization must be fully committed to diversity in all facets of institutional life in order for fundraising to be successful in diverse ethnic and racial communities. This commitment starts at the top with the board of trustees, the CEO, and senior management. In addition the organization must allocate resources to the effort—both people and money.

Consistent effort and accomplishments over time will generate trust in the organization and encourage participation by people of diverse backgrounds in the organization's programs, events, and committees. This participation, in turn, leads to commitment and support. We will discuss these concepts further in Chapter Four.

4

Building Awareness and Cultivating Prospects

The people you hope to attract must become aware of your organization and the services it provides before you can hope to involve them as volunteers or contributors. This chapter provides information about specific sensibilities and customs of each of the four broad population groups as well as examples of techniques and activities that a variety of nonprofit organizations have used successfully.

SENSIBILITIES AND CUSTOMS

Effective fundraisers in diverse cultures must be aware of varying values, meanings, and cultural sensitivities, and they must be willing to adjust fundraising strategies to meet the needs of the community. Here are some of the traditions unique to each population segment.

African Americans

Factors in successful fundraising in the African American community include (1) establishing respect and trust, (2) giving your own money before asking others, and (3) providing the opportunity to leave something lasting that will help others help themselves, according to Brenda Rayford, president of the Black United Fund of Michigan.

Potential donors may closely ally trust with participation in the governance of the organization. "I cannot emphasize enough the importance of control to black donors; the question of which entity controls the allocation of charitable dollars is a central one," writes African American philanthropist Jean Fairfax (1995, p. 14). "The amount of giving to the black church is a sign of trust in an institution that historically has been controlled by African Americans."

Pier Rogers, formerly at Associated Black Charities, pointed out that blacks like to be treated individually, not as a stereotype. She also cautioned that black people do not necessarily want public recognition; recognition is important to varying degrees to different people.

Personal interaction and group gatherings are especially important in the African American community, perhaps because of their strong oral traditions. They value face-to-face meetings where they can assess firsthand the sincerity and trustworthiness of the organization's leadership. Social events are also important as opportunities to be with family and friends and as occasions for celebration. Mark Dennis of The Alford Group Inc. describes seven steps to engage and cultivate African American donors: identify, invite, inform, interest, involve, invest, and inspire.

Asian Americans

Asian Americans take fundraising personally. "If you ask me to do something and I respond positively, I am giving you face," said Gwynne Tuan, former development director of the China Institute. "If I say no, it is taken personally. This is why it is very hard to get people to lead a campaign or event. The results are a reflection on me." In addition the leader does not want to "owe" people.

Asian reluctance to ask directly for money is another example of the importance of face. "If you ask me up front and I can't give the money, I lose face," said Vishakha Desai, senior vice president and director of the museum at the Asia Society. "I don't want to be seen as cheap, so don't ask me for too much." One approach that would be more sensitive might be to carefully put together a solicitation team of the prospective donor's peers. Plan for the context of the meeting, perhaps over lunch at a restaurant. Talk about other people who would be considered peers and what they have done for the organization. One of the peers can later ask the prospect to be part of the team.

Japanese Americans are not so direct as Western Americans, but, said Irene Hirano, president of the Japanese American National Museum, they are more direct than Chinese Americans. She reminded us that first-generation Japanese Americans built many churches and temples: "They can be pretty direct. The second generation is more Americanized and sometimes more reluctant."

After you have told a person about a philanthropic opportunity, you should wait for a response. If you call the prospective donor in a few days to remind them, that person may view you as rude. "Once a person has been told the situation, one must wait for the response," said David Baker at On Lok Senior Health Services. "Even in the case of the annual dinner, a board member might tell a friend that the dinner was taking place on a specific night, but he would not ask the friend to attend. The friend would acknowledge that the trustee had told him about the dinner and then go home and write a check."

After an Asian American agrees to chair an event or committee, that person will not volunteer whom he or she knows. You must uncover these connections and show the chair how he or she will gain prestige and recognition. You must demonstrate a benefit to both the leader and the organization.

Some Asian American immigrants are very sophisticated and westernized, perhaps having immigrated as children and been educated in the United States. They have been exposed to U.S. culture and have enjoyed the fruits of philanthropy. Others may be unsophisticated about philanthropy. Do not assume that Asian Americans are knowledgeable about U.S. philanthropic traditions or protocol. For example, they may not realize that service on a charity's board of directors or campaign committee is done without compensation or that contributors to the nonprofit organization will be listed in the annual report unless the donor requests anonymity. Expectations should be clearly stated, preferably in writing, to avoid any misunderstanding.

Memorial gifts are popular with the Chinese, particularly for organizations that serve the elderly. For example, On Lok Senior Health Services attracts about $90,000 per year in memorial gifts.

Memorial gifts are popular with the Chinese, particularly for organizations that serve the elderly.

The frequency of memorial gifts relates to the custom of the Chinese elderly to give charitable contributions in honor of changes in the lives of their families and friends, such as birthdays and anniversaries. Flowers are traditional at funerals, but families increasingly ask that mourners make monetary contributions in lieu of flowers.

Acknowledging a gift quickly is important in Chinese culture, according to Baker. If the thank-you letter comes weeks or months after donors send memorial gifts, family members may be offended that the organizations is reminding them once again of their grief. Donors who give to mainstream organizations generally want recognition from the organization. "We live in a racist society," said Gail Kong, executive director of the Asia Pacific Fund. "We want respect." Tangible evidence of that respect is a prompt and thoughtful thank-you note.

"Donors and prospective donors who are older and not American-born are sensitive to protocols and etiquette," said Margaret Fung, executive director of the Asian American Legal Defense and Education Fund. Even with younger and more westernized donors, certain protocols apply. For instance, when a board member holds a house party, having one person challenge the group by taking out a checkbook and writing a check has not worked well. It is much more effective to host the house party and follow up later individually.

Latinos

"Latinos don't ask each other for money," says Lili Santiago de Silva of El Museo del Barrio in New York City. "Latinos give money because they are very excited or because there is a deficit—either a big project or a big need. They respond to crises, rather than ongoing operations. An earthquake, for instance, really garners their support."

According to Adam Martinez at Baylor College of Medicine in Houston, it is important to Latinos that a well-respected community leader make the fundraising call. It is not as important for that person to speak Spanish as to communicate a desire to be respectful and a willingness to learn from the prospective donor.

The way in which Latinos compose letters and brochures is different from the spoken word, according to Martinez. "There is a warmth, baroqueness, sincerity, and flair to Spanish writing. The choice of words in writing is unlike the way they talk." Referring to a letter he had received from a person in Mexico, he said it could be roughly translated, "We are deeply grateful for the spirit with which your giving has touched our lives and made us all better people." He said he does not receive similarly worded or personable letters from white Americans. You will want to phrase your thank-you letters warmly—and perhaps check with a board or staff member from the same ethnic background to confirm that your message is culturally appropriate before it is mailed.

Latinos must feel an intimacy about giving so that they feel a personal connection to the cause or to the individual soliciting funds. Who is involved is almost as important as the cause. Thus testimonials are important and effective in fundraising with Latinos.

Native Americans

"If you want to organize something in Native American communities," said Tia Oros of the Seventh Generation Fund and a member of the Zuni tribe, "you would go to the elders first. Perhaps even have a ceremony."

In Native American communities, first impressions matter. At any meeting, protocol calls for having introductions first. Native Americans want to know who is in the room and who they are. White participants may become impatient to begin the formal agenda, but Native Americans know that the introductions are one of the most important parts of the meeting. Participants can form networks and begin friendships based on how people introduce themselves. For example, Oros described introductions at a recent meeting: "A Mayan from Guatemala living in the Bay Area in California described the five hundred years of exile for his people in Guatemala. A Lakota in the group of indigenous people felt the common pain. The group has now decided to include historic grief counseling in its next meeting."

The giver and the receiver are equally important in Native American cultures. When they receive a grant, Native Americans always want to give something back to the donor, so the donor can receive as well. This balance is very important. Often Native Americans make their gifts anonymously and privately. Do not ask for a gift directly; rather, explain the need and let the person choose to give of his or her free will. The degree of potential donors' exposure to white culture will make a difference in the appropriate approach to Native Americans as well.

When they receive a grant, Native Americans always want to give something back to the donor, so the donor can receive as well.

"Most Native Americans," said Carla Roberts with the Arizona Community Foundation, "want to give to directly benefit individuals in need rather than through an organization. This is changing with the increased level of sophistication."

"There seems to be a perception," said Donna Chavis, executive director of Native Americans in Philanthropy, "either that Native Americans are no different than the rest of us or that they are very exotic. Reality is somewhere in between." For example, with some tribes, it is appropriate to bring a gift of recognition with you to a meeting. In Chavis's tribe, the gift should be tobacco.

The annual report cover for the Alaska Native Heritage Center (see Exhibit 4.1) is a good example of the use of culturally appropriate images and messages. Its title, *A Gathering of Traditions*, speaks to the importance of history and culture to Alaska Native people. The photograph of the family shows members of every generation, with the elder highlighted in the center of the circle. We

Exhibit 4.1. Alaska Native Heritage Center: Annual Report Cover.

Photo source: Copyright © Chris Arend Photography 2002.

can visualize the wealth of wisdom and knowledge that generation hands down to generation by the guiding light of tradition. Yet the light from the laptop computer in this photo shows that the group also embraces modern changes in such a way that the people can be full participants in the present era as well.

Generations or Time in This Country

Immigrants, both as individuals and as communities, struggle to survive in this new and often hostile country. Barriers such as language, lack of familiarity with the new country's customs, inability to obtain housing and business financing, and blatant discrimination are common experiences for immigrants regardless of ethnicity, class, or date of entry to the United States.

As we discussed in Chapter One, the time that immigrants have spent in this country and their degree of acculturation are important indicators of readiness for philanthropy. For instance, according to Valerie Lee, former executive director of Asian American Renaissance in Minneapolis, the organization conducts two direct mail appeals for donors annually and attracts more than half of its gifts from the Asian community, primarily from Japanese Americans. Even though the Japanese Americans are a small community in Minneapolis compared to the Chinese and Southeast Asian populations, they have been in the United States longer, have fewer direct ties to the country of origin, understand philanthropy, and are extremely sensitive to issues of social justice. But the majority Asian population in Minneapolis is Hmong (Southeast Asian), young (under eighteen), newly arrived, and still at the survival stage on the continuum of philanthropy. They are less likely to be donors.

According to Penelope Haru Snipper, a Japanese American philanthropic consultant, many third- and fourth-generation Asian Americans are not yet involved with philanthropy. Yet sometimes they make charitable gifts, usually to mainstream organizations. This is because they perceive that such giving is expected of their companies and because they enjoy the mainstream recognition. It is an acknowledgment that they have made it, that they are fully accul-turated Asian Americans.

STRATEGIES TO BUILD AWARENESS

The individuals we interviewed at organizations that are success-fully raising funds from diverse donors suggested useful techniques and basic strategies to build awareness of your organization in diverse communities and to begin to cultivate the interest of eth-nically and racially diverse people.

Earn the goodwill of the community before beginning any fundraising; your organization must provide good products and needed services to earn goodwill. This concept is closely related to the ideas we discussed in Chapter Three about commitment, trust, and programs. Fundraisers often have the knee-jerk reaction that if the project involves a certain eth-nicity, then approaching members of that community for funds is appropriate. Many mainstream organizations do not understand that they must have already estab-lished a track record with the community and a relationship with the donor. Remember that

Fundraisers often have the knee-jerk reaction that if the project involves a certain ethnicity, then approaching members of that community for funds is appropriate.

your organization's purpose is to serve its constituents well, not to promote its own public relations. As Anni Chung, executive direc-tor of Self-Help for the Elderly in San Francisco, says, "Clients and donors, not the agency, are the center of our work."

Research your diverse community or communities; identify the leaders and understand cultural interests locally, regionally, and nationally. Mainstream organizations must have a genuine interest in the ethnic communities and not simply check off suggestions from a book's laundry list of ideas. People in diverse communities will quickly know if the outreach is less than sincere.

Get involved in local activities that are important to the donors' community: attend parades and festivals; learn about ceremonies and special events; go to a church picnic. Getting involved will build up your knowledge and sensitivity to other cultures. People you meet will learn more about your organization. And your presence in the community speaks volumes about your interest and commitment.

Identify a person within the potential donor group who may be willing to guide and advise you. Find someone to act as your mentor if you genuinely want to learn more about the people you serve and hope to reach as donors. A teacher, a community worker, or another established person can introduce you to other people once they trust you and your motives. Donna Chavis at Native Americans in Philanthropy, for example, relies upon her network of contacts, which she calls her "moccasin line," to advise her about specific tribes.

Ask people you talk to for the names of others you should contact. Write carefully pitched letters letting the person know that you will call them to set a time to talk. Then call the person you want to contact directly to ask for an appointment to meet. Do not ask an assistant to make the phone call; make the call yourself. Use your mentor's name, with permission, in your introductory letter and telephone call.

Seek personal meetings, preferably in the person's home or a comfortable setting (perhaps your organization or a quiet restaurant). Your first job is to get to know and trust the other person and earn trust in return. Only then can you ask for support.

If the donors you aspire to attract speak a native language at home, learn, under the tutelage of your mentor, at least some words in that language—for example, the words for *hello, please, thank you,* and *farewell.* Perhaps there is a title by which your prospective donor should be addressed. Individuals will view your efforts to use their native language as a sign of respect and will appreciate it. A note of caution: a poor attempt to speak in a native language or one in the wrong context could be seen as insulting or patronizing. For example, a second- or third-generation Japanese American might be insulted to hear a Caucasian greet them with *konichi-wa* or some similar greeting. Ask your mentor about customs and sensitivities to which you should be particularly attuned.

Systemwide Outreach: United Way of Metropolitan Tarrant County

The United Way of Metropolitan Tarrant County (Fort Worth, Texas) provides an example of integrated organizational outreach to diverse constituencies. Viney Chandler, president and CEO, described her organization's efforts to build relationships with diverse populations and bring new people into the decision-making process.

Several years ago, IBM offered to partner with this United Way by providing computers for a special community initiative. Ann Rice, senior vice president for community investment, saw this offer as an opportunity to reach out to ethnic communities by setting up community technology centers. She also saw it as a chance to bridge cultural gaps and develop meaningful relationships.

Listening Sessions

Rice asked established contacts in ethnic communities, often liaisons that were involved in numerous mainstream organizations, to arrange what she called listening sessions, which shared the following elements:

1. Begin with a meal planned and prepared by community members. (If needed, United Way supplied funds to buy supplies.)
2. Hold the listening sessions in the evening or on a weekend to accommodate working people.

3. Welcome children.
4. Include the United Way president and board chair, as well as other staff and board members.
5. Invite a variety of people from the community, not only those already in active leadership positions.
6. Use a neutral, skilled facilitator to lead the discussions.
7. Announce that the purpose of the listening sessions is to learn about the greatest concerns of the community and how the United Way can help.
8. Establish guidelines for United Way participants: listen carefully; do not defend past practices; do not make promises.

As an example, the listening session in the Native American community took place on a Sunday afternoon in a packed room. About ten United Way participants sat at different tables for the meal, which was delicious and very authentic. The conversation was frank, with people expressing much frustration about a past project (a medical center) for which the Native Americans had asked the United Way for help and been turned down. As United Way President Viney Chandler said, "We got blasted." The community expressed many needs. After listening for more than an hour, Chandler stood up and made the following points:

"This discussion is very enlightening."
"We came to listen."
"Your points are valid, and we appreciate your openness."
"We can't make promises."
"We can't undo the past."
"What can we do to help in the future?"

The discussion that followed was productive, with many constructive and creative ideas from the participants. One suggestion was to establish a technology center.

Results So Far

The organization repeated the listening sessions in many ethnic communities in the Tarrant County metropolitan area. The leaders of each of the groups then came together for listening sessions in which common concerns were aired and possible solutions were proposed. Today Tarrant County has ten community technology centers staffed with full-time VISTA workers under United Way's direction, as well as numerous projects in specific communities.

> *Today Tarrant County has ten community technology centers staffed with full-time VISTA workers under the direction of United Way, as well as numerous projects in specific communities.*

This Native American community and the United Way have for the first time an open and trusting relationship. Native Americans serve on many United Way volunteer committees. United Way always makes sure that the donor photographs in its general brochures and printed materials include persons who are clearly Native American. United Way has allocated funds to several neighborhood groups that the Internal Revenue Service has not yet recognized as 501(c)(3) organizations. Native American donors have made gifts, albeit small ones. The groundwork for larger gifts and long-term relationships is being built through these efforts in African American, Asian American, and Latino communities as well.

Lessons Learned

Chandler listed the following as lessons learned:

- People become empowered in new ways once they are gathered around the table. The organization must be ready to respond to new kinds of requests in tangible ways.

- Do not set up outside day care; let the children come to the meeting. People expect to have their children with them and are comfortable in that setting. This comfort helps them to be more forthcoming.

- Sharing a meal together is an important and effective way to lower communication barriers.

- Establish avenues to allocate resources to these groups. Some may not fit into standard operating procedures, such as community groups that don't have 501(c)(3) status.

- This may be the first time that diverse communities have discussed their common interests. For example, even though nearly all the people in a community are Spanish-speaking, they may represent many ethnicities and countries of origin. There will be great diversity of experiences and opinions. Allow plenty of time for discussion, and expect multiple meetings.

- Respect people's time. Most of them will not be accustomed to attending long meetings. Work with an experienced facilitator to make the most of limited time.

- Be sure that you clearly describe and follow the next steps that you will take.

With diverse audiences, you can effectively use techniques and activities that most nonprofit organizations use to educate members of the general public and attract their involvement—but often with a special cultural twist.

MEMBERSHIP PROGRAMS

Many organizations have established membership programs to increase involvement and to enhance the experience of visitors, neighbors, volunteers, and supporters. Not only do membership programs generate revenue (often from dues), they also encourage involvement in the organization through networking and volunteer opportunities and special events.

The United Way of Central Ohio, for example, has established a membership group called the Leaders Circle for donors who follow giving guidelines based on the donor's annual salary, said Sheryle Powell, Key Club manager for United Way. The guidelines, a sliding scale from 0.5 percent to 2 percent of annual salary, provide the opportunity to recognize all individuals who donate to United Way, at their capacity, regardless of the dollar amount that each donates to the campaign. After only two years of the Leaders Circle's existence, the number of donors giving at or above the recommended guideline levels has increased from fifty-five hundred to seventeen thousand individuals. The end-of-campaign Circle Celebration in 2001, an exclusive event for Leaders Circle members, featured entertainers like Bill Cosby and Lionel Richie and attracted twelve thousand members. Local corporations underwrote all the event's costs.

The Asian American Legal Defense and Education Fund in New York City has been a membership organization since 1986 (its twelfth year). Membership fees range from $50 to $1,000. A large percentage of the members are Asian Americans—lawyers, community members, and students. Members receive a newsletter as well as periodic one-page update sheets on recent events and legislation, both of which are also available on-line.

The Mexican Fine Arts Center Museum in Chicago has two thousand members, paying dues from $15 to $250. The members are drawn from over one hundred thousand visitors annually, 55 percent of whom are Mexican. The museum has started a support group called Opano Mexica to educate young Mexican Americans in their twenties and thirties about philanthropy. The group trains the members about their responsibility to give back to the community, not just the museum. The concept of giving to a museum is foreign to Mexican-born Americans, because arts organizations in Mexico receive all their funding from the state, according to Carlos Tortolero, the museum's executive director.

The concept of giving to a museum is foreign to Mexican-born Americans, because arts organizations in Mexico receive all their funding from the state.

Smaller organizations use membership programs as well, some for specific audiences. For example, the J. Ashburn Jr. Youth Center, a social service organization in an African American neighborhood near downtown Columbus, established a program called Community Links for local businesses. It asked successful entrepreneurs to help spread the word about the center's work with young people. The center keeps the businesses informed through regular communications, with the hope that they will serve as advocates and spokespersons and in the hope that they will eventually become donors as well. Community Links members have provided entrée for the staff to form partnerships with larger institutions such as a health care provider and others who made contributions to the center's capital campaign. Annette Jefferson, the center's development director, said, "We like to think of their involvement as a high commitment, low-cost, low-time investment for them with big results for us."

SPECIAL EVENTS

Special events are the most popular means to attract friends and publicize the mission and programs of nonprofit organizations. This is especially true in diverse communities. Although some events provide impressive net proceeds, most raise awareness rather than substantial funds. Special events come in all varieties: galas with the support of major corporations, golf tournaments with superstar hosts, and phonathons focused on reconnecting with lapsed members. The special events we discuss in this chapter serve primarily as vehicles to involve and engage constituents in the activities of the organization.

One of the advantages of a special event is that it provides a vehicle to attract the involvement of a cadre of volunteers. "I have learned from experience that the best way to encourage giving from Latinos or others is not to get in people's faces to pressure them for donations but rather to get them involved as volunteers in philanthropic organizations doing work they care deeply about. Generally, this eventually leads them to contribute not only their time but also their money," said a Cuban American accountant we interviewed in Miami.

In the late 1960s and early 1970s, the early years of San Francisco's group Self-Help for the Elderly, volunteers ran the concession stands at Golden Gate Park, selling hot dogs for Self-Help. The project did not earn much money, but it did educate people about the organization and generate goodwill. For each of the past fifteen years, Self-Help has held a walkathon with the entire community participating—from elementary schoolchildren receiving twenty cents per mile to eighty-year-olds walking only a few blocks. The young and the old can walk together. In 2000 some one thousand walked in San Francisco and six hundred in San Jose, netting $100,000 for Self-Help. "All of our events rely on volunteers," said Self-Help's executive director, Anni Chung. "Once outsiders are brought into the community, they are hooked. Each function brings more volunteers."

The organization puts these volunteers to work on many projects throughout the year. On Thanksgiving, for example, three hundred Self-Help volunteers served three thousand meals to the poor at their facilities and took food to the homebound. Self-Help now has one thousand people who are or have been involved, including many volunteers from high schools and universities.

Another example of the creative use of volunteer skills was the recruiting of sixth-grade students in Columbus to decorate commemorative shovels for the ground breaking of a new youth service facility in a predominantly African American community. Mayor Michael Coleman hung his shovel in his office, a testimonial to its attractiveness as well as publicity for the J. Ashburn Jr. Youth Center.

For thirty-three years, the Arizona group Chicanos por la Causa has held a children's Christmas party. In 2000 it attracted seventeen thousand youngsters at the elementary school across the street from the organization's offices in Phoenix. The organization also sponsors Christmas parties in Tucson and Somerton. In addition to giving holiday entertainment and gifts to local children and involving scores of volunteers, it promotes goodwill and increases people's understanding of the services that the group provides.

The Asian American Legal Defense and Education Fund hosts events such as theater parties and book readings. Summer events are held in a club or lounge to attract student law interns. Since 1981 the organization has sponsored summer internships with high school students. In 1999 and 2000 the students set up outreach tables in neighborhood and local businesses to encourage participation in the 2000 census.

Another way to involve community members in the organization is to invite them to small gatherings around topics of interest to the group. Gail Kong at the Asian Pacific Fund hosted focus groups of Asians to learn about which issues were important to them, to determine whether they wanted to support ethnic-specific programs or pan-Asian issues, and to find out which other major leaders should be involved. Individuals of all backgrounds want to be asked their opinions and to have their answers listened to respectfully. You may want to consider the kinds of information that your organization could obtain by sponsoring focus groups.

"The best way to teach people about our culture is to invite them to visit," according to Barbara Poley, executive director of the Hopi Foundation. The Hopi Foundation has no special events to raise funds, because it does not

Another way to involve community members in the organization is to invite them to small gatherings around topics of interest to the group.

want to compete with the fundraising efforts of other local organizations and because they take so much time and energy to organize. Rather, staff invite people to share everyday life and other community activities with them. Prospective donors "need to see how we interact with one another, see that we can be trusted," said Poley, who also shows visitors the foundation's strategic plan and annual report to demonstrate the organization's stability.

WHERE WE GO FROM HERE

Nonprofit organizations committed to diversifying their pool of donors must build awareness of the organizations' services and programs that are relevant to specific populations they hope to attract. They must also develop techniques to cultivate prospective donors, techniques that acknowledge and respect the communities' customs and traditions.

This chapter suggests a few of the culturally specific customs you will want to understand. We present them here not as an exhaustive list but rather as examples to whet your appetite to learn more about the rich cultural diversity in your area.

People in all four broad categories—Asian American, African American, Latino, and Native American—highly value social interaction with peers. Programs and events that bring people together are effective ways to generate interest in your organization. Chapter Five describes ways to move those who have an interest in your organization to contribute toward its future.

5

Turning Diverse Prospects into Donors

Once people of diverse backgrounds are familiar with and involved in the work of your organization, you have the opportunity to convert them into contributors. This chapter offers ideas and suggestions to customize some of the strategies you already employ to attract diverse donors—and some strategies that other organizations have used effectively. We include examples from the full gamut of activities: small gatherings of friends to major public events, direct mail addressed to thousands of prospective donors to personal notes for specific individuals, and the donation of spare change from neighborhood children to corporate sponsorships. First we look at the continuum of philanthropy to provide a context for our discussion.

Philanthropic practices primarily evolve from grassroots communal giving to individual giving that helps others in need to institutional giving aimed at solving societal problems. Moving along the continuum of philanthropy, the donor goes from a primary interest in matters close to home and immediate to more long-term issues with importance to the broader community. Likewise the charitable vehicles the donor uses evolve from personal gifts directly to the recipient to voluntary associations to more structured non-profit organizations. Mindy Berry and Jessica Chao (2001) describe this phenomenon in the publication for the Forum of Regional Associations of Grantmakers.

Causes of importance to those in the early stages of philanthropy include

- Family and friends in need

- Children, youth, and families

- Elderly in need

- Human services

- Education and scholarships

- Cultural heritage, preservation, and pride

Those in the early stages of philanthropy are likely to make remittances to the following recipients in their countries of origin: family and friends, emergency aid, disaster relief, public works, hospitals, and schools.

As individuals become more financially and socially stable, their charitable interests seem to broaden to include

- Higher education: scholarships, fellowships, ethnic studies and history, professional schools

- Youth development and precollege education: programs for at-risk children and youth, literacy, tutoring, and mentoring

- Cultural heritage, preservation, and pride: museums, celebrations, ethnic schools, arts, and cultural centers

- Civil rights, social justice, and human rights: specific to one race or ethnicity as well as across communities

- Health care and services for the elderly: access to primary and emergency care, substance abuse, diseases, and research

- Human services, including housing, economic and business development: community development, microlending, self-help, and training

Donors at the beginning of the continuum often give directly through individuals or voluntary associations. Later, donors choose more structured nonprofit organizations:

- Family and friends

- Emergency aid, loans, and human services

- Faith-based institutions: churches, temples, and mosques

- Mutual aid associations

- Fraternal, cultural, and social associations

- Alumni, professional, occupational, civic, and business associations

- Tribes, tribal organizations, enterprises, and funds

Donors at the beginning of the continuum often give directly through individuals or voluntary associations. Later, donors choose more structured nonprofit organizations.

- Community organizations, institutions, and centers

- Historically black or tribal colleges

- Health clinics, hospitals, and nursing homes

Nonprofit organizations use several strategies to encourage these gifts: (1) personal meetings, the most labor-intensive and the most effective way to solicit funds; (2) special events, also labor-intensive and an attractive way to involve volunteers; and (3) direct mail appeals, which reach many people with minimal staff time and often bring minimal returns.

PERSONAL MEETINGS
AND HOUSE PARTIES

Individuals in each diverse population treasure personal interaction and personal relationships. Latinos whom we interviewed, both those involved in fundraising and those who give, all connected *personalismo* (personalization) to giving. People need to feel a personal connection to the cause or to the persons soliciting funds (Royce and Rodriguez, 1999, p. 15).

Face-to-Face Meetings

Respondents to research conducted in 1999 in the Baltimore African American community unanimously believed that the most effective means of solicitation is a personal appeal. "We are a relationship people. I give to someone who I know and trust. We want to be asked directly—not through mail, telephone, or other more impersonal techniques" (Baltimore Giving Project, 1999, p. 4).

Lorraine Holmes Settles of The AFRAM Group names three keys to raising funds from African Americans: develop trust; meet face-to-face with prospective donors; and demonstrate that your organization meets important needs efficiently and effectively.

Face-to-face meetings, however, do not imply that you should ask directly for a gift. People of Asian American, Latino, and Native American cultures, as we discussed in Chapter Four, might consider this approach rude or inappropriate. David Baker at On Lok Senior Health Services, for example, explained that his board shies away from direct one-to-one fundraising for a couple of reasons: it is awkward and sometimes culturally inappropriate to ask for a specific gift directly, and the board members perceive that their main strength is bringing policy and program expertise to the organization, rather than fundraising. Even in the absence of face-to-face fundraising, On Lok nonetheless receives contributions from 6 percent of the Chinese population in San Francisco.

Personal Request

However, other interviewees with whom we spoke in Asian American communities said that even at lower giving levels, Asian Americans respond best to the personal request. None of the Asian American donors interviewed for *Cultures of Caring* (Council on Foundations, 1999) has made or considered making a major gift in response to a direct mail campaign. When we asked which types of fundraising appeals were most effective, Asian American donors answered emphatically, "The personal ask." Donors mentioned that a personal visit or phone call from a close friend, family member, or business associate is important. Most suggested that the person asking should be prominent within the community, have a reputation of respect, and be accomplished. A Japanese American donor said, "I give to those I know and trust."

Personal Relationship

Personal relationships with mainstream organizations are important to Asian Americans. Prospective Asian American donors want to be clear about and comfortable with the expectations of the organization. They do not want to risk losing face by not understanding U.S. practices and customs or the traditions of a specific organization. They may feel awkward if they have not been fully briefed. A personal relationship will permit them to ask questions. Once the prospective donor reaches a personally defined level of comfort, he or she will lose the reluctance to ask questions about what to expect as a donor in the mainstream culture.

House Parties

Prospective Asian American donors seem to particularly value dinners in people's homes as a form of recognition by their peers. The downside of such events from the organization's point of view is that they require considerable staff time and do not raise much money in the short run.

Prospective Asian American donors seem to particularly value dinners in people's homes as a form of recognition by their peers.

Board members of the Asian American Federation of New York host house parties throughout the year, with friends and colleagues of the host as guests, as a way to engage people in the organization. The board member then encourages these colleagues to host events for their friends. When the house party guests understand the organization's mission and activities, they are likely to write checks and donate items for the auction at the gala. (We will provide more details about this in Chapter Six.)

Involvement Before a Personal Appeal

"The traditional fundraising practice of face-to-face fundraising—an individual talking to another individual about specific gifts—can be an uncomfortable style of fundraising for many members of culturally diverse backgrounds," said Mary Kaufman-Cranney of the Greater Seattle YMCA. One example of how the YMCA involved a diverse population is its Black Achievers program, established to link junior and senior high school students with mentors who are successful African American leaders. Companies enlist employees as adult volunteers; they support their volunteer employees by giving them flextime to participate and paying the YMCA $1,000 per volunteer. An annual dinner honors outstanding students and the adult volunteers from fifteen to twenty corporations. The corporations buy tables at the event, and the YMCA raises $50,000 to $75,000 to support the following year's program. Thus the organization asks the individuals not for monetary contributions but rather for gifts of time and energy; it asks the employers for financial contributions. The adult participants in the program have become volunteer face-to-face fundraisers as their involvement with the organization has increased.

EVENTS

Events range from ethnic-specific cultural celebrations for the whole community to intimate gatherings of selected prospective donors with board members. Some special events are sporting competitions with corporate sponsors; others focus on children's activities; and many are major fundraisers (which we will discuss in more detail in Chapter Six). Nearly all the fundraisers we interviewed told us that their organizations host a broad range of events, usually with cultural components. Mainstream organizations may host events with cultural components or may partner with ethnic groups in order to attract diverse donors.

The events we describe in this chapter are primarily focused on awareness building and friend- (rather than fund-) raising. As was the case with the awareness events we described in the last chapter, a major benefit of these events is the ability to attract the involvement of numerous volunteers.

Every summer two hundred Chinese youth in San Francisco come together to do the lion dance on the streets and through the shops in Chinatown for Chinese New Year. The youth ask for donations for Self-Help for the Elderly. The young people learn the traditional dance and do something for the elderly; it is a way to bridge the generation gap. Although the event raises some money for Self-Help, its primary goals are to raise awareness about the organization and to involve local youth in its work, according to Anni Chung, Self-Help's executive director.

Carlos Tortolero of the Mexican Fine Arts Center Museum in Chicago said that his organization focuses on teaching visitors and members about how the museum operates. "We are a high quality museum. I do not play the woe-is-me game. I tell people, 'Don't save me; help me grow.'" The museum offers behind-the-scene tours and concerts on the patio to attract interest, educate visitors, and generate contributions. In addition it hosts an annual gala, an elegant dinner celebration. The cover of its 2001 invitation (see Exhibit 5.1)

Exhibit 5.1. Mexican Fine Arts Center Museum: Gala Invitation.

Source: Copyright © Mexican Fine Arts Museum, Chicago. Angelina Villanueva, Graphic Arts Director.

was a rich gold sun on a bright pink background. The inside of the invitation not only gave the program for the evening but also listed the sponsors, grouped at various levels of giving; members of the board of trustees; and the gala cochairs. The invitation told attendees what to expect and who was involved with the organization.

The J. Ashburn Jr. Youth Center in Columbus has expanded its services to include families by constructing a new facility in its predominantly African American community. Although the $2.5 million building project was achieved primarily through governmental funds and grants from local foundations and businesses, the center also encouraged local residents to contribute—even the children. The center sponsored a treasure hunt to involve neighborhood children in fundraising efforts, asking them to hunt for treasure (loose change) around their homes. Each young person received a locking plastic bag, a "treasure chest," with a colorful brochure explaining the project:

There's money to be found in unusual places,
Nooks and crannies and hidden spaces.
Collect all you can and bring it in.
You'll help build the new Center, and a treat you will win.

Staff at the center notified parents in advance that the children would be seeking spare change. Each child who brought back "treasure" received a Happy Meal, compliments of McDonald's. Development Director Annette Jefferson said, "It is important to get the kids involved so that they will take pride in the center as their own. It is not how much they give, but *that* they give." By the time the new facility was dedicated, many local young people had contributed both money and time.

"It is not how much they give, but that they give."

The Asia Foundation sponsors panel discussions at corporate breakfasts, lunches, and dinners, each one focused on particular interests and particular countries. For example, a panel from China might talk about legal aid, or a panel of experts might discuss Philippine trade regulations. The Asia Foundation hosts approximately two events in the Asian Perspective Series each month, primarily in Washington, D.C., but also in New York, Los Angeles, and San Francisco. The foundation invites important people from the appropriate communities to attend. At the event, representatives distribute materials about the organization but give no fundraising pitch.

The Asian Pacific Fund signature youth program, Growing Up Asian in America, is a forum for elementary and secondary school students in nine San Francisco Bay Area counties to share their ideas and perspectives. The program explores and celebrates the experience of Asian American children and youth through an essay and art contest and community exhibits. Postcards of the winning submissions, such as the one shown in Exhibit 5.2, are used as publicity for the next year's contest and as note cards by staff, trustees, and volunteers throughout the year. Young professional volunteers run the event with the support of many corporate sponsors. The event raises approximately $75,000 each year and introduces young professionals to the organizations. Those who screen the candidates to be honorees are members of the local media, so they also learn about the Asian Pacific Fund.

One way for mainstream organizations to attract diverse audiences is to partner with ethnic organizations in sponsoring events. For example, the Chicago Historical Society hosted the annual fundraising event of an African American youth center. The society had an exhibit of the revitalization of an African American community that particularly interested the predominantly African American guests. This saved the youth center some costs and introduced the society to a new audience of prospective donors from the African American community.

Lessons Learned

As you design events for your organization, include components that will be particularly inviting to the ethnicities you hope to attract. Be sure that people indigenous to that culture are part of the planning, execution, and evaluation processes.

Remember to treat all your guests with respect and warmly. In Asian cultures, having your name inscribed on a plaque is not so important as how you are treated in person, according to Vishakha Desai at the Asia Society. "People want to be introduced at events. They want to be part of the family, rather than feel that they are being included only for their money."

Exhibit 5.2. Asian Pacific Fund: Growing Up Asian in America.

Diwa Ng Aking Inang Bayan (Thought of My Motherland)
Jason Carpio (1999)

Interviewees in each of the ethnic and racial communities talked about the importance of introductions. Just as they want to know the other people at the event in order to develop a level of comfort, donors would like other people to know them. When many ethnic organizations host events, they take care to welcome guests individually at the door. In addition, a master of ceremonies may introduce, from the podium, the individuals on the dais, members of the board, the event planning committee, and distinguished guests. Note that we are discussing introductions at events, not special recognition reserved for major contributors. As discussed previously, people from some cultures will not want to be singled out, certainly not without their prior permission.

The Latino community has an expression that translates in English as "Clear communication conserves friendship," said Lorraine Cortés-Vasquez of The Hispanic Federation. The importance of clearly stating the purpose of each gathering is demonstrated by a story told by Cao O, executive director of the Asian American Federation of New York. In 1994 the organization conducted a pilot campaign to raise funds for services in the Chinese community. The campaign's purpose was to attract local businesses, and the Steinway Corporation kindly hosted a reception at its store. Some attendees were expecting a piano concert, not a fundraiser. The following year, the group held its first annual May Gala, which it clearly promoted as a fundraiser, and it was very successful.

ANNUAL FUND

Your annual giving program, often called the *annual fund*, introduces your organization's programs, services, and needs to the widest audience in order to seek funds for operating support on an annual basis. The annual fund is one step in a series of contacts with a donor in the hope of building a long-term relationship that may eventually lead to major planned gifts. It often uses a variety of ways to ask people for money: mail, telephone, radio and television, the Internet, and personal contact. We know that the most effective way to reach people is in person, particularly in diverse communities. Unfortunately, that is also the most time-consuming and expensive.

The annual fund is one step in a series of contacts with a donor in the hope of building a long-term relationship.

Case Statement

The case statement, often called the case for support, explains who you are, what you are trying to do, and why. Because your organization serves several different constituencies, you may need more than one case statement to effectively demonstrate your organization's ability to solve problems that are important to the interests of diverse prospective donors. Tailor your message to what the donors care about, not simply what the organization needs. The case statement must be concrete and contain specific information that prospects need to know in order to make their giving decisions. Be sure to test your case statement with actual prospects who are members of the diverse community—and listen carefully to their feedback.

For example, the United Way of Central Ohio developed a case statement for African American audiences in response to inquiries about how United Way monies were addressing African American issues. It set forth seven critical need areas and the results achieved to date. It featured African American CEOs of United Way agencies and emphasized the fact that 40 percent of the recipients of services provided by United Way agencies were African American (while 20 percent of the population is African American). According to Sheryle Powell, Key Club manager, the focused case statement helped this United Way increase African American participation in its Key Club, a group for donors of $1,000 or more, from seventy members at the end of 1999 to over four hundred members at the end of 2001 (a 471 percent increase).

Direct Mail

The solicitation of smaller donors is often relegated to direct mail efforts. Yet anecdotal evidence suggests that direct mail campaigns have produced only limited results with donors from diverse backgrounds, particularly African Americans, Latinos, and Native Americans.

Established national African American organizations have done direct mail appeals for many years, although many of the organizations (United Negro College Fund, National Urban League, NAACP, and so on) have relied heavily on mainstream corporate and individual contributions. Only in the last few years have many large African American organizations developed materials for prospective African American donors.

In The Hispanic Federation's report "Latinos and Giving, 1999," Latinos identified mail appeals as the primary way that nonreligious charities solicited them, and 24 percent of Latinos indicated that they gave because they received a mail solicitation. Yet 40 percent of the respondents did not receive any requests for monetary donations. The report also noted that mail appeals increased as education, income, and length of residence increased. It should not be a surprise that churches receive the majority of Latino giving; they ask for donations in person and ask more often than other nonprofits.

The Mexican Fine Arts Center Museum in Chicago has tried an annual fund drive three times, and these have not been successful. The past attempts have been at the end of the year when the churches are doing their campaigns. In 2002, right after the new museum expansion opens, the museum will conduct a campaign—and will not call it an annual campaign.

El Museo del Barrio's annual Christmas appeal, a form letter, generates $25,000 to $30,000 for operating expenses from donors, members, and lapsed donors. In 2000 the appeal was a personalized letter, but it did not yield more money. President Lili Santiago de Silva believes that phone calls and one-on-one conversations would make a difference. Again, personal contact rather than written solicitations is the key.

In contrast to direct mail solicitations, which receive a low response rate, appeals on television and radio seem to be remarkably effective, especially those to help victims of tragedies or disasters. Some Latino organizations have used this trend to their benefit. For example, The Hispanic Federation began its annual fund appeal in 1997 with a media campaign on radio and television. The following year, fundraisers added a mailer to appeal to those who had responded to earlier disaster relief efforts. In 1999 the media campaign continued (free of charge), and the federation sent direct mail both to its mailing list and a purchased list.

The federation was disappointed with a 1 percent return from the purchased list and is about to embark on a donor cultivation effort using small discussion groups hosted by captains of industry. The purpose is to get people engaged in issues

In contrast to direct mail solicitations, which receive a low response rate, appeals on television and radio seem to be remarkably effective.

and, secondarily and eventually, to encourage large donations. Federation staff recognize that small personal group gatherings are more likely to result in contributions than is direct mail, according to executive director Lorraine Cortés-Vasquez.

Direct mail appeals seem to have worked best in Asian American communities. On Lok Senior Health Services receives many memorial gifts each year. After a donor gives a second memorial gift, On Lok considers the giver a donor and adds the donor's name to the annual fund mailing list. On Lok sends two direct mail appeals to donors each year, said development director David Baker.

Self-Help for the Elderly mails a newsletter to volunteers and donors, according to Anni Chung, executive director. It sends an annual appeal letter, which does not include a suggested gift amount, to the donor base of seven thousand. Staff or board members personally contact donors who give more than $1,000 to thank them for their support and to ask them to consider another gift.

Yet some major Asian institutions have chosen not to conduct an annual fund. For example, Gail Kong, executive director of the Asian Pacific Fund, an Asian community foundation based in San Francisco, told us that her organization does no direct mail appeals for two reasons: (1) this positions the fund as a unique, select, and special organization, and (2) it avoids squandering resources on an expensive pursuit that achieves very little return.

Most of the gifts from Native Americans are in-kind. For example, at the Seventh Generation Fund for Indian Development, Native Americans run all projects as volunteers. "Huge amounts of personal resources and time and energy are freely given," according to Tia Oros. "These are donors. They each have a personal investment in our collective vision. . . . Most Native people cannot give more than $25. They are not asked for money, but rather for time. . . . Some will bring things to share, cultural assets more than economic—perhaps food and how to prepare it. They might make a necklace to be given away or raffled. They bring living assets to keep us alive."

The Native American Rights Fund has done direct mail fundraising since 1972 and has an active donor base of thirty-eight thousand. Traditionally the organization sent direct mail to white donors and prospective donors, but not to Native Americans, according to its development director, Mary Lu Prosser. Since 1998 it has sent tribes direct mail and has recently established a tribal honor roll. With the program still in its infancy, the fund's representatives are pleased by the response from the tribal members.

Prospect Research

We can attribute some of the low response rates for direct mail to diverse donors to the oral (rather than written) traditions of many diverse communities. The composition of the mailing lists and lack of prospect research also contribute to the general ineffectiveness of direct mail in diverse communities.

You may have heard it said that there are three ways to do prospect research: written texts, electronic searches, and word of mouth. The last is the most effective for members of diverse communities. After you have established one or more links within the local targeted community, invite them to share address lists with you (social and cultural associations, church rosters, and so on). Many other organizations have membership lists that might be helpful in your research efforts: ethnic chambers of commerce, alumni chapter members of fraternities and sororities, ethnic professional associations (Black MBAs, National Association of Hispanic Engineers, and so on), affiliated tribal associations and ethnic networks in large corporations (for example, Sears Hispanic Network, Asians at Microsoft). Ask your contacts to share such directories with you, and remind them that you want to be able to reach more people with the story of your organization and the services it provides.

Acknowledgments and Recognition

In our interviews, volunteers cited informal, intrinsic, and personal recognition, such as personalized thank-you notes, as more meaningful than receiving formal recognition at public events. Notes from the organizational leaders, especially the president and board chair, are particularly meaningful. At the same time, the public recognition programs provided validation of their work as full partners in the larger society. One form of public recognition particularly appealing to a younger generation is the children's courtyard at the Japanese American National Museum in Los Angeles, where children's names are engraved in the bricks. The National Museum of the American Indian, the addition to the Smithsonian Institution in Washington, D.C., scheduled to open in 2004, will have an "honor wall" that permanently lists the names of those who have contributed $150 or more, as well as an electronic member and donor scroll. In keeping with Native American customs, most of the Native Americans who have contributed to the museum have done so through their tribes rather than individually, in which case the tribe will be listed, not the individual.

Pledges

People who are on the continuum of philanthropy's helping stages often want to make small gifts over an extended period of time. African Americans have become accustomed to this prac-

People who are on the continuum of philanthropy's helping stages often want to make small gifts over an extended period of time.

tice through weekly gifts to the church. Black United Funds, begun in the early 1970s, are based on workplace giving primarily through the Combined Federal Campaign. According to William Merritt, president of National Black United Funds, the twenty-two local affili-

ates depend on gifts through payroll deductions and also sponsor a wide variety of other fundraising programs and events. The affiliates seek to make charitable giving affordable and easy. Your organization may want to explore ways to accommodate such giving patterns and preferences.

As part of the National Center for Black Philanthropy's efforts to promote increased giving among African Americans, the center holds the annual national Day of Celebration and Thanks for Giving on March 4. The purpose of this holiday celebration initiative is to encourage African Americans to give or pledge a charitable gift equal to at least 1 percent of their annual salary, with the motto "¾ (March 4) = 1%." The center encourages people to give to whatever organizations they choose; however, they strongly encourage giving that supports the African American community, said Rodney M. Jackson, president and CEO.

Because most gifts from diverse donors come from current income rather than accumulated assets, it is important for your organization to make large gifts affordable as well. Help the donors by allowing them to pay pledges a little each month over time. The San Francisco Public Library's capital campaign with diverse ethnic groups, which Chapter Six describes in more detail, used pledges effectively. Many individuals and families paid $50 per month on pledges of $1,000 or more; another option for some donors is to charge a small amount to their credit cards each month, thereby spreading out a donation over time. But a Latino donor reminded us, "people are reluctant to make a pledge for a certain amount because circumstances might prevent them from meeting it, and then they would have broken their word."

Fundraising Themes

The theme of the fundraising appeal is an important consideration. Make sure that your case statement speaks to the needs of your local diverse communities and that the graphics are appealing to the people you hope to attract. Using writers and graphic designers whose backgrounds are the appropriate communities can be particularly effective. Seek the advice and involvement of people you want to reach—and then listen carefully to their advice.

According to Michael Cortés (1995, p. 30), fundraisers

> must learn about and build upon Latinos' traditions of mutual assistance and trust in personal relationships in all their local variations. "Latinos helping Latinos" would be a productive theme for fundraising strategies and campaigns, for example. Political organizing in Chicago illustrates how diverse ethnic subgroups can join together with a single Latino identity. But more typical are Miami and other cities where ethnically diverse Latino populations usually call themselves Cubans, Nicaraguans, and so on. Thus, Guatemalans helping Guatemalans, Puerto Ricans helping Puerto Ricans, Tejanos del Valle del Rio Grande helping their own, and so forth, might be even more effective fundraising themes. So, too, would campaigns among immigrants that promise help to victims of misfortune in their homelands.

"Hispanics are generous by nature, but they do not give in a vacuum. They need to be targeted and approached."

"The message is key," said a Mexican American investment executive from Los Angeles in an interview for *Cultures of Caring*. "Hispanics are generous by nature, but they do not give in a vacuum. They need to be targeted and approached. It must be someone credible and culturally competent from the Latino community's perspective, who understands and can appeal to the Latino community's strong notion of family and extended family ties."

Annual Giving: St. Jude Children's Research Hospital

St. Jude Children's Research Hospital in Memphis, Tennessee, has offered services to people of many nationalities and ethnicities since its founding forty years ago, but only recently has it systematically marketed those services and development opportunities to Latinos and African Americans.

It began its first efforts to attract contributions from Latinos in 1997 when it held its first Spanish-format radio pledge drive in Modesto, California. Five years later, the program, *Promesa y Esperanza ¡para los Niños del St. Jude!* (Promise and Hope for the Children of St. Jude), is carried by forty Spanish-format radio stations across the United States in twenty markets and has generated a total of $6 million in cash and pledges from Latino communities.

The St. Jude radiothons are two-day events held during the week, broadcast from 6 A.M. to 7 P.M. The radio station keeps its regular format but breaks to broadcast patients' stories and interviews, thus providing an educational service that is very important in the Latino community. The station also provides a toll-free number listeners can call to make pledges or ask questions.

For the past five years, St. Jude has mailed appeals in both Spanish and English directly to the Hispanic community. Those who have responded to the *Promesa y Esperanza* radiothons receive stories, also printed in both Spanish and English, featuring patients of all nationalities, including Latino children. St. Jude has also invested resources in providing a toll-free Spanish hotline to service donors.

Next, according to Cecilia Villa in St. Jude's Multicultural Marketing department, St. Jude plans to launch the current English-language Web site in Spanish as a service to its Latino constituents, both in the United States and abroad. In 2001, it also began efforts to design materials and programs especially for African Americans and their health concerns.

PRINTED MATERIALS

Some nonprofit organizations have published marketing materials for specific ethnic communities. Although such publications are potentially very powerful, as Emmett Carson (1995) and others discuss, every organization producing such materials must pay particular attention to ethnic and cultural communication differences. Always involve people—writers, graphic designers, artists—from the local ethnic communities.

Another consideration, of course, is the cost of producing and distributing ethnic-specific materials. When weighing the benefits versus the price in your cost analysis, be sure to include such long-term returns as goodwill, community education, and engagement along with actual gifts that you anticipate in response to the materials.

You may want to conduct an audit of the materials you already publish . . . to determine their relevance, effectiveness, and attractiveness to diverse readers.

You may want to conduct an audit of the materials you already publish—your annual report, newsletter, annual fund appeal, and so on—to determine their relevance, effectiveness, and attractiveness to diverse readers. You may be able to make a relatively simple adjustment or addition to engage the people you hope to attract—perhaps a guest column featuring diverse points of view or a feature about relevant members of the diverse community.

The Asian American Federation of New York decided to honor Asian American philanthropists at its annual May Gala. The group asked the philanthropists to share their philanthropic stories. Their testimonials were so moving that the organization developed a brochure featuring the donors' messages of gratitude and desire to give back. Exhibit 5.3 shows a page from the brochure, demonstrating the effective use of a personal story to move others while also honoring the parents of donor Dr. Procopio Yanong.

You will need to decide in what language to write your publications. Some Latino organizations publish in both English and Spanish, but the written communications of most seem to use English alone. Of course, with Asian Americans and Native Americans, there are many different languages and dialects. Valerie Lee, former executive director of Asian American Renaissance in Minneapolis, said that they print all materials in English simply because of the large number of languages and the technical nightmares of getting inaccurate translations. "Sending something out in mangled Hmong does not make friends or generate gifts," she said. Sometimes a token gesture, such as headlines in several languages, is an effective way to recognize ethnic diversity.

CORPORATE GIFTS

Although individual giving (both current gifts and giving through estates) accounts for more than 80 percent of charitable contribu-

Exhibit 5.3. Asian American Federation of New York: New Heritage of Giving, Dr. Procopio Yanong.

Growing up in a family of sixteen children would be an adventure even under the most favorable circumstances. But in a family with very limited means in a small village in the Philippines, survival to adulthood was a real triumph of the human spirit. The best my brothers and sisters could do was to minimize expenses and fight for scholarships that were only granted to the top one or two of each class. There were no loans, no part-time jobs. Our educational expenses rested on the shoulders of my parents

"IT IS BEYOND MY COMPRE-HENSION HOW THEY DID IT. IT WAS CLEAR THAT THEY JUST COULD NOT REFUSE ANY REQUEST FOR HELP"

who, through strict discipline and very hard work, not only managed to give all of us the best education they could afford, but also managed to help put countless other children of relatives and friends through college. It is beyond my comprehension how they did it. It was clear they just could not refuse any request for help. At times, life was so unbearably hard that we complained about our parents' premature philanthropy. But each time we complained, they would get out the Bible and open to those pages of miracles — like the one with loaves and fishes. Their values influenced us throughout our lives. I always think of my father's final words, "What we get out of life is not that important. The worst tragedy is having nothing to give.

Dr. Procopio U. Yanong

What is Philanthropy?

Philanthropy is giving, sharing, helping and investing in the common good. It includes the many ways individuals, families and groups of friends take private action on behalf of public good. Philanthropy — our generosity with both those we know as well as those we do not know — strengthens our families and our communities, and helps us to persevere and overcome adversity. It relieves our loneliness and isolation. It strengthens our bonds with our families and friends in Asia. It creates bridges between generations and connects our heritage with our future.

Philanthropy builds our communities here and enables us to have a civic voice by connecting us to the broader U.S. public. It empowers us to help ourselves and to succeed, and then offers us a way to show our appreciation for our good fortune.

Philanthropy is a vehicle for investing in the future of our children — to ensure that they have a public identity and an impact on American society. Philanthropy builds shared dreams. It builds community centers, hospitals, nursing homes, places of worship, libraries and museums. It creates bonds among people and the nonprofit organizations to strengthen those bonds.

5

tions each year, corporations contributed $10.86 billion (5.3 percent of total gifts) to nonprofit organizations in 2000, according to *Giving USA 2001* (Kaplan, 2001). As African Americans, Asian Americans, Latinos, and Native Americans own more companies, and as members of these communities become more attuned to philanthropy, organizations have an opportunity to appeal to a wide range of businesses through their diverse owners. South Florida is one area of the country where this trend is apparent.

The impact of Latino corporate leadership is greater in South Florida than anywhere else in the United States. Broward and Dade counties are home to over 159,000 Hispanic-owned businesses, according to a special report based on a sample of Miami-Dade County's largest Hispanic-owned companies. More than 30 percent of the top five hundred Hispanic-owned companies in the United States is based in South Florida (Bussel, 2000).

Although the findings of this report are descriptive of the survey results only and we should take care not to draw general conclusions from them, it is interesting to note that 96 percent of the companies that responded make charitable gifts to nonprofit organizations in the community. Senior managers of 62 percent of the companies serve on the boards of nonprofit organizations. The twenty-six respondents reported making cash donations to over fifty-three organizations in the community, 66 percent of which are not typically identified as Latino charities, with hospitals, health care agencies, and educational institutions receiving the most support (Bussel, 2000).

Several executives from community-based nonprofit organizations described their limited success in attracting funds from large national corporations. For example, in 1997 McDonald's granted $10,000 to the Mexican Fine Arts Center Museum in Chicago and $300,000 to the Chicago Lyric Opera. Carlos Tortolero, executive director of the museum, asked, "How many of the Lyric Opera patrons stop at McDonald's on their way home? I can tell you lots of our visitors do." While Tortolero is understandably disappointed in the amount received from McDonald's, the museum did receive a grant from the mainstream giant and in the future can highlight the demographics of its visitors with McDonald's and other potential funders. As more ethnic businesses support your organization, you will be able to build a stronger case for support from the large national corporations.

Michael Cortés (1995, pp. 34–35) offers several ideas to foster Latino philanthropy: "First, Latino nonprofits could target wealthy

Latino entrepreneurs to encourage them to adopt the corporate contribution practices used by other successful companies. Second, Latino business and professional associations are another potential target. Expanded Latino corporate philanthropy might then be a precursor to more personal forms of giving later on. Third, Latino nonprofits could seek more donations from wealthy Latinos. Fourth, organized labor might also be a resource for increasing charitable giving."

The Mashantucket Pequot Tribal Nation's casino, Foxwood, sponsored the victory celebration for the United Way of Southeast Connecticut as a result of their longstanding relationship of trust. According to Alice Azure, vice president for service and planning at the United Way of Southeast Connecticut, Foxwood also sponsors a Christmas party in New London annually for needy children and their families, an example of the tribal enterprise's outreach to its neighbors.

Some nonprofit organizations have created new business models, sometimes called *social enterprise* or *social entrepreneurship*, which build businesses based on nonprofit causes. Chicanos por la Causa, for example, owns and manages four thousand apartments in twenty-two cities. When its president, Pete Garcia, meets with wealthy business owners about charitable giving, he talks about social investing. In Washington, D.C., the charity DC Central Kitchen serves the poor in part with revenues earned through its Fresh Start Catering business, which turns a $300,000 profit each year. The Eagle Staff Fund of First Nations Development Institute, according to vice president Sherry Salway Black, combines technical assistance and grants to tribes and rural Native nonprofits engaged in community-driven, culturally-based economic development.

Another model to attract business support is *cause-related marketing,* which links corporate advertising budgets to nonprofit causes. Such marketing relates use or purchase of a sponsor's product to contributions of the sponsor of the cause. Both the business and the nonprofit gain—a win-win strategy. This model may be attractive to both community-based businesses and mainstream corporations with large numbers of ethnic customers or consumers.

Chicanos por la Causa is one organization that has had particular success with cause-related marketing. It holds numerous events each year, both in Phoenix and Tucson, including a golf tournament, a Tex-Mex festival, and a more formal annual dinner, according to president Pete Garcia. Both national corporations and local businesses heavily sponsor the events. The organization also gives teacher awards of $3,000 each year for the teachers to spend however they want. It awarded ten grants in 2001. Sponsors include Pepsi, Bank One, IBM, and SW Supermarket.

WHERE WE GO FROM HERE

Your job as a fundraiser is to adapt your fundraising programs, methods, and appeals to the different cultures from which you hope to find supporters. You cannot expect people to adapt to your style and worldview just because your cause and organization are worthy. This chapter has offered ideas and examples of ways to attract new diverse donors to your organization and keep them engaged.

Chapter Six tackles the critical issue of helping small donors move along the continuum of philanthropy to become major donors.

6

Advancing Donor Investment
Through Major Gifts

As they travel along the continuum of philanthropy, growing in stability, wealth, and acculturation, diverse donors shift their charitable motivations from sharing to helping and eventually to investing. The ethnic community thrives because those within it share and help each other. As income levels rise and assimilation increases, some ethnic members seem to reduce their participation in voluntary associations and ethnic faith-based organizations. Philanthropy becomes giving, as opposed to sharing, where those with more give to those with less.

People with substantial wealth, or at least a personal sense of financial well-being, give to missions they want to see realized. These donors realize that although mutual aid societies and voluntary associations provide effective strategies for people needing temporary help, they are not necessarily effective in changing systems or remedying the root causes of deep social problems.

Donors who decide to make major gifts usually have a vision for the future and the passion and wherewithal to make that vision a reality. African American and Latino donors often use the word *empowerment* to describe this phenomenon; Asian Americans use the term *investing;* Native Americans speak of *renewal.* This chapter discusses the motivations and considerations of diverse donors able to make major contributions.

MAJOR GIFT DONORS

By being aware of your prospective donor's position on the continuum, you will be able to discuss the programs and services your organization offers that are most likely to engage the donor's interests. Some of the factors that will help you determine where prospective donors fall along the continuum of philanthropy include

- Where they were educated

- Where they were born

- How many years or generations they have lived in the United States

- Whether they grew up in an ethnic enclave, inner-city neighborhood, or suburban community or on a reservation

- What type of business provides their income

- Who forms the clientele of their business: ethnic, mainstream, or both

Research for *Cultures of Caring* (Council on Foundations, 1999) included interviews with eighty-seven individuals from all four ethnic communities who gave at least $10,000 per year to charitable causes. The most frequent mainstream organizations to which these individuals contributed major gifts were (1) colleges and universities: scholarships, fellowships, ethnic studies and history, professional schools; (2) hospitals and medical research: health services for youth and the elderly, research in substance abuse and specific diseases; and (3) cultural institutions and museums: collections, programs, and exhibits focusing on the history and contributions of diverse communities as well as individual donor interests.

In addition, the *Cultures of Caring* researchers identified 639 ethnically diverse funds in seventy-two community foundations across the country in 1998. Of these, 66 percent were established by individuals or families of color; 20 percent by nonprofit organizations that primarily serve ethnically diverse communities; and 14 percent by white donors to support the needs of such communities. The origins of the funds are 61 percent from African Americans, 13 percent from Asian Americans, 20 percent from Latinos, and 6 percent from Native Americans.

When researchers asked how and why the donors gave major gifts to a particular cause or nonprofit organization, individuals in all four groups responded similarly:

- They identified with the nonprofit and its cause or beneficiaries and were passionately committed to the issues.

- They had participated in the nonprofit and its cause for some time, either on a board or advisory committee or on a gala or event committee.

- They gave a major gift, particularly an endowment, that followed a sequence of increased financial commitments over time.

- They knew and trusted personally the person who asked them to contribute; most often, this person was highly respected in their community.

WORDS OF WISDOM ABOUT ASKING FOR LARGE GIFTS

Booker T. Washington, founder of the Tuskegee Institute in Alabama, pinpointed the major stumbling block to fundraising for major gifts in his autobiography *Up from Slavery* (1901, p. 122): "My experience and observation have convinced me that persistent asking outright for money from the rich does not, as a rule, secure help. I have usually proceeded on the principle that persons who possess sense enough to

"My experience and observation have convinced me that persistent asking outright for money from the rich does not, as a rule, secure help."

earn money have sense enough to know how to give it away, and that the mere making known of the facts regarding Tuskegee, and especially the facts regarding the work of the graduates, has been more effective than outright begging. I think that the presentation of facts, on a high, dignified plane, is all the begging that most rich people care for."

Dr. Washington understood the four fundraising principles we learned from the people we interviewed. Although he did not have the advantage of prospects who knew his institution well, Washington regularly traveled to northern cities for personal visits with prospective wealthy donors who were committed to the work of Tuskegee and who trusted his credibility and integrity.

Washington told this story to illustrate that the first gift received from a donor is usually not the largest or the last (1901, p. 140):

> The first time I ever saw the late Collis P. Huntington, the great railroad man, he gave me two dollars for our school. The last time I saw him, which was a few months before he died, he gave me fifty thousand dollars toward our endowment fund. Between these two gifts there were others of generous proportion which came every year from both Mr. and Mrs. Huntington.
>
> Some people may say that it was Tuskegee's good luck that brought to us this gift of fifty thousand dollars. No, it was not luck. It was hard work. Nothing ever comes to one that is worth having, except as a result of hard work. When Mr. Huntington gave me the first two dollars, I did not blame him for not giving me more, but made up my mind that I was going to convince him by tangible results that we were worthy of larger gifts. For a dozen years I made a strong effort to convince Mr. Huntington

of the value of our work. I noted that just in proportion as the usefulness of the school grew, his donations increased. Never did I meet an individual who took a more kindly and sympathetic interest in our school than did Mr. Huntington.

MAKING THE REQUEST

When seeking funds, ask first those who have the closest ties to the institution. In Fundraising 101 most of us learned that this means gaining the support of board members before asking others to contribute. Grassroots support sometimes comes from those even closer to the organization: those who have benefited from it.

Personal Commitment to the Organization

When the J. Ashburn Jr. Youth Center embarked upon a $2.5 million capital campaign to build a new family center in a central-city African American neighborhood in Columbus, development director Annette Jefferson knew that the support of local individuals and businesses was critical for success, she told us. Yes, tax money from the state and the city as well as grants from local foundations provided the bulk of the money, but the total outside funding would not support the first-class facility that the board and the residents hoped for.

Jefferson herself had participated in programs at the center as a high school student in the 1960s. Her parents were volunteers and her children later attended the center as they were growing up. Jefferson's first call as part of the capital campaign was to her working-class parents, then eighty-two years old. She wanted to start with success, and her parents pledged a gift of $1,000. The next thing she knew, the man who lived across the street from her parents came to the center with $1,000. She spoke at the meeting of a local community group of senior citizens, who gave readily and freely. A post office employee asked her to have lunch with a group of coworkers to talk about the center. A few people in the community have pledged $3,000 over three years. The Columbus chapter of Links, Inc., an African American women's service and friendship organization with chapters throughout the world, furnished the library and computer center at the new youth center.

Most contributors are long-time community residents or members of the church that started the center in the 1960s in its basement. All of these gifts have come about for three reasons: (1) Jefferson was out in the community asking; (2) the community trusts her; and (3) the youth center is well respected and provides needed services. In total the capital campaign raised more than $1.2 million, with "stretch" gifts—ones that seem to overreach the financial means of the donors—contributed by residents of this modest neighborhood who wanted to be part of the center's dream.

"What is the Native community contributing to the project?" asked a prominent banker when fundraisers came to call for a contribution to the Native Alaskan Heritage Center in Anchorage. Diane Kaplan of the Rasmuson Foundation and Roy Huhndorf, retired head of CIRI, decided to concentrate on the twelve regional corporations—of which CIRI was one—formed from the settlement of the Alaska Natives' claim to the oil lands. In less than three years they raised $12 million from the corporations, with even the smallest corporation, the Aleutians, donating $200,000. CIRI paid all fundraising expenses in addition to its capital campaign gift. Once the Native firms had contributed so substantially, convincing other funding sources to contribute was much easier, Kaplan and Huhndorf told us.

> *"What is the Native community contributing to the project?" asked a prominent banker when fundraisers came to call for a contribution.*

Association with the Organization

Some Asian American fundraisers report a different experience. Steve Suda, head of Asian development efforts at Stanford University, finds that Asian alumni do not focus on ethnic issues when making gifts but rather on "giving back" to their alma mater. "I would say that the majority of gifts from Asian American alumni at Stanford do not support Asian-specific matters," he said. He has also found that some Silicon Valley Asian American entrepreneurs who did not attend Stanford want to be involved with the institution. Suda stated that 25 percent of the CEOs in Silicon Valley are Indian or Chinese, many of them successful "serial" entrepreneurs (individuals who have started more than one successful company). Suda believes that there is a compelling case to be made to South Asian prospects (and non-Asian prospects as well) of the importance of funding programs that give Americans a better understanding of the cultures of Central and South Asia.

Face-to-Face Meetings

Many of the steps that mainstream fundraising seminars teach about cultivating and soliciting major gifts apply to diverse donors. Devote ample time to the identification, research, and cultivation stages to ensure a positive result. The face-to-face solicitation visit may seem the most daunting task, but it is also the most important. On the one hand, many ethnic-specific sensitivities preclude asking for large gifts directly (see Chapter Four); on the other hand, we found very few examples of donors making large contributions unless someone asked them to do so. The one common element across all the diverse communities in successfully cultivating major gifts is to approach the prospective donor through a trusted and respected person. The ideal person should be, among other criteria:

- A member of the same race or ethnic background who has made a personal commitment to the organization

- A respected elder or mentor in the ethnic community

- A colleague or friend of the prospective donor, involved with the organization as a board member, donor, or volunteer

- A president or board chair of the organization with knowledge of the donor's charitable interests

If the person that your organization selects to meet with the prospective donor is not of the same ethnic background, consult an adviser who can provide guidance about the most effective approach, asking questions such as these:

- Should an individual or a solicitation team meet with the prospective donor?

- What steps should the meeting take?

- Should the prospect be asked for a specific gift or dollar amount?

- How should the soliciting representative or team conclude the meeting?

- What material should the representative or team have available or leave with the prospect?

EVENTS

Special events for major donors run the gamut from small, intimate gatherings to large galas. For many diverse donors, events are particularly appealing for some or all of the following reasons:

- They provide an occasion to be with friends and colleagues.

- They acknowledge donors' leadership.

- They support an important cause or organization.

- They honor loved ones.

- They provide a tangible benefit for the expenditure.

- They are a sign of recognition by and acceptance into the broader community.

Intimate Gatherings

Small dinners or receptions are effective ways to introduce prospective donors to the institution's leadership as well as to recognize and thank major donors. Because the invitation list is by definition limited, donors often consider it as an honor to be included. The small gathering also permits in-depth conversations and relationship development. Plan such events, which may appear casual and informal, carefully, paying particular attention to the following:

- The invitation: list of invitees, design and copy for the invitation, from whom should the invitation come (the organization, board of trustees, or host family), appropriate follow-up after the invitation is sent

- The setting: headquarters of the organization, board member's home, or special location

Small dinners or receptions are effective ways to introduce prospective donors to the institution's leadership as well as to recognize and thank major donors.

- The program: welcoming remarks, introductions, printed materials, speakers, and entertainment

- The food service: seating arrangements, decorations, food and drink selection

As you begin to plan for an event that will attract people from diverse backgrounds, be sure to include their input from the beginning of the planning process. Talk with mentors you have already identified or with a respected member of the community, such as the publisher of the ethnic newspaper, clergy, or electronic media professionals. Check if it is appropriate to directly ask one of the prospective donors you want to invite to give you advice about the event. Seek the help of your organization's board members in identifying appropriate contacts.

The China Institute regularly hosts such gatherings, monthly dinners in connection with guest speakers, authors' book signings, and appearances by experts on topics of current interest to the Chinese community and to China scholars. These are exclusive dinners of thirty or fewer people that include a few trustees, prospective donors, and donors whose contributions the institute wants to acknowledge. After the dinner, all attendees receive either a follow-up letter or personal visit, depending on each circumstance. The China Institute traces many major gifts to these events.

Major Events

Some events for well-established organizations are large and complex fundraisers. Every major event requires a great deal of staff time and a cadre of volunteers, probably organized into various subcommittees. In addition to generating financial support, the successful major event can provide visibility and earn goodwill for the organization.

Asian Pacific Fund

The Asian Pacific Fund's annual dinner is a premiere Asian event that focuses on honoring outstanding individuals. In 1997 the first such dinner honored outstanding immigrants and made grants to organizations that serve immigrants, which was particularly important during immigrant reform in Congress. In 1998, during the controversy about Asian contributions to the Clinton-Gore campaign, the dinner honored people who encourage civic participation and made grants to civic programs—such as parental involvement in public schools and tenants' rights. In 2000 it focused on after-school programs and made grants to increase accessibility to them. To illustrate the level of detailed attention to cultural sensitivity, the year 2000 dinner was the organization's fourth, but this fact does not appear anywhere in the event materials, because many Asian cultures consider the number 4 unlucky, according to the Asian Pacific Fund's executive director, Gail Kong.

A friend or colleague, not a staff member, asks the event honoree to be an honoree, stressing that the person will have no duty except to attend. In Asian cultures it is important that someone of stature personally ask the honoree to attend. The organization invites the honoree's circle of friends and family. The group asks selected board members to purchase tables; it asks those whose tables are not full to be host to specific people that the organization wants to get involved. For example, a prominent Chinese American financial planner had not been involved with the group until he was honored at a dinner. The following year, he volunteered to hold two courses for prospective donors on behalf of the organization. If corporations have purchased tables but do not intend to send people to the dinner, the organization asks them to give the table back to provide seats for selected guests of the organization.

China Institute

The China Institute has successfully used its gala event to provide publicity, introduce the institute to new constituents, tell friends and supporters about its programs, and generate funds. According to Gwynne Tuan, the institute's former development director, the institute designed the gala to recognize leaders in a particular field. For example, the first gala, in 1995, recognized fashion designers at the United Nations' delegates' dining room, with over four hundred people attending. Institute staff sent invitations to twenty well-known fashion designers and had nine positive responses. The designers each contributed one outfit for the auction, and all loaned costumes for the fashion show, in which modern dancers did the modeling.

In 2001 the gala theme was families: the China Institute family, corporate families, and individual families. Anyone who bought a table could honor his or her family; the event netted $345,000. The cover of the printed program was a collage of faces. For Asian Americans the event program is an important memento of the occasion. Your organization should prepare it carefully and beautifully.

The Asian American Federation of New York

The Asian American Federation of New York has held an annual gala each May since 1995. In the past the event has honored groups of outstanding Asian Americans in different professions such as finance and sports. In 2001 it honored outstanding philanthropists, executive director Cao O told us. The event attracts about four hundred people, includes an auction, and brings in $275,000. To begin to bridge the gap between the needy and highly successful people, the gala added a community service award. After the gala a follow-up letter goes to every attendee, and the organization targets some for personal meetings or lunch with a board member or the CEO.

The Hispanic Federation

The Hispanic Federation hosts an annual gala, which netted $800,000 in 2000, according to executive director Lorraine Cortés-Vasquez. First it identifies the corporate leadership, which either has a close relationship with the federation or a strong commitment to the cause. The sponsors, at various levels, account for two-thirds of the income. The sponsors have a clear understanding of the federation's financial and other expectations: it asks each sponsor to donate from $35,000 to $50,000 and help in raising $100,000 from others. The gala has become an important event for the greater New York Latino community, not only because it is a big market but also because the federation is well respected and credible with all the stakeholders. Nearly a third of the sponsorship money comes in with the first mailing, after which the staff, board members, and corporate heads follow up with invitees who have not responded to the mailing. The gala consists of a dinner, dancing, and an awards presentation honoring a Latino individual of national status, a community agency, and a community corporation. Many of the costs, except for the hotel and food, are defrayed by in-kind contributions (of music, awards, printing of invitations and programs, lighting, centerpieces, favors, and so on).

Associated Black Charities of Maryland

Associated Black Charities of Maryland became the beneficiary of a charity National Basketball Association game. Because the charity organization had decided to pursue the involvement of athletes and entertainers, it worked with a marketing firm to find an athlete interested in community work. The firm identified Theo Ratliff, a founder of the Atlanta Hawks, as the athlete, and he arranged for the game in July 2001. The National Basketball Association's sanctioning of the game guaranteed the Associated Black Charities of Maryland net proceeds of at least $100,000. In addition the charity group hosts an annual fundraiser each year that combines blues, jazz, a comedy routine, mock casino, and other entertainment. It attracts fifteen hundred people who pay $150 per person, plus corporate underwriting. Although this event generates a considerable net profit each year, it also attracts newcomers to the organization and educates those in attendance about the organization's programs. "It is the place to be in Baltimore," said Erika Seth, director of major gifts and planned giving for the group.

Koahnic Broadcast Corporation

The Koahnic Broadcast Corporation in Anchorage, Alaska raised $140,000 from its art auction in 2001. Native organizations and companies purchased about half

The Koahnic Broadcast Corporation in Anchorage, Alaska raised $140,000 from its art auction in 2001.

the $1,000 tables, even though only about 7 percent of the Anchorage population is Native. "It is," said Diane Kaplan, president of the Rasmuson Foundation, "the primo arts auction."

Native American Rights Fund

The Native American Rights Fund hosted an auction in 2000 that generated $100,000, which included an honoring dinner with a drum group. The master of ceremonies individually announced each major donor of the past thirty years, said Mary Lu Prosser, the fund's development director. Each donor received a special gift, such as a blanket, and attendees sang an honoring song. After dinner the group held a community powwow.

Mainstream Organizations

Many mainstream organizations hold fundraising events with multicultural components to attract diverse constituents. It is critically important to include members of diverse communities in the early stages of planning the event (and on all subcommittees) if you hope to have more than token participation from the ethnic community. Partnerships with ethnic-specific organizations are often effective ways to reach expanded audiences and broaden the experience of traditional participants.

VOLUNTEER INVOLVEMENT LEADING TO GIFTS

Events usually attract more volunteers than any other activity. Once people are involved and active, the organization has the opportunity to convert that interest to other volunteer activities and perhaps to future contributions.

At Self-Help for the Elderly in San Francisco, computer entrepreneurs in their twenties and thirties help with the group's technology center. One such volunteer gave $25,000 from his private foundation for a new senior center. "We touch their hearts, then their minds, then their pocketbooks," says Anni Chung, executive director.

Pete Garcia at Chicanos por la Causa in Phoenix involves employees of small businesses and companies in hands-on projects, such as painting a building. This develops the volunteer workers' sense of ownership and pride in the organization. When meeting with wealthy business prospects, Garcia talks about social investments. He finds out what the prospective donor is interested in and talks about how to invest in that segment.

One way to engage diverse people in your organization is to involve them on committees and councils. Here are some important considerations in attracting people from diverse backgrounds to serve on volunteer committees:

- Make sure that the committee has direct bearing on their lives.

- Understand the time commitment the work requires and keep the meetings short.

- Define your expectations clearly.

- If you expect committee members to make a financial contribution, inform them in advance of appointing them to the board or committee.

- Provide a committee assignment that is an avenue for the person to grow.

MAJOR GIFT CAMPAIGNS

People are more likely to be generous when the issues and the organization truly engage them, when they understand the results that their gifts can help achieve, and when the organization has standards of high quality and substance.

The Asian Pacific Endowment for Community Development at the Saint Paul Foundation needed to raise $11,000 in a very short time to meet a challenge grant, according to Norman Harrington Jr., director of development for the foundation's Diversity Endowment Funds. The group did so by having board members write letters to supporters who had made modest donations in the past. Each board member made follow-up calls to approximately twenty-five assigned people. The group exceeded its goal in less than two months.

For the twenty-fifth anniversary of the Asian American Legal Defense and Education Fund, the board attempted to raise twenty-five gifts of at least $25,000—and did not succeed, said executive director Margaret Fung. Its efforts did get previous donors of smaller gifts ($1,000 to $5,000) to increase the amount of their contributions (to $5,000 to $10,000). Some people have started to give stock rather than cash. Board and staff members feel that they have learned valuable lessons from this experience: (1) major gift fundraising is a long-term effort; (2) donors must be cultivated incrementally over time; (3) opportunities for multiyear pledges might have produced better results; (4) options for various gift planning vehicles should be offered; (5) selected individuals must call on prospective major donors individually; and (6) the fundraising goal should be based on prospective donors' interests rather than the organization's dreams.

All of the fund's major donors are immigrants. Their gifts are a means to establish that they are fully acculturated Americans.

Gail Kong at the Asian Pacific Fund calls major donors "close-in donors." She meets individually with people only when she has something to say, not just to ask for money. She uses these meetings as opportunities to inform donors about what the organization is achieving. All of the group's major donors are immigrants. Their gifts are a means to establish that they are fully acculturated Americans.

Adam Martinez of Baylor College of Medicine has had limited success with major gift solicitations of wealthy Latinos: "When I talk about the importance of major gifts, the whole process is foreign. Hispanics are more likely to help with immediate needs rather than long-term solutions."

Lili Santiago de Silva of El Museo del Barrio in New York City says that it is hard to get Latinos to commit to a larger gift because of the quid pro quo nature of Latino fundraising. The board member does not want to ask a friend to up the ante because he or she knows the friend will come right back with another charity.

An effective fundraising professional in the Latino community listed the following steps to motivate donors: (1) bring them into the decision-making process; (2) keep the gift close to home and family (such as a gift in memory of the grandmother); (3) show the donor how his or her gift has made a difference; and (4) thank the donor personally and publicly.

Major Gifts from African Americans: United Way of Greater St. Louis

In 2001 a total of 503 African American donors gave $1,000 or more (for a total of $1.4 million) to United Way of Greater St. Louis. Thirty-three of these donors are members of the Alexis de Tocqueville Society, each contributing $10,000 to $50,000 annually.

In 1994 Dr. Donald Suggs, a member of the United Way's executive committee and the publisher of the largest African American newspaper in St. Louis, decided to increase African American leadership giving. He gathered together a group of colleagues to plan a recruitment campaign. By 1997 they had generated $560,000 in gifts of $1,000 or more from African Americans, and expectations increased.

They developed a case statement especially for the African American community, focusing on an area of importance to this population: the inclusive practices of both the United Way (board, staff, programs, and so on) and the United Way–funded agencies that primarily serve the African American community. Out of a total of $64 million raised in 2000, African American agencies (those whose clients are more than 50 percent African American) received $18 million; they also, of course, gave money to agencies whose clients were less than 50 percent African American. The focused case statement helped the volunteers articulate the most compelling reasons for support. Gary Dollar, president and CEO of the St. Louis United Way, said, "Two factors were key to our success: great leadership and our record of serving the community."

The Charmaine Chapman Society, named after the woman who was the organization's president and CEO from 1994 to 2001, honors African American donors of $1,000 or more. Its leadership team of thirty to forty volunteers, the Chapman Cabinet, hosts a series of special events and personal meetings. The cabinet is divided into constituency groups (such as people in education, entertainment, business, financial services, media, medicine, and so on), each of which focused on a particular segment of the African American population. The annual campaign begins with a kick-off event in June, followed by a series of meetings called Pace Setter Luncheons to bring together prospective donors and lapsed donors. At the end of the campaign, the group holds a thank-you celebration at a prestigious location.

David Steward, CEO of Worldwide Technology, and his wife, Thelma, hosted a special reception for the

African American Alexis de Tocqueville Society's members and prospective members in February 2001. Afterward, a Chapman Cabinet member called personally on every person who attended the reception. These one-on-one contacts resulted in six new society members in 2001.

GIVING CIRCLES

Giving circles—sometimes called donor circles—are becoming favorite vehicles to encourage diverse individuals to make larger and more consistent gifts. A *giving circle* is a group of individuals that creates a pool of money dedicated to a specific issue, region, or population. Empowered by the ability to make grants beyond the means of one individual, the group then engages in a process—often including research, site visits, and meetings—to decide together how they should use the money, or the money's earnings.

> A giving circle *is a group of individuals that creates a pool of money dedicated to a specific issue, region, or population.*

The Baltimore Giving Project, a four-year initiative to promote organized philanthropy in greater Baltimore, has produced what it calls the Giving Circle Tool Kit. It states: "Giving Circles are an enormously powerful way to impact social change and pave the way for a new frontier in philanthropy. In the same way that venture capital supports innovation in the business world, Giving Circles use a model of 'venture philanthropy,' infusing nonprofits with financial and intellectual capital, resources and contacts. Joining or forming a Giving Circle provides you with a hands-on opportunity to explore and collaborate with others who share the desire to make focused, social investments with impact" (Baltimore Giving Project, 2000).

Giving circles have the potential to assist diverse donors as they move on the continuum of philanthropy toward a desire to effect long-term change. For those who may not have the wealth or sophistication to make a lasting impact on their own, giving circles are vehicles for joint efforts. African Americans, Latinos, and Native Americans, as we have seen, often prefer working with peers and community members rather than alone. Giving circles can provide the following advantages:

- Pooled dollars invested toward a key issue can have a far greater impact than smaller individual gifts.

- The group's collective know-how adds value and impact to volunteerism and philanthropic investment.

- Creating partnerships with a small number of nonprofits allows individuals a deeper level of involvement and helps them to better gauge return on charitable investments.

- Participating is an excellent way to deepen understanding of issues important to the circle members.

One individual may invite friends and colleagues to form a giving circle; nonprofit organizations may sponsor them as well. Members can customize their circle's formation, purpose, practices, and governance to their interests. For example, the Twenty-First Century Foundation in New York has established the African American Women's Fund to support programs for girls and women. They sponsor annual fundraising events, distributing the proceeds to selected nonprofit organizations and adding to its growing endowment fund. Its members, from Atlanta, New York, and Washington, D.C., raised $67,000 and gave away $11,000 in 2000, according to Erica Hunt, the foundation's executive director.

The Fund for Harlem is another program of the Twenty-First Century Foundation. Its goal is to attract one hundred people to contribute $1,000 each per year for five years. The fund sent out invitations to forty people, twelve of whom agreed to participate at the full level, which entitles them to vote on a screened docket of proposals. Others contributed at more modest levels. The fund offers a credit card deduction program at $80 per month, which provides a way for people of relatively modest means to participate. In the near future the organization will reach out to additional people through professional associations and clubs. It also hopes to attract matching gifts to leverage additional funds. Its motto is "connecting community assets with community needs." The Fund for Harlem has already done the following: (1) demonstrated that ordinary people can be philanthropists, (2) introduced the concept of giving grants, (3) shown what small grants can achieve, (4) spread the word about the Twenty-First Century Foundation, and (5) provided a new grantmaking vehicle to meet needs in Harlem.

STEWARDSHIP

In the fundraising context, *stewardship* is the "process whereby an organization seeks to be worthy of continued philanthropic support, including the acknowledgment of gifts, donor recognition, the honoring of donor intent, prudent investment of gifts, and the effective and efficient use of funds to further the mission of the organization" (Ciconte and Jacob, 2001, p. 417). Stewardship fosters strong relationships between an organization and the people who support it. From the institution's point of view, the desired outcome of such a relationship is the supporter's continued and increased involvement as well as another gift. The first gift, as we know, is seldom the largest. Sometimes the gift is one by which the donor tests the waters, a way for the donor to judge whether the organization applies the gift as the donor requested and whether the group recognizes the donor appropriately.

Sometimes the gift is one by which the donor tests the waters.

Stewardship techniques, in addition to the important thank-you letter, include a regular schedule of mailings to donors: newsletters, annual reports, copies of interesting articles, and cards for special occasions. Most organizations host special events to recognize donors and look for ways to put benefactors in touch with the recipients of their generosity. Each institution tailors its stewardship activities to its own special circumstances.

Honoring loved ones and paying tribute to family members are customs for people of all ethnic backgrounds. The gift acknowledgment card from the Native American Rights Fund in Exhibit 6.1 encourages tribute gifts while also explaining Native American traditions.

The most important aspect of stewardship is a philosophical commitment to accountability. Once you receive a gift, urged Margaret Fung at the Asian American Legal Defense and Education Fund, call and thank the donor for the gift. Then send a letter of appreciation. "Our donor programs are just like anyone else's: look at the donors, send special mailings, eventually arrange to meet one-on-one. Find out what is important to them. Send personal letters with clippings about issues of importance. The ethnicity of the person doing the calls is important, but issues are the most important," said Fung.

Major Gifts from Asian American Donors: Japanese American National Museum

The Japanese American National Museum in Los Angeles provides an outstanding example of a major gifts campaign that was appealing to the interests of Japanese American donors. It included a program to permanently recognize donors for their gifts—both large and small—that in turn encouraged larger gifts. The museum, established in 1985, opened its first building in 1992 in a former Buddhist temple donated by the city of Los Angeles, and it

Exhibit 6.1. Native American Rights Fund: Gift Acknowledgment Card.

In the *Journals of Lewis and Clark* it is noted that the Sioux had a custom of giving gifts in the names of those they wished to honor.

This custom is referred to as **Otu'han** (ō-tū-han) — a Lakota word literally translated as "giveaway." Items of value such as shawls, quilts and household items are gathered over a long period of time to be given away during pow-wows or celebrations in honor of births, anniversaries, marriages, birthdays, and other special occasions. The **Otu'han** is also customary in memory of the deceased. The custom of giving in honor or memory of someone is still very much alive among Indian people today.

The Native American Rights Fund has just received your contribution in the name of

This contribution to NARF enables us to continue to work towards equality and long-overdue justice for the First Americans — including the right of self-determination necessary to preserve our traditional lifestyles, beliefs and customs.

Notice of this gift has been mailed to the designee as requested.

Pila'Mayan
(Thank you)

completed a massive expansion in 1999. It is now in the midst of a campaign to raise $50 million in endowment over ten years. A group with fifty-five thousand members and donors, 60 percent of the museum's annual budget of $9 million comes from individuals.

The museum documents Japanese American heritage and families, which became the focus of its fundraising campaign. It encouraged multiple generations of families and extended families to pool their donations to create one gift larger than any could have given alone. This provided a connection to their common heritage: although the youngest members' contributions might be small, given perhaps in the names of their grandparents, the gifts provide a connection with the next generation. The museum recognizes donors by providing family windows in the museum's outer walls engraved with the family name.

The museum reached its fundraising goals through a series of campaigns to involve people in personal solicitations. It held twenty-six minicampaigns, each with a goal in excess of $100,000. Each minicampaign was composed of twenty-five or more volunteers organized into teams by community affiliations such as veterans, various professions, company employees, geographic areas, and so on. For example, the campaign for the museum's docents, with thirty-five volunteers, originally had a goal of $150,000. The docent group ended up increasing the goal to $250,000 after six months; the docents raised $1.25 million in total. The museum trained docents to reach out to family members and friends, whom they educated about the museum and various methods of charitable giving. They found that although most prospective donors regularly gave to their churches and temples, very few had ever thought about giving large gifts to the museum.

The minicampaigns provided a great sense of accomplishment for the volunteers and the donors. Irene Hirano, executive director and president of the Japanese American National Museum, believes that the fundraising efforts, which flowed naturally from the institution's mission and programs, provided a way for people to get involved and closely linked with the museum.

The museum has found that recognizing donors in a public way has been very important for the vast majority of donors. Peer and community recognition motivates the donors, so the institution is public about acknowledging contributions. Such recognition shows respect, honors the donors, and creates new traditions. Donor recognition also serves to move people up to the next level of giving and to develop long-term relationships. Of course, requests for anonymity were respected.

WHERE WE GO FROM HERE

Major gift fundraising from diverse populations follows many of the same principles as does fundraising from mainstream donors, with some caveats and fine tuning. Through examples and stories, we have explored some of the often mysterious and hidden nuances of successfully seeking large gifts. We learned that diverse donors enjoy and support special events of all kinds, particularly favoring small

Major gift fundraising from diverse populations follows many of the same principles as does fundraising from mainstream donors, with some caveats and fine tuning.

intimate gatherings. They expect immediate and personal acknowl-edgments, even for modest gifts.

Even among the affluent of diverse cultures, major gift cam-paigns are relatively rare. Organizations that have found ways to make large gifts affordable—through such vehicles as multiyear pledges and giving circles—have attracted considerable support. Fundraising campaigns that relate to the organization's mission and the donor's interests are the most successful.

Major gift cultivation also provides an opportunity to discuss gift planning and endowment building with prospective donors, a topic we take up in Chapter Seven.

7

Encouraging Gift Planning
and Endowment Building

At the far end of the continuum of philanthropy are the experienced and visionary donors who want to invest in a better future, who want to transform the world—or at least a portion of it. These extraordinary donors are the subject of this chapter.

For many organizations serving diverse populations, the decision to build an endowment requires a shift from focusing on the organization's operations and survival to paying greater attention to long-term goals and permanence. These organizations understand that intractable problems demand ongoing and creative solutions that can be implemented only by a stable institution committed to the issues for the long haul. They are dedicated to becoming such institutions.

The donors and nonprofit organizations that make gift planning and endowment building a priority share a philanthropic maturity. They understand that complex issues require long-term solutions. They know that remedying the root causes of entrenched social problems calls for secure and durable charitable institutions. And they are willing and able to invest financially to accomplish important dreams.

Some nonprofit organizations are not yet ready to begin gift planning programs. Lorraine Cortés-Vasquez at The Hispanic Federation told us that the federation's lack of an endowment or a planned giving program is due to several factors: the organization is only ten years old; the Latino community is young; and planned giving is a foreign concept to many of her donors. "Most Latinos believe that when you die, you leave what you have to your family," said Cortés-Vasquez. "Latinos give because they are drawn to a cause or an issue rather than to an organization."

Few prospective donors are at the "invest" stage on the continuum, and few nonprofit organizations are equipped to provide appropriate gift planning services to them. This chapter is about those few—and how to recognize them, learn from them, and attract them to your organization.

New Heritage of Giving: Philanthropy in Asian America is a publication by the Asian American Federation of New York (2001b) featuring comments of prominent Asian Americans. Francis Y. Sogi summarizes the investment point of view succinctly in the excerpt in Exhibit 7.1, where he states, "I began to realize that giving is not just charity, but really about investing in the future."

GIFT PLANNING

Charitable gift planning, also called *planned giving*, is the designing of charitable gifts so as to maximize the benefits (financial, social, emotional, and spiritual) to the donor. It includes both present gifts (cash, securities, real estate, tangible property such as art and jewelry, and so on) and deferred gifts (bequests, death proceeds of life insurance, gift annuities, charitable remainder trusts, and residual interests). Donors usually make planned gifts from accumulated assets rather than from current income.

Through planning their charitable giving, usually with the help of trusted advisers, donors become the producers of solutions rather than supporters of projects. "People want to give back," said Erica Hunt, executive director of the Twenty-First Century Foundation. "They now need to give to more than individuals—they need to move to transformative giving."

Lorraine Holmes Settles, founder of The AFRAM Group in Washington, D.C., believes that trust is the primary issue in rais-

Exhibit 7.1. Asian American Federation of New York: New Heritage of Giving, Francis Y. Sogi.

> At first, we set up our family foundation purely for tax reasons, but as time went on, I became a convert. I was really influenced by my wife who was always devoted to the YWCA and was extremely active. Then over time, I became more and more moved by the power of the private voluntary sector. I began to realize that giving is not just charity, but really about investing in the future. Asian Americans must learn this important role they can play in America. We can be leaders, but only if we know how to participate in all sectors of American life.
>
> By understanding our past through our own eyes and telling our own story, we will be able to control our destiny within the American culture that is constantly changing. Our diversity is our strength, not our weakness. This is a critical mission for me and motivates all of my volunteerism and philanthropy. Whether it's the Japanese American National Museum, the Asian American Federation, the Japanese American Memorial Foundation, or my alma mater, I am dedicated to building bridges among people, both nationally and internationally.
>
> *Francis Y. Sogi, life partner, Kelley, Drye & Warren*

"I BEGAN TO REALIZE THAT GIVING IS NOT JUST CHARITY, BUT REALLY ABOUT INVESTING IN THE FUTURE"

How can you enhance your charitable giving?

Many charitable donations have no tax benefit for the donor. Many of us are well-aware of this and give regardless of this technical issue. Only cash and assets (i.e., marketable or closely held securities, artwork, life insurance policies, real estate, jewelry, etc.) donated to qualified nonprofit charities, trusts and foundations, recognized by the Internal Revenue Service, offer tax deductibility. The level of deductibility and the valuation of donated assets vary from instrument to instrument, but can be quite advantageous to the donor and the nonprofit beneficiary, in effect making the gift larger and more beneficial than would be possible without such tax advantages.

If you are interested in long-term financial support of a nonprofit, but would also like to integrate this support with a long-term financial plan for your family, you may consider various planned giving vehicles, such as charitable remainder or lead trusts. You can also create a family legacy in your will in the form of a bequest to a nonprofit. Major gifts, planned gifts or bequests to a nonprofit can memorialize a loved one in perpetuity by setting up a named fund. Family or friends may continue the legacy or tradition by adding their contributions to this fund.

You and your colleagues and friends can also set up a named fund with contributions raised by your donor circle for specified purposes or nonprofits. It may be named for your association, for your cause or for a respected community leader or teacher.

Learning about how tax, estate and financial planning can enhance your individual and family philanthropy may help you make a bigger financial difference to the nonprofits and causes you care about most.

ing funds from African Americans. She quipped that her African American mother initially had more trust in a local Jewish lawyer she didn't know than in an African American financial planner with whom she was acquainted because she assumed that the Jewish person would have more experience with money.

Trust is the primary issue in raising funds from African Americans.

Reasons to Establish Gift Planning Programs

Gift planning programs are important for both mainstream non-profit institutions and ethnic-specific or pan-ethnic organizations for similar reasons:

- They attract gifts that are generally larger than outright cash donations.

- They often tap new and different donors for support, people who give gifts that are often from accumulated assets rather than income.

- They permit individuals of modest wealth to make meaningful gifts, often larger than the individuals had anticipated.

- They help individuals who want to leave lasting legacies beyond gifts to family members.

- They provide valuable services that strengthen relationships with donors.

- They expand the income and resources of the organization and provide a pipeline of future gifts.

- They position the organization to receive increasingly larger and more complex gifts in the future.

Disincentives to Gift Planning

What are some considerations that negatively affect gift planning in diverse cultures? One is the perception that charitable giving will automatically decrease the amount of money that the donors' children will inherit. "Hispanic donors' biggest concern," said a Cuban American tax attorney from Miami, "is that a charitable gift will take from family members. This is a huge disincentive to Hispanic charity."

Another impediment to gift planning is the long timeline until the organizations can use the gifts. "It will be a very long time," said Vishakha Desai of the Asia Society, "before some seeds bear fruit." For organizations with limited staff and resources, assigning significant resources to efforts that may take years to yield tangible results is difficult.

Lili Santiago de Silva said that El Museo del Barrio in New York City does not contemplate doing planned giving for at least five years because such an effort will take too many resources (both people and money). El Museo has grown from a mom-and-pop operation that began in 1970 to promote Puerto Rican arts and culture to a major institution representing all Latino cultures, with a budget of $3.2 million and facilities that include a museum, theater, gift shop, and café. Before planning an endowment drive, Santiago wants to increase the gala proceeds, attract more members, and increase grants from family foundations. She expects money for the immediate future to come from increased memberships, the appeal of the new theater to new supporters, and the expansion of the museum, which will attract more people through its new café and concerts in the courtyard.

Sensitive Topics

Another difficulty in establishing and growing gift planning programs in diverse populations is the sensitivity of the subject matter. Discussing money, death and dying, illness, and aging is difficult for people of all cultural backgrounds. Yet those are the very topics that estate and charitable gift planning deal with. Fundraisers must understand some of the culturally specific sensitivities around these issues.

In Asian American cultures, talking about death is considered bad luck. The prospective donor may think that the person bringing up the topic is "wishing" death on him or her. Gwynne Tuan, former development director at the China Institute, told of one development person she knows who approached an Asian donor to explain how the donor might benefit from a planned gift by increasing lifetime income and saving estate taxes. The prospective donor was upset and never returned to the organization.

Money is also a taboo subject in Asian cultures, which have an unspoken courtesy of not bringing up the subject. According to Anni Chung of Self-Help for the Elderly, many older Chinese believe that mentioning money may bring bad luck. Chinese people in their fifties and sixties are more open. Self-Help is considering forming what it calls a Legacy Circle in the near future, because many of its board members have arranged planned gifts for the organization. The group will ask board members who have made a commitment to talk with friends and associates in the fifty- to seventy-year-old range about considering a planned gift.

Another issue for members of all ethnicities is privacy. David Baker at On Lok described a major donor who permitted the organization to use his gift as an example in a newsletter but did not want staff to identify him as the donor. Baker's predecessor started a planned giving program with the standard committee of the board and a high-quality brochure. According to Baker, creating "buy-in" was difficult; the trustees found three aspects of the program unpleasant:

1. On Lok asked board members to ask for money.

2. On Lok asked board members to ask for lots of money.

3. On Lok asked board members to ask for lots of money in connection with the critical event of death.

Despite limitations, the organization's planned giving has had some notable successes. Between July 2000 and December 2001, On Lok learned of six gifts with a total value of $1.7 million. One donor had given one gift before and left $1.2 million in his will. None of the donors had previously given a gift in memory of a loved one, which surprised Baker because many of the organization's gifts come in the form of memorials.

Irene Hirano of the Japanese American National Museum in Los Angeles agrees that cultural issues exist but feels that they are not insurmountable. With sensitive education and the right messages, she said, people are moved to act. She believes the messages that will appeal to her constituents are the following: (1) the museum can be a way for people to provide for themselves and their families, and (2) the museum can be a medium by which to share the experience of Japanese Americans with an international audience.

Gail Kong at the Asian Pacific Fund believes that some people overstate the perception that Asian Americans do not want to talk about estate planning. "The subject is personal," said Kong. "Asians with wealth are serious about assets and want to plan what will happen to them and their children. Values are important to them." She believes that listening to people is the most important thing the staff can do. "When people have assets, they plan."

Some people overstate the perception that Asian Americans do not want to talk about estate planning.

People in Latino cultures face some of the same issues but for different reasons. "Discussing planned giving is considered rude in the Mexican culture," according to Carlos Tortolero at the Mexican Fine Arts Center Museum. "I would be seen as money-grubbing if I brought up the subject of estate planning. *Ambition* is not a positive term in our culture." He stated that most wealthy Mexicans in Chicago have not yet been affected by the U.S. estate taxes and have no interest in talking about a will or charitable estate planning.

But Adam Martinez at Baylor University has found that Latinos are very attuned to tragedy and hard times and thus used to the concept of death and dying. He has found that Latinos are more comfortable with the concept than are most planned giving officers.

"The concept of endowments," said Donna Chavis of Native Americans in Philanthropy, "brings up the subject of death, which is taboo. Endowment also smacks of hoarding rather than distributing. Yet all tribes have some aspect of responsibility and stewardship—the seventh generation concept. Therefore, don't talk about death, but rather talk about sustaining a way of life." Many Native Americans believe that one's life today will influence the next seven generations, just as one's life today is influenced by the past seven generations. This long view of life helps Native Americans understand the value of endowment funds.

African Americans are also reluctant to talk about death. "We say that a person has passed on, not died," said Jean Fountain, a consultant for the Minneapolis Foundation. "We refer to home-going celebrations instead of funerals."

Gift Planning Strategies

Planned gifts are an extension of major gifts. People we interviewed, particularly African Americans, repeatedly mentioned four ingredients critical to the success of gift planning programs in diverse communities: personal meetings, appropriate language and analogies, policies and guidelines, and professional advisers.

Personal Meetings

One-to-one meetings with people with whom the prospective donor already has a trusted relationship are the most effective method of attracting a planned gift. The courtesies and techniques we mentioned in Chapter Four are important to consider. Seek the guidance of a mentor who is a member of the community you want to attract to help you decide which strategies to employ.

The Diversity Endowment Funds of the Saint Paul Foundation in Minnesota, established in 1992 "to enhance the philanthropic capacity of Minnesota's richly diverse communities of color" (Saint Paul Foundation, 2000), have generated most of their funds through personal meetings. Director Norman W. Harrington Jr.

has found that it is more effective to market the cause and the value than the technical aspects of planned giving. In other words market the why rather than the how—and create a sense of urgency. Harrington explained that at first, many donors expect an event in connection with charitable giving: a dinner, a raffle, or a social occasion. Gift planning is raising the bar to focus on the donor's passions, causes, and service. "The most effective way to reach prospective donors," said Harrington, "has been through one-on-one contact."

Appropriate Language and Analogies

Use language and analogies familiar to the prospective donor. For example, Wenda Weekes Moore, a Kellogg Foundation board member and speaker at the Third National Conference on Black Philanthropy in 2001, favors the use of a banking analogy with African Americans to explain the concept of endowment: "Think of an endowment as your savings account for the future and annual fundraising as the checking account you use to cover immediate needs. Organizations need both." Weekes Moore helped raise money from the local Minneapolis Links chapter for the National Links Endowment, estimated at $1.2 million in 1998.

"What would you want written on your tombstone?" a black attorney said he asks clients. "What do you want to be remembered for?" Another attorney asks clients: "Have you thought about all the wonderful things that have happened to you and how you might see that it continues?"

Carla Roberts's experience with many artists and cultural centers has taught her to discuss endowment building in "terms of seed corn and making sure that the cycles continue."

Adam Martinez at Baylor College of Medicine suggests that planned giving officers talk with Latino prospects about the importance of the family name, carrying forth traditions, and building a legacy.

Carla Roberts, formerly the executive director of Atlatl (a Native American arts organization), has found that mainstream ways of explaining fundraising do not resonate with Native Americans. Her experience with many artists and cultural centers has taught her to discuss endowment building in "terms of seed corn and making sure that the cycles continue."

The Native American Rights Fund has developed a program to recognize and honor donors who have included it in their wills and estate plans, the Circle of Life. According to Mary Lu Prosser, the fund's development director, each Circle of Life member receives a handmade porcupine quill medicine wheel, a Lakota symbol of spirituality and well-being, as a token of appreciation for the donor's lasting legacy to Native Americans throughout the country.

Policies and Guidelines

People considering a planned gift to your organization must have confidence in the organization's credibility, management, trustworthiness, and long-term viability. Some of the indicators of stability that investors look for are

- Clear mission and vision statements

- Trustee selection practices and criteria

- Investment guidelines and vehicles

- Gift acceptance and valuation procedures

- Planned gift vehicles

- Standards for establishing an endowment fund

- Criteria for the donor to establish and name a separate fund

Review each of these documents for language reflecting sensitivity to diverse cultures. For example, the investment guidelines should contain provisions that include firms owned by members of the ethnicities you hope to attract.

Professional Advisers

Your organization will want to establish relationships with diverse legal and financial advisers—attorneys, accountants, insurance agents, brokers, trust officers, financial planners, and others—just as you already have with mainstream advisers. In addition members of diverse communities often seek legal and financial advice from people who may not immediately come to a Caucasian fundraiser's mind: pastors and spiritual leaders, tribal and clan leaders, mentors, revered elders, and others. These advisers need to know about your organization, the needs its addresses, and the people it serves.

Financial planning helps people organize personal and financial affairs, identify what they own, and decide what they want to do with it. James Ellis, an African American estate and tax attorney from Detroit, said that financial and estate planning is important to blacks. "Many blacks are not financially savvy. They need to understand the concept of compound interest and how it can work for them." Ellis said that blacks don't need a lot of money, but they do need to know what to do with the money they have.

Even though such advice is important, many individuals with considerable assets rarely seek professional services. People in each of the diverse communities are more likely to talk informally with respected extended family members and mentors. Broadcast and share with the community information about charitable estate planning. Chapter Eight will provide some strategies for doing this.

Characteristics of Planned Gift Prospects

In the course of our research for *Cultures of Caring* (Council on Foundations, 1999), we interviewed more than eighty diverse donors who each give $10,000 or more annually to charitable causes. These wealthy donors often share certain characteristics that you will want to take into consideration as you approach them to become involved in your organization.

The donors and their families or tribes have accumulated their wealth in their lifetimes; it is first-generation wealth. They have often earned the wealth through entrepreneurial activities. African Americans have been successful in a broad range of businesses: food, personal care products, real estate, construction, insurance, and banking, as well as entertainment and sports. Asian Americans have traditionally achieved financial stability in real estate and food industries, but they have created more recent wealth in the high-tech, communications, financial services, and venture capital industries. Food and real estate businesses have produced many wealthy Latinos, although the range of industries is now much wider. Native American tribes have gained wealth through natural resources and gaming, among other enterprises.

These highly successful individuals function and flourish in multicultural environments. They participate in mainstream and ethnic cultures for both professional success and personal satisfaction. Although some are more comfortable than others in multicultural settings, all have learned to navigate multiple networks.

Many of these donors support nonprofit organizations and charitable programs that serve their particular racial or ethnic community, but they also support mainstream nonprofits.

Most are reluctant to commit to long-term philanthropic planning, for a wide range of reasons. Diverse donors face many financial responsibilities to extended family members both locally and abroad. Some consider personally driven interests in philanthropy inappropriate when compared to their obligation to help less fortunate family and friends. Many are still in the stage of producing and accumulating wealth, and they consider philanthropy a luxury

Some diverse donors consider personally driven interests in philanthropy inappropriate when compared to their obligation to help less fortunate family and friends.

they cannot yet afford. Many have seen wealth created and lost (or taken away) in their lifetimes. Others believe that only their children should (and will) inherit their wealth in the future. Still others simply do not want to face their own mortality.

Examples of Programs That Encourage Gift Planning

In the African American population, innovative work has begun to educate broad segments of the community about gift planning and endowment building. Here are two approaches.

African American Legacy Program

The African American Legacy Program, a partnership with the Community Foundation of Southeastern Michigan, is a comprehensive educational and technical assistance program for nonprofit organizations and their constituents in Detroit's black community. Its goals are to strengthen the local African American community by

- Increasing awareness of charitable giving options among individuals, organizations, and religious groups

- Increasing financial capital for new programs and projects to meet the needs of the community

- Creating permanent endowments for future generations to build upon as a legacy for the future

The African American Legacy Program is not a fundraising or fund-development program. Its focus is on education, outreach, and community building that emphasizes the importance of sound asset management and the use of resources to strengthen the community. Its interactive Web site, http://www.africanamericanlegacyprogram.org, is a national resource for philanthropy and allows interested organizations to gain access and insight into the charitable giving patterns of African Americans.

Associated Black Charities of Maryland

"African American organizations are the first to go under in bad economic times," according to Donna Stanley, executive director of Associated Black Charities of Maryland, "and thus need endowments the most." This Baltimore organization is an example of an organization that has made the transition from thinking solely about current operations to preparing for the future. It is educating organizations as well as individuals about strategic giving to increase organizational capacity. That requires spending resources for both today and the future. Stanley does not believe that endowment building should or will ever replace existing fundraising but rather that it can augment current fundraising strategies with multiple vehicles. It is also a way to gain access to additional resources such as property, stocks, and insurance.

Associated Black Charities formed a partnership with an African American financial services company to demonstrate ways that the adviser, the donor, and the community can all benefit. According to Erica Seth, director of major gifts and planned giving, through this program the client establishes a donor advised fund at the charity through the financial planner, who continues to manage the assets. The charity charges a modest fee to manage the fund and makes distributions from the fund at the donor's recommendation and the board's approval. Should the donor not suggest a distribution from the fund for more than one year, the charity may make a distribution in the donor's name. Each fund starts with a minimum of $5,000 that must build to $10,000 before making grants. The group had six named donor advised funds at the end of 2000.

One donor has established a $15,000 fund, with plans to increase it to $100,000. This individual has been close to the organization since 1997 and chose to give the money without restriction to provide ongoing support for the organization. Few donors are so farsighted and magnanimous. Associated Black Charities has several prospective donors who know they want to make a gift but have not yet decided what to give. Executive director Donna Stanley sends these prospective major donors articles about the organization and personal notes, and she keeps in touch by phone to continue building their trust and confidence in the organization.

The group is preparing to offer what it calls Field of Interest Funds as well. It used to have priority funding areas, where the majority of discretionary grants were applied, but is now converting them into fields of interest: economic empowerment, community revitalization, youth development, and family preservation. This forward-thinking organization has addressed the need for prospective donors to have

This forward-thinking organization has addressed the need for prospective donors to have a menu of program options from which to choose. . . .

a menu of program options from which to choose, rather than the traditional approach of seeking unrestricted endowment funds.

ENDOWMENTS

Endowments are permanent funds invested for long-term growth whose earnings support ongoing and special projects. Traditionally many organizations have viewed them as the exclusive purview of large established mainstream institutions, primarily hospitals and universities. Since the 1990s, however, smaller nonprofit organizations—neighborhood associations, social service agencies, poverty programs, arts organizations, community colleges, churches, synagogues, and mosques—are establishing endowments.

The organization's board may establish an endowment with reserve funds or a windfall gift from a donor. Or a donor may contribute a gift restricted for endowment only.

Permanent Endowments Versus Current Needs

The concept of a permanent endowment is new to most ethnically diverse community members, many of whom neither understand nor accept it. With the number of critical current needs in diverse

populations, many individuals and organizations find it incongru-
ous to raise money to save for the future. Donors of diverse ethnicities are accustomed to immediately responding to such needs, and
they are well aware that these needs far exceed their resources. Generally they prefer to give direct support to individuals rather than
to give to or through institutions. This frame of reference makes it
difficult for them to consider large irrevocable gifts, planned gifts,
or endowments.

Moreover those diverse individuals and organizations that set a
course for endowment building generally establish relatively minimal fundraising goals. With few exceptions organizational endowments for ethnic-specific causes generally have assets of less than $1
million, and some individual endowments are as small as $5,000.

The Houston Hispanic Chamber of Commerce sponsored a program to help its members learn about investing and saving. It
expected about 250 attendees; six people showed up. When asked,
members of the chamber said that they were concerned about getting through tomorrow, not investing for the future.

Scholarship funds seem to have the most appeal and the greatest
potential to break down the reluctance to establish endowment
funds. Donors of diverse ethnic backgrounds have established more
scholarship endowments than any other kind of fund, indicating
the high value that ethnic communities place on education. Many
ethnic-based civic and social organizations sponsor scholarships,
generally raising funds annually through special events. By adding
a portion of each year's net proceeds to an endowment, the organization can decrease its reliance on annual fundraising and eventually accumulate a permanent fund to provide ongoing scholarships
from the fund's annual earnings.

The Importance of Endowments

Endowments can provide a firm foundation for established organizations. The earnings of the endowment can sustain the organization
in lean years or during unexpected financial downturns. As the orga-

nization matures and diversifies its funding base, the endowment can provide support for operational expenses, freeing annual fundraising proceeds for new and innovative programs. An endowment provides an additional option for memorial contributors and planned gift donors. In addition outside funders—corporations, foundations, and governmental agencies—often consider the size of the organization's endowment as an indicator of the nonprofit's stability.

Concerns About Endowments

Some people and organizations question the value of endowments. For instance, Anni Chung at Self-Help for the Elderly in San Francisco is not eager to build an endowment, unless a donor so designates a gift, for at least two reasons. First, Chung remembers when funds were tight in the early 1980s. Critics questioned why other health and human service organizations were cutting back on services and laying off staff while holding large endowments in the bank. Second, Chung's board wants access to the principal in extraordinary circumstances. Her organization has $800,000 in restricted funds for contingencies but does not plan to convert any of those funds into permanent endowment.

New Economics for Women, a Los Angeles organization "birthed" by a Latina feminist organization of professional women to promote economic development and affordable housing, is not interested in promoting sustainability. Its CEO, Beatriz Olvera Stotzer, said it wants to remain flexible and innovative and will sustain the organization by other strategies, perhaps by starting a business. Its board would, however, like to establish an endowment to provide risk capital for creative ideas.

"It is easier to raise funds for tangible projects than for endowment," said Diane Kaplan of the Rasmuson Foundation in Alaska. With proceeds from its casino, the Tohono O'odham Nation in Arizona amassed $15 million and planned to build a cultural center. When Kaplan consulted for the Tohono O'odham recently, she advised the group to put the $15 million into an endowment and

"It is easier to raise funds for tangible projects than for endowment." raise the money for the new center from federal agencies and vendors in the majority community near the reservation. Kaplan knew that it would be easier to raise funds for the construction of the building than for its upkeep.

Others think that endowment building may detract from raising current operating funds, although no evidence supports this claim. "It is generally accepted that endowment building is critical to supporting long-term capital needs of our community," said Norman W. Harrington Jr. at the Saint Paul Foundation's Diversity Endowment Funds. "The challenge is meeting immediate and long-term needs at the same time."

Impediments to Endowment Building

Endowment gifts, like other major gifts, require the donor to irrevocably give up control and ownership of assets, either now or at a future time. Donors do not make the decision to take that step lightly.

It is likely that the donor has recently become financially secure. Virtually all of the top one hundred black businesses listed in *Black Enterprise* magazine in June 2001 were organized within the two preceding decades (Edmond, 2001). This is true of nearly all the enterprises in each of the four broad diverse populations. Wealthy people of diverse backgrounds well remember scrambling to provide for their families in the past.

"The income of today's affluent blacks is earned by several workers in the household," according to Phoenix philanthropist Jean Fairfax (1995, p. 16). "Many of these homes are the first in their family history to be rich. They perceive their affluent status to be fragile."

In addition many wealthy people have multiple responsibilities for large and extended families. Nonprofit organizations frequently ask them to assume leadership roles and contribute financially. And many are still actively working to expand their businesses.

Another impediment to endowment building is the lack of experience and expertise in charitable gift planning among legal and financial professionals from diverse backgrounds. For instance, 20 percent of Michigan's white attorneys are members of the probate and estate section—the group that specializes in writing wills and planning charitable gifts—of the Michigan Bar Association, according to Robin Ferriby (2001), vice president of the Community Foundation for Southeast Michigan, whereas only 3 percent of the African American attorneys are members of that section.

Building Endowments

Despite the concerns about endowments and impediments to building them, they are growing rapidly in diverse populations, particularly in African American communities.

"We have to go beyond annual funds," said Ronald Goldsberry (2001), CEO of CarStation.com and a major donor to scholarship programs at Michigan State University. "The paradigm has to shift from 'Help me' to 'Help ourselves.' There are too many well-heeled blacks out there for us not to have more endowments and foundations." He said that the biggest challenge for black philanthropy is not attracting resources but garnering endowment funds that can generate their own wealth.

Endowment building in diverse communities relies on the gift planning strategies we described earlier in this chapter and on incentives and challenge grants. Here are some examples of the many ways to structure such incentives.

Asian Pacific Fund

The Asian Pacific Fund passed a significant benchmark in 1998: a donor announced that he had put the organization in his will, and another established a charitable remainder trust naming the group as the remainder beneficiary. (A charitable remainder trust pays the donor—or a person designated by the donor—a fixed percentage of the trust's value for a number of years or the person's lifetime. At the end of that period, the remainder in the fund is given to the charity named by the donor.) Written acceptance and investment policies and procedures are now in place, said executive director Gail Kong. With a grant from the California Endowment, the organization has recently hired an Asian American attorney to begin a planned giving program.

Chicanos por la Causa

Chicanos por la Causa has an endowment of $6.1 million from an original $2.5 million grant from the Ford Foundation. President Pete Garcia, who started with the organization in 1972, has learned on the job how to meet with wealthy prospective donors and excite them about the organization's future. He believes that personal relationships with a few committed individuals are the key to building the endowment.

> *Garcia has learned on the job how to meet with wealthy prospective donors and excite them about the organization's future.*

Mexican Fine Arts Center Museum

The Mexican Fine Arts Center Museum in Chicago has a $1 million endowment, begun with a challenge grant from the National Endowment for the Humanities and the support of board members and private foundations. It has recently announced a campaign to raise an additional $6 million, according to executive director Carlos Tortolero.

Hopi Education Endowment Fund

"Establishing the Education Endowment Fund," said Hopi Tribal Council Chairman Wayne Taylor Jr., "has created a perpetual source of funding upon which we can rely even when the tribal government's main source of revenue, coal royalties, runs out" (Hopi Tribe, 2001). Begun in 2000 with $10 million from the council, the Hopi Tribal Education Endowment will provide scholarships for local youth. The council established the Hopi Education Endowment Fund under Internal Revenue Code Section 7871, which permits the tribal government to retain control as a sovereign nation.

In 1987, Hopi community members in northern Arizona also established the Hopi Foundation, which affiliated with the Arizona Community Foundation in 1998. It distributes grants to such reservation-based organizations as Native Sun, a solar electric enterprise; KUYI, the Hopi radio station; and Gentle Rain Design, an earth-friendly clothing company that gives new life to recycled plastic bottles and creates employment for community members. Barbara Poley, executive director of the Hopi Foundation, said that as their endowment grows, the majority of the earnings will be for programs that serve youth rather than for economic projects.

"Foundations are becoming the wisdom keepers," according to Donna Chavis at Native Americans in Philanthropy. The oldest Native-initiated funds were started in the mid-1980s, such as the First Nations Development Institute, the American Indian College Fund, and the Seventh Generation Fund for Indian Development. In addition nine tribal colleges have established endowments even though many of the colleges are relatively young, having been formed in the 1980s and 1990s, and have a limited number of alumni. As of September 1998, we learned in our research for *Cultures of Caring*, Native Americans had created endowed funds at sixteen community foundations spread across the country from North Carolina to Hawaii.

African American Community Fund

The Community Foundation of St. Joseph County in Indiana (South Bend) established the African American Community Fund in 1999, which has leveraged additional funds from corporations and foundations. It started with one African American couple who pledged $10,000 over two years. That couple attracted nine other families to join in, each establishing a separate named donor advised fund. The foundation asked corporations to match each dollar from the African American community with four additional dollars. The fund had assets of more than $1 million in early 2001 and has committed to raise the second million dollars. Rose Meissner, president of the Community Foundation, said that the money was the smallest part of the story. Members of the grants committee for the fund, who are all African Americans, visit sites and recommend organizational recipients. "The exciting thing about the fund is how the money meets the road," according to Meissner. In St. Joseph County the grant's focus is to increase the capacity of local African American nonprofit organizations.

Boulé

The fraternity Sigma Pi Phi, usually called Boulé, will celebrate its one hundredth anniversary in 2004. Started in Philadelphia, Boulé is a nationwide professional fellowship and social organization of approximately four thousand African American men. The group established the Boulé Foundation in the mid-1990s to foster educational excellence in the African American community. Its endowment was $6 million at the end of 2000; the goal is to reach $10 million by 2004. Each member must contribute $50 of his annual dues to the endowment, and most members have not given more than that amount, according to president-elect Calvin Pressley.

The national president requested that each member give a one-time gift to the foundation of $1,000 to become a Minton Fellow; 435 members have done so. More recently, Boulé has established giving levels, named for well-known and respected members, at $2,500, $5,000, $10,000, and $25,000. President-elect Pressley says the group will establish a $100,000 category in the near future. The Detroit Boulé chapter has 100 percent participation as

The national president of Boulé requested that each member give a one-time gift to the foundation of $1,000 to become a Minton Fellow; 435 members have done so.

Minton Fellows and has challenged the other local chapters to equal their accomplishment.

Methods to raise funds for the Boulé Foundation do not yet include a planned giving component, primarily because staffing is limited. Once a full-time executive director is in place, the organization plans to begin a gift planning effort.

Delta Sigma Theta

Patricia Solomon in Detroit discussed her sorority's involvement in building an endowment. Delta Sigma Theta has participated in the VanDussen challenge grant program through the African American Legacy Program since 1994. It now has a $200,000 endowment fund for last-dollar scholarships for African American youth and distributes $40,000 per year. (Last-dollar scholarships permit students to receive the maximum federal, state, and private grants for which they qualify and then provide the funds necessary to fill any remaining financial gap.) Eight donors have their own named funds in the endowment. The sorority raises $10,000 per year, all of which it adds to the principal of the fund. Each of its twenty board members has pledged at least $500. Solomon said the sorority's annual volunteer activities are as important as the money. For example, it arranged to take thirty-eight youth on a college tour in May 2001.

Twenty-First Century Foundation

The Twenty-First Century Foundation in New York functions as an African American community foundation in many ways. Started in 1971 by an economist who inherited $1 million from a friend to expand black philanthropy, the foundation provides seed funding and operating support to promote community empowerment. Since Erica Hunt became executive director in 1998, the foundation has attracted grants from private foundations to strengthen giving vehicles and encourage black donors to establish donor advised funds; by 2001 the foundation had two fully funded donor advised funds at $50,000 each. An anonymous donor provided the funds to develop a business plan for the foundation to become self-sufficient, according to Hunt.

Gift Planning:
The Greater New Orleans Foundation

Numerous community foundations have raised endowment funds and generated planned gifts from diverse donors, in part because endowment building is one of their primary missions. The Greater New Orleans Foundation is an example of a community foundation that has proactively reached out to diverse donors and continues to do so.

In 2001 the twenty-nine-member board of trustees included nine African Americans, one Latino, and one Asian American; the staff of nine included three African Americans and one Latino. The foundation has provided training for professional advisers in diverse communities. According to vice president Margaret Epstein, one fund was established by a Japanese American who learned about the foundation from his Japanese American stockbroker. He established a fund in his family's name at the foundation in conjunction with selling his business—and substantially decreased his capital gains taxes at the same time. An African American established a $1 million endowment fund for dyslexia with a life insurance policy upon the advice of his insurance agent. The policies of the foundation, such as setting a low minimum to establish a named fund, encourage new donors to become involved. The stories and pictures in the annual report and other materials demonstrate broad ethnic and racial diversity. Yet possibly the most important activities have been those that the program staff has undertaken.

For example, in partnership with the Annie E. Casey Foundation, the Greater New Orleans Foundation began a program to revitalize a once-vibrant black neighborhood. Making Connections: Transforming Neighborhoods and Strengthening Families is the name of a small grants program for local grassroots organizations. Program Officer Deborah Thomas went into the neighborhood to explain the program and solicit applications. She held both morning and evening workshops. The foundation streamlined the application process into a series of straightforward questions and allowed applicants, who did not need to have a fiscal agent or 501(c)(3) status, to write responses by hand.

The organization created a grants committee composed of two foundation board members and seven community residents. In the first grants cycle, the committee recommended eighteen $1,500 grants to neighborhood programs focused on such topics as economic development, job training, conflict resolution, and after-school programs. After announcing the grants, the foundation held a congratulatory breakfast to discuss expectations, answer questions, and give a participant from each recipient organization the chance to describe his or her program to the group.

According to Margaret Epstein, vice president for donor relations, programs such as Making Connections have demonstrated to diverse populations that the foundation is truly open to all the community.

WHERE WE GO FROM HERE

Individuals and nonprofit organizations in diverse populations have not fully embraced gift planning and endowment building. Many community members do not understand or accept the reasons to

Individuals and nonprofit organizations in diverse populations have not fully embraced gift planning and endowment building.

establish planned giving programs. Obstacles to gift planning and the sensitivity of the subject matter often deter boards of trustees from initiating such programs. Nonetheless several gift planning tactics have been effective, especially with African American donors, and fundraisers have identified characteristics of planned gift donors.

The concept of permanent endowment funds is counterintuitive for diverse donors accustomed to providing immediate help for current needs. In addition many affluent donors are not yet ready to consider irrevocable gifts of their newly acquired wealth. Yet some donors who have reached the "invest and empower" stage on the continuum of philanthropy have begun to establish endowments through major ethnic and mainstream institutions, as well as private foundations. The institutions have assisted the donors by providing a variety of incentives and opportunities to leverage additional funds from individuals, corporations, and foundations.

Many of the people we interviewed for this book, both individual donors and leaders of nonprofit organizations, are grappling with long-term financial stability, even if they are not currently building endowments or offering gift planning programs. Chapter Eight describes some collaborative educational efforts with specific diverse populations around the United States.

8

Achieving Success
Through Collaboration

Fundraising in diverse populations provides many opportunities
for collaboration: with organizations serving the same population; among organizations dealing with similar issues; and with
individuals, businesses, and nonprofit organizations interested in
promoting philanthropy.

PARTNERSHIPS WITH
EXISTING DIVERSE GROUPS

Partnerships with appropriate associations and organizations in diverse
populations can develop mutual respect and understanding with new
constituents. Partners can include mutual aid associations, fraternities
and sororities, Native American tribes and organizations, churches
and other faith-based organizations, historically black and Native
American colleges, business and professional associations, and so
forth. Joint projects can include celebrations, fundraising events,
health fairs, educational seminars and workshops, neighborhood
clean-up campaigns, lobbying efforts, disaster relief, and others.
Choose both the partners and the joint project with care. We discussed several effective programming partnerships in Chapter Three.

When challenges and opportunities emerge during the development of relationships with selected leaders in the specific cultural

community, seek community members' advice about possible joint solutions and strategies. As they realize that your organization offers value to the collaboration and that they can count on you to honor your commitments, their initial reluctance or suspicion will lessen.

After your mentor has agreed to introduce your joint program ideas to the group, provide the information and materials the mentor requests and follow that person's lead. He or she may not want you at initial meetings with the new organization. Trust the mentor's advice. As both organizations participate in the development of the project, the original concept will change and evolve, often into a far better one than either organization could have envisioned or accomplished alone.

Sometimes the project will disband for lack of funds, interest, time, or opportunities, and you may need to find another partner. Be not discouraged. The initial stages of reaching out to diverse populations can be slow and frustrating at times, but the long-term benefits usually outweigh temporary setbacks. Remember that you are not only doing the specific project but also building trusted relationships for the future.

ENTRÉE TO NEW DONORS AND THE MAINSTREAM

Community-based organizations may be interested in partnerships with established institutions because they perceive the larger group as providing a seal of approval to the smaller organization. For example, the Mexican Fine Arts Center Museum is a member of the Chicago Arts Consortium, a group of nine institutions on public property that share in a $37 million-per-year pot of operating support from the city of Chicago. The museum receives $1.2 million annually. The nine partners meet monthly to share common concerns and run two joint programs: Park Voyagers (a group membership program) and MAPS (Museums and Public Schools, which offers tours to school groups).

The Mexican Fine Arts Center Museum is one of two museums in the consortium that is not located downtown, so Director Carlos

Tortolero said that being a member of the consortium provides status for his museum. He wants to position it in two worlds: as (1) a major cultural institution that is also (2) based in the Mexican neighborhood. Tortolero says that sometimes he feels that the museum is like a platypus—a mammal that lays eggs—an unknown and unusual hybrid that very few funders understand. He believes that his museum's membership in the arts consortium adds legitimacy and credibility with mainstream corporations and foundations.

Usually celebrated in May, Asian American history month is an opportunity to build cultural awareness and celebrate cultural traditions and practices. Many communities across the United States hold a festival or a series of special events. Often a collaboration of local organizations plans and hosts the local celebration, making it larger and attracting more participants than any one organization or nationality could on its own. Such recognized months of cultural heritage may provide opportunities for mainstream and community organizations to form new partnerships.

Such recognized months of cultural heritage may provide opportunities for mainstream and community organizations to form new partnerships.

Anni Chung at Self-Help for the Elderly cautions that some collaborations can take a great deal of staff time for minimal return. For example, Self-Help once participated with two or three other organizations in a charitable sporting event with a professional sports team foundation. The event generated limited net revenue and consumed a great amount of staff and volunteer resources. The experience demonstrated to Chung the importance of clearly defining responsibilities and expectations for all parties involved.

Another way to collaborate with local diverse populations is to hold functions at facilities located in a particular neighborhood. For example, the Houston chapter of the Association of Fundraising Professionals held its annual conference in the center of Houston's African American community in 2000. Adam Martinez of Baylor College of Medicine said it attracted four hundred people, the largest attendance at any Houston conference for this organization, introducing veteran members to an unfamiliar location and African American nonprofit executives to the organization.

The Mexican American Legal Defense and Educational Fund is one community organization that provides resources for many other local nonprofits while also contributing to its own operating expenses. The fund completed a six-year, $7.5 million capital campaign to support the purchase and renovation of the organization's headquarters in Los Angeles. By providing office space for other charitable groups in the twelve-story building, the fund generates revenue for its own operations and offers a "professional environment for other nonprofits organizations that provide assistance to minority or other underserved communities" (2002).

The Asian Pacific Fund has formed strategic alliances with Asians who are networked or with Asian networks, such as with the Asian Bar Association. Gail Kong, its executive director, says she has found that other pan-Asian organizations make good partners; they are usually large, well established, and supportive of each other, and they do more than ask for money.

Donors seem to appreciate collaborative efforts as well. "We could leverage much better if the African American organizations were to do more collaboration," a Baltimore donor stated during research for the Baltimore Giving Project. "Right now I see a lot of independent, fledgling organizations doing their own thing" (Winters, 1999, p. 6). Joint efforts to seek funds with organizations that have similar missions or are addressing common issues can be beneficial to both the organizations and the donors.

CHALLENGE GRANTS

Challenge grants can be very effective in inspiring contributions from diverse donors. People understand the value of leveraging additional money, particularly for causes dear to their hearts.

With a grant it received from the Ford Foundation's Rural Development and Community Foundations Initiative in 1997, the

Montana Community Foundation offered a challenge grant to the Blackfeet tribe to build a permanent endowment. For every three dollars that the Blackfeet raised, the Montana Community Foundation added another dollar. When the foundation first offered the challenge grant, the tribe had few financial resources and no experience with formal philanthropy or endowment building.

According to Sidney Armstrong, former executive director of the foundation, the Blackfeet arranged with the administration of Yellowstone National Park, adjacent to their reservation, to hold the Harvest Moon Ball, a dinner, dance, and auction featuring the work of local artists. Following the third annual ball, the Blackfeet Foundation held assets of nearly $200,000. The endowment supports a youth art camp and has started a minibank system to teach youth about finance and money. The Montana Community Foundation oversees the administration and investment of the funds and provides technical assistance about planned giving and endowment building. The Blackfeet effectively used their primary assets—talented artists and volunteers—to match the challenge grant and increase the economic security of tribal members.

Through the involvement of the Ford and Mott Foundations in South Africa, the Blackfeet reservation has hosted two visits of trustees from start-up community foundations in Botswana, a rural area with similar geography and native communities.

PAN-ETHNIC AND INTERNATIONAL COLLABORATIONS

Collaborative programs promote understanding and activities across ethnic and international boundaries as well.

Saint Paul Foundation's Diversity Endowment Funds

The Diversity Endowment Funds of the Saint Paul Foundation have adopted the motto, "Many faces, one heart, one voice . . . building community." The Diversity Endowment Funds are composed of five major funds, one for each broad segment—African American, Asian

American, Latino, and Native American—and the Common Fund, which is multicultural. With assets of $6.5 million at the end of 2000, the funds are a partnership between the Saint Paul Foundation and the ethnic communities to provide a mechanism for fundraising, identification of interest areas, and allocation of charitable capital. Each fund has its own advisory board, conducts its own fundraising efforts, and awards grants to the specific community.

Two members of each of the four funds' advisory councils make up the Diversity Endowment Funds Council, a multicultural group that allocates earnings from the Common Fund. When India had an earthquake in 2000, the Asian Fund decided to contribute $5,000 to Indian relief efforts. Norman Herrington Jr., director of Diversity Endowment Funds, reports that the council contributed an additional $5,000, and each individual fund discussed sending money as well. As a result of this first jointly funded project, the members of the council, after a one-hour discussion, decided to earmark 20 percent of its discretionary funds for emergency grants in the future. That amounts to about $20,000 per year. This was their first major pan-ethnic collaborative decision. Also in 2000 the council combined funds to support the Racism in the Media project, an initiative that the Saint Paul Foundation began in the late 1990s to create a nonracist community.

When India had an earthquake in 2000, the Asian Fund decided to contribute $5,000 to Indian relief efforts. The council contributed an additional $5,000.

Herrington lists six lessons participants have learned from the partnership so far:

1. Involvement of stakeholders from the beginning is essential to structuring and implementing the partnership.

2. All the members of the partnership are valued resources.

3. Two-way communication, particularly listening, is important.

4. As walls and barriers break down, trust develops.

5. Agreement is necessary on the need for the endowment and what the organizations want it to achieve.

6. The partners must be willing to change and take risks.

Such a partnership requires a long-term commitment, sensitivity to cultural differences, committed and dynamic leadership, and community ownership. The benefits to the partners include

- The development of culturally appropriate business practices, marketing, and development strategies

- Better understanding and articulation of immediate and long-term needs

- Awareness of the impact of each community's values and beliefs regarding money and wealth

- A growing trust in individuals and confidence in organizations

The Asia Foundation

The Asia Foundation, begun as a public charity in 1954 to develop leadership and focus on public policy issues in Asia, now has a network of fifteen offices in Asia and experience in working with local Asian organizations and U.S. government agencies, private foundations, and corporations. Although the foundation is the U.S.-based organization that grants the largest amount to Asia (the Ford Foundation is second), its executive vice president, Barnett Baron, told us that its most important role to the Asians is not to make grants but rather to convene, give access, broker, network, bridge gaps, and cofund local programs with others.

The Asia Foundation has recently established a separate supporting organization, Give2Asia, which offers a menu of donor services designed to meet a variety of charitable interests and financial planning goals. Its experience with local Asian organizations gives it a unique position in formulating grantmaking plans, mobilizing the most effective partners, and identifying timely grantmaking opportunities. Through Give2Asia, the Asian Foundation has elevated the concept of remittances to a new level and established a comprehensive vehicle to serve Asian American donors interested in international grantmaking.

Hispanics in Philanthropy

The Funders' Collaborative for Strong Latino Communities is administered by Hispanics in Philanthropy, an association of more than 450 U.S. and Latin American grantmakers and nonprofit leaders. The goal of the five-year, $16.5 million effort is to build capacity among Latino-run, Latino-serving nonprofits through technical assistance and a matching grants program (Hispanics in Philanthropy, 2001). By 2001 the collaborative had attracted the support of forty-two funders and had selected twelve grant disbursal sites (geographical areas in which local Latino nonprofit organizations, working together, have pledged to raise at least $250,000 to be matched dollar for dollar by the collaborative).

The first grants were awarded in 2001 to local programs in California and Colorado. The Northern California–Central Valley site, for example, raised $400,000 from local foundations and individuals, generating a match of $400,000 from the collaborative, distributed to the local organizations for their capacity-building programs. An additional benefit to the participating organizations has been the formation of a network of colleagues and funders who have learned to work together on the local committee.

The international collaborative plans to hold a leadership training institute in the spring of 2003 to offer hands-on training to local sites and serve as a forum for grantees to share their work and learn from one another.

COMMUNITYWIDE EDUCATIONAL COLLABORATIONS

Each broad population segment can benefit from education and training about gift planning. Several organizations have begun such efforts.

African American Philanthropy Initiative

The African American Philanthropy Initiative, a partnership between the Baltimore Giving Project and the Associated Black Charities of Maryland, seeks to strengthen philanthropy through education, outreach, and fund development in the Baltimore region's African American community. The initiative is helping to develop a fund or series of funds, part of which will be endowed, that leaders in the African American philanthropic community will spearhead to benefit the African American population.

The partnership has published the *Giving Circle Tool Kit* (Baltimore Giving Project, 2000), has provided a program for the Chesapeake Planned Giving Council on new trends in African American philanthropy, started a speaker's series, and has hosted a breakfast for African American financial advisers, all in collaboration with other community-based organizations. African American churches and social service organizations widely distributed its simple and appealing cover letter (see Exhibit 8.1) and its *Giving Circle Tool Kit.*

African American Legacy Program

"As a result of finding that misunderstanding about various philanthropic options are widespread," said Patricia Solomon, president of Detroit's Minerva Education and Development Foundation, an offshoot of the Delta Sigma Theta sorority, "we formed the African American Legacy Program to set up education sessions and speakers, and to develop materials." Chapter Seven describes the program in more detail. "It continues to grow in the African American community and is now collaborating with Leave A Legacy, Touch the

Exhibit 8.1.   African American Philanthropy Initiative.

African American Philanthropy Initiative

"Giving has been a gift…."
Eddie and Sylvia Brown,
Eddie C. and C. Sylvia Brown Family Foundation
Baltimore, Maryland

There are as many motivations for a person's charitable giving as there are people — giving resources and time to help others is one of the most personal acts you can take. **The Baltimore Giving Project (BGP)** came into being to articulate the benefits of organized philanthropy to specific audiences, to increase the number of philanthropic dollars at work in our community by bringing new donors into organized philanthropy, and to promote the concept of philanthropy to the public as often and in as many ways as possible. **The African American Philanthropy Initiative (AAPI)** developed as one of many strategies to reach these goals.

The AAPI, a partnership between Baltimore Giving Project and the Associated Black Charities (ABC), seeks to strengthen philanthropy through education, outreach and fund development for the **Greater Baltimore African American Community**.   The Initiative seeks to:

- Develop and deliver education and outreach to targeted sections of the African American community, which identifies the specific benefits and vehicles of organized philanthropy, and addresses financial management for wealth accumulation;
- Increase the number of philanthropic dollars strategically generated and strategically allocated for maximum impact in the black community;
- Assist Associated Black Charities to enhance its capacity to act as a catalyst for more effective leveraging of resources in the black community.

The AAPI has created this **"Giving Tool Kit"** as a "one stop shop" for information on charitable giving and financial planning.   As we further develop this kit, also included will be a history of black giving in the Greater Baltimore region, profiles of local African American philanthropists and much more.   AAPI's other outreach vehicles include: an **African American Philanthropy E-Newsletter**, a bi-weekly email that keeps you informed on the activities of the AAPI, as well as current trends and best practices in local, regional and national African American philanthropy; and a **Speaker's Series** bringing in national and regional experts to discuss hot topics in African American philanthropy.

For more information on the efforts of the AAPI, to receive additional copies of the Giving Tool Kit and/or to sign up for the E-Newsletter, **please contact Lea Gilmore at (410) 727-1205 or via email at lgilmore@abagmd.org.**

Thank you for your interest!

African American Philanthropy Initiative

ASSOCIATED
BLACK CHARITIES
1114 Cathedral Street
Baltimore, MD 21201
Phone 410-659-0000
Fax 410-659-0755
www.abc-md.org

BALTIMORE
GIVING PROJECT
2 East Read Street
8th Floor
Baltimore, MD 21202-2470
Phone 410-727-0719
Fax 410-727-7177
bgp@abagmd.org
www.baltimoregivingproject.org

Future, and other initiatives designed to promote philanthropy to diverse populations."

Make a Will Campaign

The Minneapolis Foundation has initiated a campaign it calls Make a Will, aimed at educating people, especially those in diverse communities, about the value of making a will. The inspiration to begin this campaign began at a regional black philanthropy conference in Minneapolis in 2000. A speaker asked audience members to indicate whether they had wills; only 20 percent of those in attendance—professionals in fields related to philanthropy—answered

The Minneapolis Foundation has initiated a campaign aimed at educating people, especially those in diverse communities, about the value of making a will.

yes. "This was a real wake-up call," said Jean Fountain, a consultant for the Minneapolis Foundation. "It is estimated that less than 50 percent of the general population has a will, but our audience was far below that. We decided to do something tangible."

Working with key stakeholders—members of the clergy, media, financial planners, and foundation executives—and an advertising agency, the foundation came up with a concept that was both sensitive to the reluctance of African Americans to face death and also creative and fresh. Focusing on the state's right to appoint a guardian for minor children, the brochures and posters featured children's faces with a bright orange stamp proclaiming "Property of Government." Smaller type proclaims: "You may think when you leave this Earth your things will go to a loved one who can care for them. Not true. If you don't protect your things with a will, the government could take them and do with them what they want. Your House. Your car. Your money. Even your kids. Protect your family. Get a will" (Minneapolis Foundation, 2001). The piece also gave a checklist to start down the path of writing a will and the phone number for an attorney referral service.

The awareness campaign included public service announcements on radio and television, posters at bus stops, newspaper stories, and widely distributed brochures. Local clergy preached sermons on stewardship and wills; legal aid attorneys gave two Saturdays of pro bono work. Probate and estate planning experts from major law firms provided continuing education training for general practice attorneys.

The campaign's toll-free telephone number received an average of twenty calls per day after airing a series of public service announcements on local television. It has received more than two thousand calls for more information.

Leave A Legacy

Leave A Legacy, a program of the National Committee on Planned Giving, is an example of a recently established national program that is adaptable to diverse populations. Begun in Columbus in 1996 as a local collaboration of charitable organizations and legal and financial advisers, it is an education campaign designed to encourage people, regardless of their income, to leave charitable gifts to their favorite causes or organizations in their wills and estate plans.

The mission of Leave A Legacy is to increase the number of planned charitable gifts. It is already proving to be an exciting vehicle to bring the diverse interests of scores (often hundreds) of local nonprofit and for-profit organizations together to jointly promote a program that benefits the entire community.

Local Leave A Legacy programs offer attractive and basic turnkey materials about gift planning, inspirational videos featuring stories of people who have made planned gifts, speaker's bureaus to make presentations to civic and social groups, Web sites, public relations campaigns, and educational events for professionals who may be new to or very experienced in planned giving programs.

Leave A Legacy has grown into an international initiative, with more than 150 programs across the United States and Canada, working to change how people think about philanthropy and charitable gift planning. Several local programs have established focused efforts to reach specific ethnic populations.

WHERE WE GO FROM HERE

Collaborative efforts and partnerships are particularly appropriate to the work of diversifying fundraising efforts to include all local populations. Your organization will reach a wider pool of donors if it

Your organization will reach a wider pool of donors if it collaborates with groups within specific ethnic or racial communities.

collaborates with groups within specific ethnic or racial communities.

Whether an organization is seeking new donors, access to mainstream organizations, access to diverse groups, ways to reach additional clients and audiences, or strategies to promote philanthropy, joint efforts provide opportunities for nonprofit organizations to work together and with professional advisers, corporations, foundations, and governmental entities.

In Chapter Nine, we will list strategies for working with diverse populations, reviewing the primary steps along the pathways to diverse donors: awareness, interest, trust, involvement, support, appreciation, recognition, and inclusion as insiders.

9

Realizing the Potential
of Diverse Donors

As we have seen, Asian Americans, African Americans, Latinos, and Native Americans represent more than 30 percent of the population of the United States and substantial amounts of untapped wealth. Traditional fundraising programs have largely ignored this significant pool of prospective donors. We must recognize and respect the rich and growing diversity in the United States, for each of us is diminished as long as others are deprived of their full participation in philanthropy and the nonprofit sector. The vitality of our local communities depends upon our willingness and ability to create philanthropic strategies attractive to new and diverse populations.

PHILANTHROPIC TRAINING

During our interviews for this book and *Cultures of Caring* (Council on Foundations, 1999), we heard time and again about the importance of and need for increased training for members of diverse populations.

"Fundraising in the black community must not be a one-shot drive for the big gift," writes Jean Fairfax (1995, p. 18), an African American philanthropist. "It must be part of a long-range coordinated effort involving many agencies in the nonprofit world to educate communities of color about philanthropy and planned giving."

The Baltimore Giving Project reported key barriers to giving: "lack of knowledge of how to leverage charitable dollars; lack of trust in traditional institutions; and a consumption versus accumulation mindset among first-generation affluent African Americans" (Winters, 1999, pp. 5–6). The placement of lack of knowledge as the first item in this list suggests its importance.

"Most Hispanics do not realize the most effective and efficient ways to leverage opportunities into tax breaks," according to Adam Martinez, director of development for Baylor College of Medicine. "We are way behind in educating the Hispanic community to consider tax consequences."

"Because wealth is new to Native Americans, they have a tendency to spend it," said Carla Roberts, former executive director of Atlatl and current vice president of affiliates for the Arizona Community Foundation. "Their most widespread model of what to do with money is the media: new cars and wide-screen TVs. They have not seen examples of financial security, don't know about options, and don't understand the power of compound interest."

Nonprofits can teach the dynamics of philanthropy by providing hands-on experiences such as involvement on boards and participation as donors. Those dynamics can also be the subject of formal educational opportunities and training sessions.

The National Center for Black Philanthropy in Washington, D.C., was begun in 1999 for this purpose. Its stated mission is "to educate the public about the importance of black philanthropy; promote full participation by African Americans in all aspects of philanthropy; strengthen and support institutions involved in black philanthropy; and conduct research into the contributions of black philanthropy to the social and economic well-being of all Americans."

The center has sponsored two national and three regional conferences on black philanthropy, begun a national campaign to promote giving, developed a membership base and various public education vehicles, and started a program to encourage philanthropy by black businesses. And it has accomplished all this in just a few years.

Similar organizations for other diverse populations are on the horizon, and mainstream institutions should encourage and support them.

STRATEGIES FOR WORKING WITH DIVERSE POPULATIONS

Your organization may want to take a leadership role in encouraging charities to promote philanthropy in diverse local communities, which are often not part of traditional philanthropic networks. The Forum of Regional Associations of Grantmakers suggest some strategies for working with diverse communities:

- Develop collaborative programs with local organizations that primarily serve diverse populations.

- Develop relationships with and serve as a resource to local ethnic organizations, associations, and clubs— business councils, faith-based groups, professional associations, chambers of commerce, sororities and fraternities, and so on—that represent or have interests in diverse communities.

- Offer your library of materials and resources to relevant groups.

- In partnership with other organizations, develop educational programs for wealthy individuals from ethnic communities that discuss philanthropic topics relevant to the population.

- Invite leaders from minority communities to participate, both as presenters and attendees, in programs about philanthropy.

- Host meetings or workshops for and by donors of specific ethnic cultures.

- Support the development of local affinity groups or giving circles for specific populations.

- Provide assistance and support on philanthropic options to those who advise wealthy ethnically diverse individuals and families.

Your organization may want to take a leadership role in encouraging charities to promote philanthropy in diverse local communities.

- Offer internships to students from groups historically underrepresented in your organization.

- Partner with organizations representing ethnic groups, local affinity groups, and community foundations to develop initiatives to reach diverse populations.

- Design and implement research projects, perhaps in conjunction with local colleges and universities, that explore the giving patterns and charitable motivations of a specific community.

PATHWAYS TO DIVERSE DONORS

Pathways to diverse donors are composed of many steps and stepping-stones—not in a straight line, not equally spaced, and not always in the same order. But the basic steps that we have discussed in this book are all important to a firmly grounded fundraising program.

As you travel along your own route to attracting new and diverse supporters to your nonprofit organization, do not give in to the temptation to skip steps or take shortcuts. Although you may come to a detour or even a dead end occasionally, find your way back on the road to diversifying your donor base.

Awareness

Once the mission, policies, and practices of your organization clearly include the full breadth of diversity in your local population, as described in Chapter Three, your first step is to make diverse prospective donors aware of your charitable organization and the outstanding programs it offers. The best public relations tools—in both diverse and mainstream communities—are word-of-mouth testimonials from trusted family members, friends, or colleagues. Do not hesitate to ask your constituents to tell their friends and associates about you.

The second most frequent way that people learn about nonprofit organizations is by reputation—the overall quality of the programs as judged by the general public. Your organization must have a reputation for top-notch services that are relevant and accessible to the prospective donor.

The prospective donor will look for people associated with the organization—clients, students, participants, patients, visitors, volunteers, staff members, and trustees—who have interests and backgrounds similar to his or her own. The closer the prospect's relationship to a person involved with your organization, the more likely that he or she will give a first gift and successive gifts. Even a large organization's high-quality, exciting public relations efforts will fall on deaf ears if the prospective donor perceives that the organization is not open to participation by people of his or her ethnicity in every facet of its work. Traditional printed materials, such as annual reports and newsletters, may not be effective methods for public awareness in some diverse communities. Instead arrange for the more influential oral testimonials in public venues—social gatherings, special events, radio and television interviews, and so on—by trusted community members.

Interest

Next your organization must develop the prospective donor's interest in its mission and work. Find ways to make your work relevant to the people you hope to attract. For example, if you work for a social service agency,

- Know how many clients are of the prospect's ethnicity.

- Discuss the programs you offer to children, families, and the elderly (important issues for people of all backgrounds).

- Talk about the ways your organization increases educational opportunities (another important issue for all ethnicities).

- Describe how your organization promotes self-sufficiency and empowerment (important issues for African American and Latinos in particular).

Other strategies to develop interest in your organization include hosting neighborhood gatherings, making radio and television advertisements and public service announcements, distributing flyers by direct mail, and sponsoring educational events for particular constituencies.

Find ways to make your work relevant to the people you hope to attract.

Trust

The people you attract will have attained a level of stability and acculturation appropriate to your organization. As diverse donors become more informed about what your organization does and more comfortable with who you are, they will begin to develop trust. The consistent high quality of your organization's programs, products, and services will give credence to the organization's trustworthiness and standing in the community.

Because people in diverse cultures have in the past trusted mainstream organizations and people that later proved to be unworthy, they may be wary of your good intentions. A trusted relationship requires both parties to have confidence in the other's character, strength, and truthfulness. Such confidence develops over time and cannot be rushed.

Involvement

You may want to invite the prospective donor to volunteer in some capacity: to serve on a committee, to provide direct service, or to give advice. Be sure to do your homework and know the donor's particular skills and interests.

As you work with prospects, encourage their involvement in many facets of the organization. This will benefit the organization and deepen the prospects' commitment to your vision. Be sure to invite prospective donors to special events; social interaction is important to members of all four major ethnic and racial groups. Ask an appropriate friend or colleague to talk personally with the prospect about the format and protocols of the event.

Depending on the prospect's financial stability, multiple responsibilities, and other factors, this may be as far along the path as the prospect is willing or able to go. Celebrate the gifts of time and expertise that the donor has given and will give in the future. Pressuring people to give more or differently than they are willing to can backfire. Continue the relationship with the prospective donor even if he or she does not give the organization the funds you seek.

Support

Some prospective donors will want to support your organization financially. Be sure that members of their ethnic groups are on all development committees: special events, annual fund campaigns, and major and planned gift cabinets. Again, prospective donors want to know that they are represented at every level of the organization.

Studies have not established the effectiveness of direct mail with people from diverse backgrounds. Personal contact by people they trust is important, even for small gifts. The donor's first contribution will probably be small, perhaps even a test to determine whether your organization acknowledges the gift properly and uses it as he or she requested. We are not suggesting that you should make a personal call for every $10 gift. However, the more personal your acknowledgment, the more likely it is that the donor will send additional contributions.

APPRECIATION

Do not send a form acknowledgement, even for a small gift. An immediate phone call upon receipt of the gift, followed by a personal letter from the executive director or trustee is appropriate. Some board chairs write personal notes to donors, something that donors appreciate. Remember to let the person who solicited the gift know that the organization has received a gift, and encourage that person to write a thank-you note as well.

Recognition

Publicly recognize all donors in your normal fashion, unless they ask for anonymity. You may want to ask diverse donors for permission to tell the story of their involvement with your organization in order to encourage others to become involved. Donors of major gifts should receive special recognition, which you will want to discuss with the donor in advance.

You may want to ask diverse donors for permission to tell the story of their involvement with your organization in order to encourage others to become involved.

Inclusion as Insider

Your organization should also accept major donors into an insiders' group of advisers from whom the executive director and board chair seek guidance on strategic issues. As the donors become aware of trends and issues affecting the philanthropic sector in general and your organization's niche in particular, the donors on the "invest and empower" side of the continuum of philanthropy will begin to visualize solutions to intractable problems. And they will discover ways that they can significantly affect solutions. You want to be there to help them through this exciting process.

THE BROAD VIEW

Throughout this book we have used the term *diversity* to highlight the rich heterogeneity of the United States population. The work of diversifying fundraising practices will position nonprofit organizations to better serve their increasingly diverse constituents and will also increase charitable giving to those organizations. In addition this work will provide broader benefits to our society as we undertake the difficult task of transforming our institutions and attitudes. Paul Ong, associate professor of urban planning and the chair of the interdepartmental program in Asian American studies at the University of California, Los Angeles, states this problem well: "Given our diverse population, the United States has the potential of developing an understanding of multiculturalism—different ways of knowing, interacting, communicating, and governing—unmatched by other nations. The policy of embracing differences in language, values, and cultural practices as opposed to homogenizing everyone . . . [provides] domestic benefits derived from a cultural richness rooted in diversity in the arts, entertainment, food, and other areas of daily life. . . . Ultimately, promoting diversity is not so much about preserving any one particular culture as it is about creating a positive multiethnic society" (Ong and Umemoto, 1994, p. 273).

Finally, remember that changing your fundraising practices and the composition of your donor base will require patience and constant vigilance on your part and by the board, CEO, and staff. The work of diversifying your donor pool is ongoing. It is also rewarding, both personally and professionally.

References

Adamson, R. "A River So Wide: Considering the Limits on Native American Use of Formal Philanthropy." *Indian Giver,* 1999, 5(3), 7–9. Copyright © 1999/2000 by First Nations Development Institute, Fredericksburg, Va.

Ascencio, F. L. *Bringing It Back Home: Remittances to Mexico from Migrant Workers in the United States.* Monograph Series, 37. San Diego: Center for U.S.-Mexican Studies, University of California, 1993.

Asian American Federation of New York. *New Census Estimates Tell Two Stories About Asian and Pacific Islander Students.* Press release. Mar. 23, 2001a.

Asian American Federation of New York. *New Heritage of Giving: Philanthropy in Asian America.* New York: Asian American Federation of New York, 2001b.

Baltimore Giving Project. *Research Findings: African American Segment.* Baltimore: Associated Black Charities of Baltimore and Association of Baltimore Area Grantmakers, 1999.

Baltimore Giving Project. *Giving Circle Tool Kit.* Baltimore: Associated Black Charities of Baltimore and Association of Baltimore Area Grantmakers, 2000.

Berry, M. "Native-American Philanthropy: Expanding Social Participation and Self-Determination." In Council on Foundations, *Cultures of Caring: Philanthropy in Diverse American Communities.* Washington, D.C.: Council on Foundations, 1999.

Berry, M. L., and Chao, J. *Engaging Diverse Communities for and Through Philanthropy.* Washington, D.C.: Forum of Regional Associations of Grantmakers, 2001.

Black, S. S. "Native American Philanthropy." In P. C. Rogers (ed.), *Philanthropy in Communities of Color: Traditions and Challenges.* Indianapolis, Ind.: Association for Research on Nonprofit Organizations and Voluntary Action, 2001.

Bussel, D. *The Corporate Giving of Hispanic-Owned Companies in Miami-Dade County: An Occasional Report by the Donors Forum, Inc.* (J. C. Bander, ed.). Miami: Donors Forum, 2000.

Campoamor, W., Diaz, A., and Ramos, H. A. J. (eds.). *Nuevos Senderos: Reflections on Hispanics and Philanthropy.* Houston, Tex.: University of Houston/ Arte Público, 1999.

Campoamor, D. *2001 Annual Report for Hispanics in Philanthropy.* Berkeley, Calif.: Hispanics in Philanthropy, 2002.

Carson, E. D. "Black Philanthropy: Shaping Tomorrow's Nonprofit Sector." *Journal: Contemporary Issues in Fund Raising,* Summer 1989, pp. 23–31.

Carson, E. D. "Understanding Cultural Differences in Fundraising." In R. C. Hedgepeth (ed.), *Communicating Effectively with Major Donors.* New Directions in Philanthropic Fundraising, no. 10. San Francisco: Jossey-Bass Publishers, 1995.

Chao, J. "Asian-American Philanthropy: Expanding Circles of Participation." In Council on Foundations, *Cultures of Caring: Philanthropy in Diverse American Communities.* Washington, D.C.: Council on Foundations, 1999.

Chao, J. "Asian American Philanthropy: Acculturation and Charitable Vehicles." In P. C. Rogers (ed.), *Philanthropy in Communities of Color: Traditions and Challenges.* Indianapolis, Ind.: Association for Research on Nonprofit Organizations and Voluntary Action, 2001.

Ciconte, B. L., and Jacob, J. G. *Fundraising Basics: A Complete Guide.* (2nd ed.) Gaithersburg, Md.: Aspen, 2001.

Conley, D. "The Racial Wealth Gap: Origins and Implications for Philanthropy in the African American Community." In P. C. Rogers (ed.), *Philanthropy in Communities of Color: Traditions and Challenges.* Indianapolis, Ind.: Association for Research on Nonprofit Organizations and Voluntary Action, 2001.

Cortés, M. "Three Strategic Questions About Latino Philanthropy." In C. H. Hamilton and W. F. Ilchman (eds.), *Cultures of Giving II: How Heritage, Gender, Wealth, and Values Influence Philanthropy.* New Directions for Philanthropic Fundraising, no. 8. San Francisco: Jossey-Bass, 1995.

Cortés, M. "Do Hispanic Nonprofits Foster Hispanic Philanthropy?" In L. Wagner and A. F. Deck (eds.), *Hispanic Philanthropy: Exploring the Factors That Influence Giving and Asking.* New Directions for Philanthropic Fundraising, no. 24. San Francisco: Jossey-Bass, 1999.

Cortés, M. "Fostering Philanthropy and Service in U.S. Latino Communities." In P. C. Rogers (ed.), *Philanthropy in Communities of Color: Traditions and Challenges.* Indianapolis, Ind.: Association for Research on Nonprofit Organizations and Voluntary Action, 2001.

Cortés-Vasquez, L., and Miranda, L. A., Jr. "Latinos and Giving, 1999." In *Hispanic New Yorkers on Nueva York: Ayúdenos a Ayudar* [Help Us Help]. Seventh Annual Report. New York: Hispanic Federation, 1999.

Council on Foundations. *Cultures of Caring: Philanthropy in Diverse American Communities.* Washington, D.C.: Council on Foundations, 1999.

Dennis, M. A., Jr. "Black Philanthropy and the Black Church." Presentation at the Third National Conference on Black Philanthropy, Detroit, May 2001.

Edmond, A. A., Jr. "The B. E. 100s Overview: Built to Last." *Black Enterprise,* New York, June 2001.

Estrada, L. F. "Hispanic Evolution." *Foundation News,* May–June 1990, pp. 34–36.

Fairfax, J. E. "Black Philanthropy: Its Heritage and Its Future." In C. H. Hamilton and W. F. Ilchman (eds.), *Cultures of Giving II: How Heritage, Gender, Wealth, and Values Influence Philanthropy.* New Directions for Philanthropic Fundraising, no. 8. San Francisco: Jossey-Bass, 1995.

Ferriby, R. Presentation at the Third National Conference on Black Philanthropy, Detroit, May 2001.

"Foundations of Diversity: An Interview with Wilma Mankiller." *Indian Giver,* 1995, *1*(3), 1, 8–9.

Goizueta, R. *Caminemos con Jesus* [Let Us Walk with Jesus]. Maryknoll, N.Y.: Orbis, 1995.

Goldsberry, R. E. Presentation at the Third National Conference on Black Philanthropy, Detroit, May 2001.

Hall-Russell, C., and Kasberg, R. H. *African-American Traditions of Giving and Serving: A Study of Ethnic Philanthropy in the Midwest.* Indianapolis: Indiana University Center on Philanthropy, 1997.

Hispanics in Philanthropy. *2001 Annual Report.* Berkeley, Calif.: Hispanics in Philanthropy, 2001.

Hopi Tribe. "Hopi Education Endowment Fund Moves Closer to Disbursing Funds." *Hopi Tutuveni,* newspaper of the Hopi Tribe, Apr. 17, 2001.

Joseph, J. A. "Black Philanthropy: The Potential and Limits of Private Generosity in a Civil Society." Paper presented at the first annual Lecture on Black Philanthropy sponsored by the Association of Black Foundation Executives and the Smithsonian Institution, Washington, D.C., June 3, 1991.

Joseph, J. A. *Remaking America: How the Benevolent Traditions of Many Cultures Are Transforming Our National Life.* San Francisco: Jossey-Bass, 1995.

Kaplan, A. E. (ed.). *Giving USA 2001: Annual Report for Philanthropy.* New York: AAFRC Trust for Philanthropy, 2001.

Lewis, D. E. "Institutions Vying for Black Philanthropy." *Boston Globe,* June 23, 2000.

"Market Research: News You Can Use." *United Way of America Research Services*, July 22, 1996.

Mexican-American Legal Defense and Educational Fund. "MALDEF Introduces the Nonprofit Support Center" [http://www.maldef.org/about/nonprofit.htm]. 2002.

Minneapolis Foundation. *Where There's a Will, There's a Way*. Minneapolis, Minn.: Minneapolis Foundation. 2001.

Minority Executive Directors Coalition. *The Minority Executive Directors Coalition's Working Definition of Cultural Competency*. Seattle: Minority Executive Directors Coalition, 2001.

Miranda, J. "Religion, Philanthropy, and the Hispanic People in North America." In L. Wagner and A. F. Deck (eds.), *Hispanic Philanthropy: Exploring the Factors That Influence Giving and Asking*. New Directions for Philanthropic Fundraising, no. 24. San Francisco: Jossey-Bass, 1999.

National Indian Gaming Association. *Survey Results of Indian Gaming Nations Charitable Giving*. Washington, D.C.: National Indian Gaming Association, in conjunction with the First Nations Development Institute, 2001.

Oliver, A. L. "Strengthening African American Philanthropy: Individual Giving." In R. M. Jackson (ed.), *At the Crossroads: The Proceedings of the First National Conference on Black Philanthropy*. Oakton, Va.: Corporation for Philanthropy, 1998.

Ong, P., and Hee, S. J. "Economic Diversity." In P. Ong (ed.), *The State of Asian Pacific America: Economic Diversity, Issues, and Policies*. Los Angeles: LEAP, Asian Pacific American Public Policy Institute, and UCLA Asian American Studies Center, 1994.

Ong, P., and Umemoto, K. "Diversity Within a Common Agenda." In P. Ong (ed.), *The State of Asian Pacific America: Economic Diversity, Issues, and Policies*. Los Angeles: LEAP, Asian Pacific American Public Policy Institute, and UCLA Asian American Studies Center, 1994.

Parra, O. V. "Hispanic Women: Nurturing Tomorrow's Philanthropy." In L. Wagner and A. F. Deck (eds.), *Hispanic Philanthropy: Exploring the Factors That Influence Giving and Asking*. New Directions for Philanthropic Fundraising, no. 24. San Francisco: Jossey-Bass, 1999.

Partnership for African American Endowment Development. *Final Report 1999*. Detroit: Partnership for African American Endowment Development, 1999.

Ramos, H.A.J. "Latino Philanthropy: Expanding U.S. Models of Giving and Civic Participation." In Council on Foundations, *Cultures of Caring: Philanthropy in Diverse American Communities*. Washington, D.C.: Council on Foundations, 1999.

Rivas-Vazquez, A. G. "New Pools of Latino Wealth: A Study of Donors and Potential Donors in U.S. Hispanic/Latino Communities." In D. Campoamor, W. A. Diaz, and H.A.J. Ramos (eds.), *Nuevos Senderos: Reflections on Hispanics and Philanthropy*. Houston, Tex.: University of Houston/Arte Público, 1999.

Rodriguez, C. G. "Education and Hispanic Philanthropy: Family, Sacrifice, and Community." In L. Wagner and A. F. Deck (eds.), *Hispanic Philanthropy: Exploring the Factors That Influence Giving and Asking*. New Directions for Philanthropic Fundraising, no. 24. San Francisco: Jossey-Bass, 1999.

Royce, A. P., and Rodriguez, R. "From Personal Charity to Organized Giving: Hispanic Institutions and Values of Stewardship and Philanthropy." In L. Wagner and A. F. Deck (eds.), *Hispanic Philanthropy: Exploring the Factors That Influence Giving and Asking*. New Directions for Philanthropic Fundraising, no. 24. San Francisco: Jossey-Bass, 1999.

Saint Paul Foundation. *The Diversity Endowment Funds of the Saint Paul Foundation*. Saint Paul, Minn.: Saint Paul Foundation, 2000.

Sanchez, D., and Zamora, R. "Current Issues Affecting U.S. Hispanic Foundation and Nonprofit Directors/Trustees: A Survey of the Field." In D. Campoamor, W. A. Diaz, and H.A.J. Ramos (eds.), *Nuevos Senderos: Reflections on Hispanics and Philanthropy*. Houston, Tex.: University of Houston/Arte Público, 1999.

Schervish, P. *Major Donors, Major Motives: The People and Purposes Behind Major Gifts*. Boston: Social Welfare Research Institute, Boston College, 1997.

Shao, S. "Asian American Giving: Issues and Challenges (A Practitioner's Perspective)." In C. H. Hamilton and W. F. Ilchman (eds.), *Cultures of Giving II: How Heritage, Gender, Wealth, and Values Influence Philanthropy*. San Francisco: Jossey-Bass, 1995.

Shinagawa, L. H. "The Impact of Immigration on the Demography of Asian Pacific Americans." In B. Ong, H. Lee, and R. Lee (eds.), *The State of Asian Pacific America: Reframing the Immigration Debate*. Los Angeles: LEAP Public Policy Institute and UCLA Asian American Studies Center, 1996.

Smith, B., Shue, S., Vest, J. L., and Villarreal, J. *Philanthropy in Communities of Color*. Bloomington: Indiana University Press, 1999.

Therrien, M., and Ramirez, R. "The Hispanic Population in the United States: March 2000." *U.S. Department of Commerce News* [http://www.census.gov/Press-Release/www/2001/cg01-41.html]. Mar. 2001.

U.S. Bureau of the Census. *We the Americans: Asians*. Washington, D.C.: U.S. Bureau of the Census, 1993a.

U.S. Bureau of the Census. *We the First Americans*. Washington, D.C.: U.S. Bureau of the Census, 1993b.

U.S. Bureau of the Census. *American Indian and Alaska Native Populations: Characteristics of American Indians by Tribe and Language*. Washington, D.C.: U.S. Bureau of the Census, 1995a.

U.S. Bureau of the Census. *Asset Ownership of Households, 1995*. Washington, D.C.: Housing and Household Economic Statistics Division, U.S. Bureau of the Census, 1995b.

U.S. Bureau of the Census. *Annual Projections of the Resident Population by Age, Sex, Race, and Hispanic Origin: Middle Series, 2041–2050*. Washington, D.C.: Population Projection Program, Population Division, U.S. Bureau of the Census, 2000a.

U.S. Bureau of the Census. *Asian- and Pacific Islander-Owned Businesses Number 900,000+: California, New York, Texas Leading States, Bureau of the Census Reports*. Press release. May 22, 2000b.

U.S. Bureau of the Census. *Asian and Pacific Islander Population in the United States, March 2000*. Washington, D.C.: U.S. Bureau of the Census, 2000c.

U.S. Bureau of the Census. *Census Bureau Says Nation's Educational Attainment Keeps Rising*. Press release, Public Information Office, Dec. 19, 2000d.

U.S. Bureau of the Census. *Educational Attainment in the United States, March 2000*. Washington, D.C.: U.S. Bureau of the Census, 2000e.

U.S. Bureau of the Census. *Housing Vacancies and Homeownership Annual Statistics, 2000*. Washington, D.C.: U.S. Bureau of the Census, 2000f.

U.S. Bureau of the Census. *Population Projections for States by Age, Sex, Race and Hispanic Origin, 1995 to 2025*. Washington, D.C.: Population Projection Program, Population Division, U.S. Bureau of the Census, 2000g.

U.S. Bureau of the Census. *Projections of the Resident Population by Race, Hispanic Origin, and Nativity: Middle Series, 2050–2070*. Washington, D.C.: Population Projection Program, Population Division, U.S. Bureau of the Census, 2000h.

U.S. Bureau of the Census. *Survey of Minority- and Women-Owned Business Enterprises: Economic Census of 1997*. Washington, D.C.: U.S. Bureau of the Census, 2000i.

U.S. Bureau of the Census. *African American Homeownership Rate: Third Quarter, 2000*. Washington, D.C.: U.S. Bureau of the Census, 2001a.

U.S. Bureau of the Census. *American Indian- and Alaska-Owned Businesses Near 200,000: California, Texas, Oklahoma Head States*. Press release, May 22, 2001b.

U.S. Bureau of the Census. *Census Bureau Releases Update on Country's African American Population*. Facts for Features, Feb. 22, 2001c.

U.S. Bureau of the Census. *Employed White, Black and Hispanic-Origin Workers by Sex, Occupation, Class of Worker and Full- or Part-Time Status.* Washington, D.C.: U.S. Bureau of the Census, 2001d.

U.S. Bureau of the Census. *Hispanic and Non-Hispanic Population by Race for the United States, 2000.* Washington, D.C.: U.S. Bureau of the Census, 2001e.

U.S. Bureau of the Census. *The Hispanic Population, 2000.* Washington, D.C.: U.S. Bureau of the Census, 2001f.

U.S. Bureau of the Census. *Household Wealth and Asset Ownership, 1995.* Washington, D.C.: U.S. Bureau of the Census, 2001g.

U.S. Bureau of the Census. *Median Income by Selected Characteristics, Race, and Hispanic Origin, 2000, 1999, and 1998.* Washington, D.C.: U.S. Bureau of the Census, 2001h.

U.S. Bureau of the Census. *Money Income in the United States, 2000.* Washington, D.C.: U.S. Bureau of the Census, 2001i.

U.S. Bureau of the Census. *Population by Race and Hispanic or Latino Origin for the United States, 1990 and 2000.* Washington, D.C.: U.S. Bureau of the Census, 2001j.

U.S. Bureau of the Census. *Resident Population Estimates of the United States by Sex, Race, and Hispanic Origin, April 1, 1990, to July 1, 1999, with Short-Term Projection to November 1, 2000.* Washington, D.C.: Population Projection Program, Population Division, U.S. Bureau of the Census, 2001k.

U.S. Bureau of the Census. *Survey of Minority-Owned Business Enterprises: Economic Census of 1997.* Washington, D.C.: U.S. Bureau of the Census, 2001l.

Wagner, L., and Deck, A. F. (eds.). *Hispanic Philanthropy: Exploring the Factors That Influence Giving and Asking.* New Directions for Philanthropic Fundraising, no. 24. San Francisco: Jossey-Bass, 1999.

Washington, B. T. *Up from Slavery: An Autobiography.* New York: Doubleday, 1901.

Wells, R. A. *The Honor of Giving: Philanthropy in Native America.* Indianapolis: Indiana University Center on Philanthropy, 1998.

Winters, M. F. "Reflections on Endowment Building in the African-American Community." In Council on Foundations, *Cultures of Caring: Philanthropy in Diverse American Communities.* Washington, D.C.: Council on Foundations, 1999.

Resources

NONPROFIT ORGANIZATIONS
SERVING DIVERSE POPULATIONS

African American

Associated Black Charities
105 East 22nd Street, Suite 915
New York, NY 10010
Tel.: (212) 777-6060
Fax: (212) 777-7904
http://www.assocblackcharities.com

Associated Black Charities of Maryland
1114 Cathedral Street
Baltimore, MD 21201
Tel.: (410) 659-0000
Fax: (410) 659-5121
http://www.abc-md.org

Association of Baltimore Area Grantmakers
Baltimore Giving Project
2 East Read Street, 8th fl.
Baltimore, MD 21202
Tel.: (410) 727-1205
Fax: (410) 727-7177
http://www.baltimoregivingproject.org

Community Foundation for Southeastern Michigan
African American Legacy Program
333 West Fort Street
Detroit, MI 48226
Tel.: (313) 961-6675
Fax: (313) 961-2886
http://www.cfsem.org
http://www.africanamericanlegacyprogram.org

Congress of National Black Churches
1225 Eye Street NW, Suite 750
Washington, D.C. 20005
Tel.: (202) 371-1091
http://www.cnbc.org

National Black United Funds
40 Clinton Street, 5th fl.
Newark, NJ 07102
Tel.: (973) 643-5122
Fax: (973) 648-8350
http://www.nbuf.org

National Center for Black Philanthropy, Inc.
1110 Vermont Avenue NW, Suite 405
Washington, D.C. 2005
Tel.: (202) 530-9770
Fax: (202) 530-9771
http://www.ncfbp.org

Twenty First Century Foundation
666 West End Avenue, Suite 1D
New York, NY 10025
Tel.: (212) 249-3612
http://www.21cf.org

United Negro College Fund
8260 Willow Oaks Corporate Drive
Fairfax, VA 22031
Tel.: (703) 205-3400
http://www.uncf.org

Asian American

Asia Foundation
465 California Street, 14th fl.
San Francisco, CA 95104
Tel.: (415) 743-3336
http://www.asiafoundation.org

Asia Society
725 Park Avenue
New York, NY 10021
Tel.: (212) 288-6400
http://www.asiasociety.org

Asian American Federation of New York
120 Wall Street, 3rd fl.
New York, NY 10005
Tel.: (212) 344-5878
Fax: (212) 344-5636
http://www.aafny.org

Asian American Legal Defense and Education Fund
99 Hudson Street, 12th fl.
New York, NY 10013
Tel.: (212) 966-5932
http://www.aaldef.org

Asian Americans/Pacific Islanders in Philanthropy
225 Bush Street, Suite 580
San Francisco, CA 94104

Tel.: (415) 273-2760
Fax: (415) 273-2765
http://www.aapip.org

Asian Pacific American Community Fund
225 Bush Street, Suite 590
San Francisco, CA 94104
Tel.: (415) 433-6859
Fax: (415) 433-2425
http://www.asianpacificfund.org

Latino

Chicanos por la Causa
1112 East Buckeye Road
Phoenix, AZ 85034
Tel.: (602) 257-0700
http://www.cplc.org

Greater Kansas City Hispanic Development Fund
2500 Holmes Street
Kansas City, MO 64108
Tel.: (816) 474-3350
Fax: (816) 221-1636
http://www.gkccf.com

The Hispanic Federation
84 William Street, 15th fl.
New York, NY 10038
Tel.: (212) 742-0707
Fax: (212) 742-2313
http://www.hispanicfederation.org

Hispanics in Philanthropy
5950 Doyle Street, Suite 7
Emeryville, CA 94608
Tel.: (510) 420-1011

Fax: (510) 420-0387
http://www.hiponline.org

Mexican American Legal Defense and Educational Fund
634 South Spring Street
Los Angeles, CA 90014
Tel.: (213) 629-2512
http://www.maldef.org

National Council of La Raza
111 19th Street NW, Suite 1000
Washington, D.C. 20036
Tel.: (202) 785-1670
http://www.nclr.org

United Latino Fund
315 West 9th Street, Suite 709
Los Angeles, CA 90015
Tel.: (213) 236-2929
Fax: (213) 236-2930
http://www.unitedlatinofund.org

Native American

American Indian Business Leaders
Gallagher Business Building, Suite 257
University of Montana
Missoula, MT 59812
Tel.: (406) 243-0211
http://www.umt.edu/aibl

American Indian College Fund
8333 Greenwood Boulevard
Denver, CO 80221
Tel.: (303) 426-8900
Fax: (303) 426-1200
http://www.collegefund.org

American Indian Higher Education Consortium
121 Oronoco Street
Alexandria, VA 22314
Tel.: (703) 838-0400
Fax: (703) 838-0388
http://www. aihec.org

First Nations Development Institute
Stores Building
11917 Main Street
Fredricksburg, VA 22408
Tel.: (540) 371-5615
Fax: (540) 371-5615
http://www.firstnations.org

Hopi Foundation
P.O. Box 169
Hotevilla, AZ 86030
Tel.: (520) 734-2380
Fax: (520) 734-9520
http://www.hopifoundation.org

Intertribal Council of Arizona
Southwest Coalition on Native American Philanthropy
2214 North Central Avenue, Suite 100
Phoenix, AZ 85004
Tel.: (602) 258-4822
Fax: (602) 258-4825
http://www.itcaonline.com

National Indian Gaming Association
224 Second Street SE
Washington, D.C. 20003
Tel.: (202) 546-7711
http://www.indiangaming.org

Native American Rights Fund
1506 Broadway
Boulder, CO 80302
Tel.: (303) 447-8760
Fax: (303) 443-7776
http://www.narf.org

Native Americans in Philanthropy
123 West Fourth Street
P.O. Drawer 1429
Lumberton, NC 28358
Tel.: (910) 618-9749
Fax: (910) 618-9839
http://www.nativephilanthropy.org

Seventh Generation Fund for Indian Development
P.O. Box 4569
Arcata, CA 95518
Tel.: (707) 825-7640
http://www.7genfund.org

Other Philanthropic and Fundraising Organizations

Association for Research on Nonprofit Organizations and
    Voluntary Action
550 West North Street, Suite 301
Indianapolis, IN 46202
Tel.: (317) 684-2120
Fax: (317) 684-2128
http://www.arnova.org

Association of Fundraising Professionals
1101 King Street, Suite 700
Alexandria, VA 22314
Tel.: (703) 684-0410
Fax: (703) 684-0540
http://www.afpnet.org

Center for the Study of Philanthropy
Graduate School and University Center
City University of New York
365 Fifth Avenue, Room 5116
New York, NY 10016
Tel.: (212) 817-2010
http://www.philanthropy.org

Council on Foundations
1828 L Street NW
Washington, D.C. 20036
Tel.: (202) 466-6512
Fax: (202) 785-3926
http://www.cof.org

Forum of Regional Associations of Grantmakers
1828 L Street NW, Suite 300
Washington, D.C. 20036
Tel.: (202) 467-0472
Fax: (202) 835-2972
http://www.rag.org

Indiana University
Center on Philanthropy
550 West North Street
Indianapolis, IN 46202
Tel.: (317) 274-4200
http://www.philanthropy.iupui.edu

National Center for Family Philanthropy
1220 19th Street NW, Suite 804
Washington, D.C. 20036
Tel.: (202) 293-3424
Fax: (202) 293-3395
http://www.ncfp.org

National Committee on Planned Giving
233 McCrea Street, Suite 400
Indianapolis, IN 46225
Tel.: (317) 269-6274
Fax: (317) 269-6276
http://www.ncpg.org

Saint Paul Foundation
Diversity Endowment Funds
600 Norwest Center
55 East Fifth Street
Saint Paul, MN 55101
Tel.: (651) 224-5463
Fax: (651) 224-8123
http://www.tspf.org

NEWS SOURCES

A Magazine: Inside Asian America
677 Fifth Avenue, 3rd fl.
New York, NY 10022
Tel.: (212) 593-8089
Fax: (212) 593-8082
http://www.amagazine.com

Black Enterprise
130 Fifth Avenue, 10th fl.
New York, NY 10011
Tel.: (212) 242-8000
Fax: (212) 886-9615
http://www.blackenterprise.com

Chronicle of Philanthropy
1255 23rd Street NW, Suite 700
Washington, D.C. 20037

Tel.: (202) 466-1200
Fax: (202) 466-2078
http://philanthropy.com

Hispanic Business
425 Pine Avenue
Santa Barbara, CA 93117
Tel.: (805) 964-4554
Fax: (805) 964-5539
http://www.hispanicbusiness.com

Indian Giver and *Business Alert*
First National Development Institute
Stores Building
11917 Main Street
Fredricksburg, VA 22408
Tel.: (540) 371-5615
Fax: (540) 371-3505
http://www.firstnations.org/publications/indian_giver.htm

U.S. Census Bureau
Director of Race and Ethnicity
Tel.: (301) 457-1305
http://www.census.gov

FURTHER READING

These reading recommendations are presented in five categories:
(1) all races and ethnicities, (2) African American, (3) Asian
American, (4) Latino, and (5) Native American.

All Races and Ethnicities

Council on Foundations. *Cultures of Caring: Philanthropy in Diverse American Communities*. Washington, D.C.: Council on Foundations, 1999.

Hamilton, C. H., and Ilchman, W. F. (eds.). *Cultures of Giving II: How Heritage, Gender, Wealth, and Values Influence Philanthropy.* New Directions for Philanthropic Fundraising, no. 8. San Francisco: Jossey-Bass, 1995.

Saint Paul Foundation. *Creating New Models of Philanthropy with Communities of Color.* Saint Paul, Minn.: Saint Paul Foundation's Diversity Endowment Funds, 1997.

Skriloff, L. (ed.). *The Source Book of Multicultural Experts.* New York: Multicultural Marketing Resources, 1999.

Spann, J. *The Value of Difference: Enhancing Philanthropy Through Inclusiveness in Governance, Staffing, and Grantmaking.* Washington, D.C.: Council on Foundations, 1993.

Winters, M. F. *Donors of Color: A Promising Frontier for Community Foundations.* Washington, D.C.: Council on Foundations, 1993.

Wittstock, L. W., and Williams, T. *Changing Communities, Changing Foundations: The Story of the Diversity Efforts of Twenty Community Foundations.* Minneapolis, Minn.: Rainbow Research, 1998.

African American

Anderson, B. E. *Philanthropy and Charitable Giving Among Large Black Business Owners.* Philadelphia: Association of Black Foundation Executives, 1993.

Carson, E. D. *Black Volunteers as Givers and Fundraisers.* Center for the Study of Philanthropy Working Papers. New York: Center for the Study of Philanthropy, City University of New York, 1990.

Carson, E. D. "Understanding Cultural Difference in Fundraising." In D. A. Brehmer (ed.), *Communicating Effectively with Major Donors.* New Directions for Philanthropic Fundraising, no. 10. San Francisco: Jossey-Bass Publishers, 1995.

Hall-Russell, C., and Kasberg, R. H. *African-American Traditions of Giving and Serving: A Study of Ethnic Philanthropy in the Midwest.* Indianapolis: Indiana University Center on Philanthropy, 1997.

Jackson, R. M. (ed.). *At the Crossroads: The Proceedings of the First National Conference on Black Philanthropy.* Oakton, Va.: Corporation for Philanthropy, 1998.

Jackson, R. M. (ed.). *Moving the Agenda Forward: The Proceedings of the Second National Conference on Black Philanthropy.* Washington, D.C.: National Center for Black Philanthropy, 2000.

Palmer, C. *Topics in Black American Philanthropy Since 1785.* Multicultural Philanthropy Curriculum Guide, no. 3. New York: City University of New York Graduate Center for the Study of Philanthropy, 1998.

Palmer, C. *A Graduate Curriculum Guide to Topics in Black American Philanthropy Since 1785*. New York: City University of New York, 1999.

Asian American

Chan, S. *Asian Americans: An Interpretive History*. Boston: Twayne, 1991.

Chao, J. *Topics in Asian American Philanthropy and Voluntarism: An Extension Course Guide*. Multicultural Curriculum Guide, no. 10. New York: City University Graduate Center for the Study of Philanthropy, 2000.

Espiratu, Y. L. *Asian American Panethnicity: Bridging Institutions and Identities*. Philadelphia: Temple University Press, 1992. (See particularly chap. 3, "Electoral Politics," and chap. 4, "The Politics of Social Service Funding.")

Wei, W. *The Asian American Movement*. Philadelphia: Temple University Press, 1993.

Latino

Campoamor, D., Diaz, W. A., and Ramos, H.A.J. (eds.). *Nuevos Senderos: Reflections on Hispanics and Philanthropy*. Houston, Tex.: University of Houston/Arte Público, 1999.

Cortés-Vasquez, L., and Miranda, L. A., Jr. *Hispanic New Yorkers on Nueva York: Ayúdenos a Ayudar*. Seventh Annual Report. New York: Hispanic Federation, 1999.

Miller, E. D. *Latinos and the Development of Community Philanthropy, Associations, and Advocacy*. Multicultural Philanthropy Curriculum Guide, no. 7. New York: City University of New York Center for the Study of Philanthropy, 1999.

Native American

American Indian Research and Policy Institute. *To Build a Bridge: An Introduction to Working with American Indian Communities*. Saint Paul, Minn.: American Indian Research and Policy Institute, 1999.

Council on Foundations. *Giving with Honor: A Legal Reference on Charitable Activities of American Indian Tribes*. Washington, D.C.: Council on Foundations, 1998.

Ewen, A., and Wollack, J. *Survey of Grantmaking by American Indian Foundations and Organization*. Lumberton, N.C.: Native Americans in Philanthropy, 1996.

O'Donnell, M., and Ambler, M. "Endowments: Investing in the Future." *Tribal College Journal*, Winter 1995–1996, pp. 17–21.

Index

A

Accessibility, 79–80
Acknowledgments, 121–122, 153*e*
Adamson, R., 13, 56, 58, 62
The AFRAM Group, 14, 158
AFRAM Group, 108
African American Alexis de Tocqueville Society, 149
African American Community Fund,
177–178
African American Legacy Program
(Detroit), 32, 169, 179, 191, 193
African American Muslims, 34–35
African American philanthropy: banking analogy used for endowment, 165;
the black church and, 33–34; donors
of, 37–39; eight characteristics of,
32–33; history of, 35–37; how the
giving occurs during, 38–39; motivations of, 37–38; Muslims and, 34–35;
philosophy of, 31–33; role of spirituality in, 33–35; when/where giving
occurs during, 38
African American Philanthropy Initiative, 191, 192*e*
African American Women's Fund
(Twenty-First Century Foundation),
150
African Americans: business ownership
by, 29*t*; demographic data (U.S. Census 2000/2001) on, 5; education
level/home ownership by, 27*t*; indica-

tors of wealth for, 31; major gifts by,
147–149; median household income
of, 26; sensibilities/cultural customs
of, 85–86; U.S. Census (1999) on, 4;
U.S. Census projections for future of,
9–11, 10*t*
Age: Latino philanthropy by, 53–54; of
U.S. ethnic/racial population (2000),
12*t*
Alaska Native Claims Settlement Act
(1971), 60
Alaska Native Heritage Center, 91–92
Alaskan regional corporations, 60–61
The Alford Group, Inc., 32, 86
American Baptist Foundation, 34
American Indian College Fund, 57, 177
Annie E. Casey Foundation, 181
Annual fund, 116–117
Appreciation, 204–205
Arizona Community Foundation, 90,
177, 198
Armstrong, J., 58
Armstrong, S., 187
Ascencio, F., 51
Asia Foundation, 113, 189–190
Asia Pacific Fund, 88
Asia Society, 44, 86, 114, 161
Asian American Federation of New
York, 116, 126, 127*e*, 142, 158, 159*e*
Asian American Legal Defense and
Education Fund, 88, 99, 102,
146, 152

Asian American philanthropy: donors of, 42–46; how it occurs, 44–45; kinds of gifts given during, 42–43; motivations of, 43–44; philosophy of, 40–42; when/where it occurs, 44

"Asian American Philanthropy" (Chao), 40

Asian American Renaissance (Minneapolis), 126

Asian Americans: business ownership by, 29t; Census (2001) on population growth of, 39; concept of "face" and, 41–42; death as culturally sensitive topic to, 161–164; demographic data (U.S. Census 1993/2000), 5–7; education level/home ownership by, 27t; encouraging prospective donors among, 109–110; by ethnicity, 6; immigrants, 87–88; indicators of wealth for, 40; median household income of, 26; sensibilities/cultural customs of, 86–88; U.S. Census (1999) on, 4; U.S. Census projections for future of, 9–11, 10t

Asian Bar Association, 186

Asian Fund, 188

Asian Pacific Endowment for Community Development, 41, 146

Asian Pacific Fund, 43, 102, 113–114, 120, 140–141, 146, 175–176, 186

Asian Perspective Series (Asia Foundation), 113

Associated Black Charities of Maryland, 143, 170–171, 191

Associated Black Charities of New York City, 68

Association of Fundraising Professionals (Houston), 185

Association motivation, 21

Atlatl, 166, 198

B

Baker, D., 87, 88, 108, 119, 162, 163

Baltimore Giving Project, 15, 108, 149, 186, 191, 198

Bank One, 130

Baron, B., 189

Baylor College of Medicine (Houston), 89, 147, 163, 165, 185

Berry, M., 38, 43, 44, 46, 54, 55, 63, 105

The black church, 33–34

Black Enterprise magazine, 174

Black, S. S., 55, 57, 58, 129

Black United Fund of Michigan, 85

Black United Fund of Texas, 37

Black United Funds, 36, 122

Blackfeet Foundation, 187

Boston Foundation, 80

Boulé Foundation, 178–179

Bratone, B., 57

Building awareness: future possibilities for, 103; membership programs for, 99–100; sensibilities/cultural customs and, 85–93; special events for, 100–103; strategies for, 93–99; by United Way of Metropolitan Tarrant County, 95–98

Business ownership, 28, 29t

Bussel, D., 128

C

Campbell, A. R., 125

Campoamor, D., 49

Carnegie, A., 12

Carollton School of the Sacred Heart (Miami), 71

Carroll, Sis. M., 73

Carson, E., 31, 35, 125

Case statement, 117

The Catholic Church, 46, 49, 52

Caucasian population: U.S. Census projections for, 9–11, 10t; U.S. segment (U.S. Census 2001) of, 2, 3, 4–5

Cause-related marketing, 130

Challenge grants, 186–187

Chandler, V., 96, 98

Chao, J., 6, 18, 38, 40, 43, 44, 46, 54, 55, 63, 105

Charitable gift planning: characteristics of prospective donors, 167–169; described, 158–160; examples of programs encouraging, 169–171. *See also* Gift planning programs; Gifts

Charmaine Chapman Society, 148

Chavis, D., 58, 90, 94, 164, 177

Cherokee Nation of Oklahoma, 71

Chesapeake Planned Giving Council, 191

Chicago Arts Consortium, 174
Chicago Civic Orchestra, 75
Chicago Historical society, 114
Chicago Lyric Opera, 128
Chicago Symphony Orchestra, 75–77
Chicanos por la Causa (Arizona), 102,
129, 130, 145, 176
China Institute, 86, 140, 141–142, 161
Chinese Americans, 87, 88. *See also*
Asian Americans
Chung, A., 93, 101, 111, 119, 145, 162,
173, 185
Ciconte, B. L., 151
Circle Celebration (United Way), 99
Circle of Life (Native American Rights
Fund), 166
CIRI, 60–61, 136
Coleman, M., 102
Collaborations. *See* Partnerships
Combined Federal Campaign, 122
Common fund, 188
Community Foundation of St. Joseph
County (Indiana), 177–178
Community Foundation for Southeast
Michigan, 175
Community Foundation of Southeast-
ern Michigan, 169
Community Links (Columbus), 100
Communitywide educational collabora-
tions: African American Legacy Pro-
gram, 191, 193; African American
Philanthropy Initiative, 191, 192e;
Leave A Legacy, 194–195; Make a
Will Campaign, 193–194
Conley, D., 28
Continuum of philanthropy model:
designed for immigrants, 18, 22; giv-
ing to help phase of, 20; investment
in philanthropy phase of, 20–21;
motivations in, 21; phases of, 19fig;
survival phase of, 18, 20
Corporate gifts, 126–130
Cortés, M., 54, 72, 123, 128
Cortés-Vasquez, L., 17, 50, 51, 116, 119,
142, 157, 158
Cosby, B., 99
Council on Foundations, 13
Council on Foundations panel (1999),
18

Cultural issues: of African Americans,
85–86; of Asian American, 86–88;
disincentives to gift planning and,
160–161; gift planning programs and,
161–164; of Latinos, 72, 89, 163–164;
of Native Americans, 89–92; sensitive topic of death as, 161–164. *See
also* Diverse donors
Cultures of Caring (Council on Foundations), 14, 18, 25, 40, 52, 53, 109,
124, 132, 167, 177, 197
Cycles of giving (Native American
model), 22, 23fig

D
DC Central Kitchen, 129
Deck, A. F., 7
Delta Sigma Theta, 179
Dennis, M., 32, 86
Desai, V. N., 41, 44, 86, 114, 161
Direct mail, 118–120
Diverse donors: bringing awareness to,
201; building trust with, 202–203;
catching interest of, 201–202; creat-
ing involvement of, 203; getting
support of, 203–204; giving apprecia-
tion, recognition, inclusion as insider
to, 204–205; pathways to, 200–204;
philanthropic training of, 197–199;
strategies for working with, 199–200.
See also Cultural issues; Embracing
diversity
Diversity Endowment Funds, 188
Diversity Endowment Funds Council,
188
Diversity Endowment Funds (Saint Paul
Foundation), 164–165, 174
Dollar, G., 148
Donor circles, 149–151
Donor pyramid of giving model,
16fig–17
Donors: of African American philanthropy, 37–39; of Asian American
philanthropy, 42–46; benefits of
engaging diverse, 2–3; demographics
of nonprofit, 1–2; fundraiser focus on
their same ethnicity/race of, 26; giving circles of, 149–151; indicators of
wealth and, 26–30, 29t; of Latino

philanthropy, 50–55; major gift, 132–133; of Native Americans philanthropy, 61–65; partnerships as entrée to new, 184–186; philanthropy as articulation of values of, 13; strategies for working with diverse populations of, 199–200. *See also* Gifts; Prospective donors

E

Eagle Staff Fund of First National Development Institute, 129
Earth Service Corps (Seattle YMCA), 77–78
Eastern Star, 36
Edmond, A. A., Jr., 174
Education level, 27–28
Egyptian Arabic Order, 36
El Museo del Barrio (New York City), 89, 118–119, 147, 161
Ellis, J., 32, 167
Embracing diversity: accessibility and, 79–80; inclusivity strategies for, 80–82; mission statement on, 69–70; organization internal diversity and, 74–76; organizational commitment to, 68–72; organizational policies/operations and, 70–72; programs which encourage, 76–79; trust and, 72–73. *See also* Diverse donors
Empowerment, 49–50, 131
Endowment building: by African American Community Fund, 177–178; by Asian Pacific Fund, 175–176; by Boulé Foundation, 178–179; by Chicanos por la Causa, 176; by Delta Sigma Theta, 179; future trends in, 181–182; by Greater New Orleans Foundation, 180–181; by Hopi Tribal Education Endowment, 176–177; impediments to, 174–175; by mature nonprofit organizations, 157–158; by Mexican Fine Arts Center Museum, 176; by Twenty-First Century Foundation, 179–180
Endowments: concerns of, 173–174; described, 171; importance of, 172–173; permanent vs. current needs, 171–172

Engaging Diverse Communities for and Through Philanthropy (Berry and Chao), 46
Epstein, M., 180, 181
Estrada, L., 74
Ethnic/racial population: age of U.S. (2000), 12t; Asian groups by ethnicity, 6; fundraisers focus on donors of their own, 26; new fundraising models needed for, 17; Pacific Islander groups by ethnicity, 6; U.S. Census (1999) on, 4; U.S. Census (2001) on, 2, 3, 4–5; U.S. Census projections on U.S., 9–11
Events: major gift solicitation and, 138–144; prospective donors and, 111–116

F

"Face" concept, 41–42
Face-to-face meetings: major gift solicitation and, 137–138; prospective donors and, 108–110
Fairfax, J., 13, 31, 34–35, 35, 74, 86, 174, 197
Ferriby, R., 175
Field of Interest Funds (Associated Black Charities), 171
First Nations Development Institute, 13, 56, 58, 60, 61, 177
Ford Foundation, 176
Ford Foundation's Rural Development and Community Foundations Initiative (1997), 186
Formal philanthropy, 12
Forum of Regional Associations of Grantmakers, 199
Fountain, J., 164, 193
Foxwood casino (Mashantucket Pequot Tribe), 129
Fresh Start Catering (DC Central Kitchen), 129
Fund for Harlem (Twenty-First Century Foundation), 150–151
Funders' Collaborative for Strong Latino Communities, 190
Fundraising models: continuum of philanthropy, 18–22, 19*fig*; Native Amer-

ican, 22, 23fig; need for new models
for diverse ethnicities, 17; traditional
pyramid of giving, 16fig–17. See also
Philanthropy
Fundraising themes, 123–124
Fung, M., 88, 152

G
Gala, M., 116
Garcia, P., 129, 130, 145, 176
A Gathering of Traditions (Alaska Native
Heritage Center), 91e–92
Gentle Rain Design, 177
Gift planning programs: cultural issues
regarding, 161–164; disincentives to,
160–161; examples of successful,
169–171; future trends in, 181–182;
by mature nonprofit organizations,
157–158; personal meetings strategy
of, 164–165; policies/guidelines of,
166–167; using professional advisers,
167; reasons to establish, 160; using
appropriate language/
analogies, 165–166. See also Planned
giving
Gifts: of African American philan-
thropy, 37; of Asian American philanthropy, 42–43; Chinese Americans
memorial, 88; corporate, 126–130; of
Native Americans philanthropy, 62.
See also Donors; Major gifts
Give2Asia, 189–190
Giving Circle Took Kit (Baltimore Giv-
ing Project), 149, 191
Giving circles, 149–151
Glen-Johnson-McLaughlin, C., 37
Goizueta, R., 48
Goldsberry, R., 175
Grassroots philanthropy, 15
Greater New Orleans Foundation,
180–181
Greater Seattle YMCA, 77–78, 110
Growing Up Asian in America (Asian
Pacific Fund), 113–114, 115e

H
Hall-Russell, C., 39
Harrington, N. W., Jr., 146, 164–165, 174

Hee, S. J., 26
Herrington, N., Jr., 188
Hirano, I., 87, 163
The Hispanic Federation, 17, 51, 71,
116, 118, 119, 142–143, 157–158
Hispanics: education level/home owner-
ship by, 27t; fundraising targeting of,
124; median household income of,
26; U.S. Census (1999) on, 4. See also
Latino philanthropy
Hispanics in Philanthropy, 190
Home ownership, 27t
"Honor walls," 121
Hopi Education Endowment Fund, 60
Hopi Foundation, 103, 177
Hopi Tribal Council, 60
Hopi Tribal Education Endowment,
176–177
House parties, 109–110
Houston Association of Fundraising
Professionals, 185
Houston Hispanic Chamber of Com-
merce, 172
Huhndorf, R., 136
Hunt, E., 150, 158, 179
Huntington, C. P., 134–135
Hyperagency motivation, 21

I
IBM, 95, 130
Identification motivation, 21
Immigrants: Asian American, 87–88;
continuum of philanthropy model
and, 18–22, 19fig; cultural barriers
faced by, 92–93; tradition of informal
ways of helping others, 14; U.S. Cen-
sus (1999) on children of, 4
Immigration Act of 1965, 6
Improved Benevolent Protection Order
of Elks, 36
Inclusion as insider, 204–205
Inclusivity strategies, 80–82
Indian Tribal Governmental Tax Status
Act (1982), 60
Indicators of wealth: among African
Americans, 31; among Asian Ameri-
cans, 40; business ownership, 28, 29t;
education, 27–28; home ownership,

27t; median house income, 26; for
Native Americans, 55–56; net worth,
28, 30t
Institutional philanthropy: defining,
12–13; valuing both personal and, 15
International/pan-ethnic collaborations,
187–190
Intimate gatherings, 139–140
Investing, 131
IRS Code Section 7871, 60, 177

J
J. Ashburn Jr. Youth Center, 100, 102,
112–113, 135
Jackson, R. M., 31, 122
Jacob, J. G., 151
Japanese American National
Museum (Los Angeles), 87, 121, 152,
154–155, 163
Japanese Americans, 87, 92–93, 95. *See
also* Asian Americans
Jefferson, A., 113, 135–136
Joseph, J. A., 31, 56

K
Kaplan, D., 1, 59, 127, 136, 144,
173–174
Kasberg, R. H., 39
Kaufman, Cranney, M., 110
Kellogg Foundation, 165
Key Club (United Way), 117
Koahnic Broadcast Corporation,
143–144
Kong, G., 43, 88, 102, 120, 141, 146,
163, 176, 186
KUYI (radio station), 177

L
Latino philanthropy: donors of, 50–55;
fostering, 128–129; gift planning
and cultural issues of, 163–164; how
donors give, 54–55; nonprofit organizations and empowerment of, 49–50,
131; philosophy of, 47–48; remittances of, 51; role of religion in, 49;
strategies for endowment, 165; trust
issues and, 72; when/where giving
occurs during, 53–54

Latinos: business ownership by, 29t; cor-
porate leadership by, 128–129; demo-
graphic data (U.S. Census 1990/2000)
on, 7–8; home ownership by, 27t;
indicators of wealth for, 46–47; sensi-
bilities/cultural customs of, 89; U.S.
Census (1999) on, 4; U.S. Census
projections for future of, 9–11, 10t
"Latinos and Giving, 1999" (Cortés-
Vasquez and Miranda), 51, 53, 118
Leave A Legacy, 191, 194–195
Lee, V., 126
Legacy Circle (Self-Help), 162
Lewis, D. E., 33
Listening sessions (United Way of Metro-
politan Tarrant County), 95–98

M
McDonald's, 113, 128
Macedonia Baptist Church (Denver),
34
Macedonia Village Project, 34
Major events, 140–144
Major gifts: by African Americans,
147–149; campaigns to solicit,
145–149; donors of, 132–133; giving
or donor circles and, 149–151;
making request for, 135–138; moti-
vations for, 136, 147; stewardship
and, 151–152; volunteer involve-
ment leading to, 144–145; words of
wisdom about asking for, 133–135.
See also Gifts
Make a Will Campaign, 193–194
Making Connections, 181
Mankiller, W., 71
MAPS (Museums and Public Schools)
[Chicago Arts Consortium], 184
Martin, P., 34
Martinez, A., 15, 89, 147, 163, 165,
185, 198
Mashantucket Pequot Tribal Nation, 61,
73, 129
Masons, 36
Meissner, R., 178
Memorial gifts, 88
Merriam-Webster's Collegiate Dictionary,
11–12

Merritt, W., 122
Mexican American Legal Defense and
  Education Fund, 49, 186
Mexican Fine Arts Center Museum
  (Chicago), 100, 176, 51, 111–112e,
  118, 128, 184
Michigan Bar Association, 175
Michigan State University, 175
Midwest Council of La Raza, 47
Minerva Education and Development
  Foundation (Detroit), 191
Minneapolis Foundation, 164, 193
Minority Executive Directors Coalition
  (Washington), 68
Minton Fellows (Detroit Boulé Founda-
  tion), 178–179
Miranda, J., 50, 51
Mission statement, 69–70
Mohegan tribe, 73
Montana Community Foundation, 187
Moore, W. W., 165
Motivations: of African American phil-
  anthropy, 37–38; of Asian American
  philanthropy, 43–44; hyperagency,
  identification, association, 21; for
  major gifts, 136, 147; Native Ameri-
  can model mutual support, 22; of
  Native Americans philanthropy,
  63–64; religious, 33–34, 46, 49, 52.
  See also Prospective donors
Mott Foundation, 187
Mutual support motivation, 22

N
NANA Corporation, 59
National Association for the Advance-
  ment of Colored People, 36
National Basketball Association, 143
National Center for Black Philanthropy,
  31, 122, 198–199
National Council of La Raza, 49
National Council of Negro Women, 36
National Indian Gaming Association, 61
National Links Endowment, 165
National Museum of the American
  Indian, 121
National Urban League, 36
Native Alaskan Heritage Center, 136

Native American fundraising model,
  22, 23fig
Native American philanthropy: donors
  of, 61–65; how giving occurs during,
  64–65; kinds of gifts given during, 62;
  motivations for, 63–64; mutual
  responsibility/reciprocity/redistribu-
  tion values of, 58; philosophy of,
  56–59; strategies for gift planning/
  endowment, 166; tribal gaming and,
  61; unique structures of, 59–61;
  when/where giving occurs during, 64
Native American reservations, 56
Native American Rights Fund, 120,
  144, 152, 153e, 166
Native Americans: business ownership
  by, 29t; demographic data (U.S.
  Census 1990-2001) on, 8–9; education level/home ownership by, 27t;
  indicators of wealth for, 55–56; interdependence values of, 56–57; median
  household income of, 26; sensibili-
  ties/cultural customs of, 89–92;
  United Way of Metropolitan Tarrant
  County and, 95–98; U.S. Census projections for future of, 9–11, 10t
Native Americans in Philanthropy, 58,
  90, 94, 164, 177
Native Sun, 177
Net worth, 28–30t
New Economics for Women (Los Angeles), 48, 73, 173
New Heritage of Giving: Philanthropy
  in Asian America (Asian American
  Federation of New York), 158
Noblesse oblige, 13
non-Hispanic whites: education
  level/home ownership by, 27t; median
  household income of, 26; U.S. Census projections for future of, 9–11, 10t
Nonprofit organizations: benefits of
  engaging diverse donors to, 23;
  building awareness strategies used by,
  85–103; commitment to embracing
  diversity by, 68–72; demographics on
  donors to, 1–2; diversity of trustees/
  volunteers/staff of, 74–76; empowerment of Latino philanthropy and,

49–50, 131; gift planning/endowment building by mature, 157–158; major gifts and association with, 136–137; major gifts and commitment to, 135–136; mission statement of, 69–70; multicultural events by mainstream, 144; pros/cons of gift planning programs by, 160–161; strategies to encourage prospects, 107. *See also* Partnerships

O

O, C., 116
On Lok Senior Health Services, 87, 88, 108, 119, 162–163
Ong, P., 26, 205
Opano Mexica, 100
Organized philanthropy, 12
Oros, T., 62, 89, 90

P

Pace Setter Luncheons (Chapman Cabinet), 148
Pacific Islanders: by ethnicity, 6; U.S. Census projections for future of, 9–11
Pan-ethnic/international collaborations, 187–190
Park Voyagers (Chicago Arts Consortium), 184
Parra, O. V., 47
Partnership for African American Endowment Development, 36
Partnership Fellows Program, 80
Partnerships: challenge grants and, 186–187; communitywide educational, 191–195; entrée to new donors/mainstream through, 184–186; with existing diverse groups, 183–184; future trends in, 195; pan-ethnic/international, 187–190. *See also* Nonprofit organizations
Pearce, J., 73
Pepsi, 130
"Perpetual foreigner" syndrome, 6
Personal appeal: effectiveness of, 109; involvement before a, 110
Personal relationship, 109
Philanthropic training, 197–199

Philanthropy: African American, 32–39; Asian American, 40–46; components of, 22–24; defining, 11–12; gift, 37, 42–43, 62, 88, 126–130; Latino, 47–55, 72, 128–129, 131; major gift, 132–152; multiple meanings of, 12–13; Native American, 56–65; traditions of, 14–15. *See also* Endowment building; Fundraising models; Gift planning programs
Philanthropy in Communities of Color (Smith, Shue, Vest, and Villareal), 13
Planned giving: characteristics of prospective donors, 167–169; described, 158–160; examples of programs encouraging, 169–171. *See also* Gift planning programs; Gifts
Pledges, 122–123
Poley, B., 103, 177
Powell, S., 99, 117
Pressley, C., 178
Prince Hall Masons, 36
Printed materials, 125–126
Prospective donors: annual fund and, 116–117; case statement and, 117; causes/interests in early states of philanthropy, 106–107; characteristics of planned gift, 167–169; corporate gifts and, 126–130; direct mail to, 118–120; events and, 111–116; house parties and, 109–110; impact of acknowledgments/recognition on, 121–122, 153e; moving along continuum of philanthropy, 105; pathways to diverse, 200–204; personal meetings/house parties to encourage, 108–110; personal relationship encouraging, 109; philanthropic training of, 197–199; pledges made by, 122–123; printed materials aimed toward, 125–126; research on, 120–121; strategies by nonprofit organizations for, 107. *See also* Donors; Motivations
Prosser, M-L., 120, 166
Puerto Rican Day Parade (New York), 17

Puerto Rican Legal Defense and Education Fund, 49–50

R

"The Racial Wealth Gap: Origins and Implications for Philanthropy in the African American Community" (Conley), 28
Ramirez, R., 11
Ramos, H.A.J., 46, 50
Rasmuson Foundation (Alaska), 136, 144, 173
Rayford, B., 85
Recognition, 121–122, 204
Religious motivation: The black church and, 33–34; The Catholic Church and, 46, 49, 52
Remittances, 51
Renewal, 131
Rice, A., 95
Richie, L., 99
Rivas-Vazquez, A. G., 71–72
Roberts, C., 90, 165, 166, 198
Rockefeller, J. D., 12
Rodriguez, R., 48, 108
Rogers, P., 68, 86
Royce, A. P., 48, 108
Rural Development and Community Foundations Initiative (1997) [Ford Foundation], 186

S

St. Elizabeth's School (Chicago), 73
St. Jude Children's Research Hospital, 124–125
Saint Paul Foundation (Minnesota), 146, 164–165, 174, 187–189
San Francisco Museum of Modern Art, 76
Sanchez, D., 74
Santiago de Silva, L., 89, 118–119, 147, 161
Schervish, P., 21
Scholarship endowments, 172
Section 7871 (IRS Code), 60, 177
Self-Help for the Elderly (San Francisco), 93, 101–102, 111, 119–120, 144–145, 162, 173, 185

Sensibilities/cultural customs: of African Americans, 85–86; of Asian Americans, 86–88; of Latinos, 89; of Native Americans, 89–92
September 11, 77
Seth, E., 143
Settles, L. H., 14, 108, 158–160
Seventh Generation Fund, 62, 89, 120, 177
Shakopee Mdewakanton, 61
Shao, S., 40, 43
Shue, S., 13
Sigma Pi Phi, 178
Smith, B., 13
Smithsonian Institution, 121
Snipper, P. H., 41, 92
Social enterprise/entrepreneurship, 129
Sogi, F. Y., 158, 159
Solomon, P., 32, 179, 191
Special events, 100–103
Staff: diversity of organization, 74–76; inclusivity strategies involving, 80–82
Stanford University, 136
Stanley, D., 170–171
Steinway Corporation, 116
Steward, D., 148
Steward, T., 148
Stewardship, 151–152
Stotzer, B. O., 48, 73, 173
Strengthening Native American Philanthropy, 60
Suda, S., 43, 136–137
Suggs, D., 147
SW Supermarket, 130

T

Taylor, W., Jr., 176
Therrien, M., 11
Third National Conference on Black Philanthropy (2001), 32, 165
Thomas, D., 181
Tithing, 34
Tohono O'odham Nation (Arizona), 173–174
Tortolero, C., 51, 111, 128, 184–185
Touch the Future, 191, 193
Tribal gaming, 61

Trinity United Church of Christ (Chicago), 33
Trust: as African American philanthropy issue, 158–159; built with diverse donors, 202–203; embracing diversity and, 72–73; as Latino philanthropy issue, 72
Tuan, G., 86, 141, 161–162
Twenty-First Century Foundation (New York), 150, 158, 179–180

U
"Ultra Baroque: Contemporary Voices in Latin Art" (San Francisco Museum of Modern Art), 78–79
Umemoto, K., 205
United Negro College Fund, 36
United States: age of population by race/ethnicity (2000), 12t; amount of remittances sent to Mexico from, 51; demographic data on African Americans in, 5; demographic data on Asian Americans in, 5–7; demographic data on Latinos in, 7–8; demographic data on Native Americans in, 8–9; increasing diversity in, 3–11; U.S. Census population projections for, 9–11
United Way of Central Ohio, 99, 117
United Way of Greater St. Louis, 147–148
United Way of Metropolitan Tarrant County, 95–98
United Way of Southeast Connecticut, 73, 129
University of Texas Health Science Center (San Antonio), 48
Up from Slavery (Washington), 133
U.S. Bureau of Census (1993): on Asian American household income, 40; demographic data on Asians in, 7
U.S. Bureau of Census (1999), 7
U.S. Bureau of Census (2000): African American demographic data in, 5;
on Asian American indicators of wealth, 40; current population makeup according to, 2; demographic data on Asians in, 5–7; demographic data on Latinos in, 7–8
U.S. Bureau of Census (2001): African American demographic data in, 5; on Caucasian population, 2, 3, 4–5; current population makeup according to, 4–5; on growth of Asian American population, 39; on indicators of wealth, 26, 28, 29t, 30; on Latino indicators of wealth, 46–47; Native American demographic data from 1990 to, 8–9; on Native American indicators of wealth, 55–56

V
VanDussen challenge grant program (African American Legacy Program), 179
Vest, J. L., 13
Villarreal, J., 13
VISTA workers, 97
Volunteers: diversity of nonprofit organization, 74–76; involvement leading to gifts, 144–145

W
Wagner, L., 7
Washington, B. T., 133–135
Wells, R. A., 58
white, non-Hispanic. See Caucasian population
Winters, M. F., 31, 34, 38, 186, 198
World Vision, 49
Wright, J. A., Jr., 33
Wyss, D., 61, 63

Y
Yanong, P., 126

Z
Zamora, R., 74